Sven Hedin (1865–195
explorers. His travels thro
Asia, China and Tibet

MW00774669

discoveries and achievements of their kind. He produced the
first detailed maps of vast parts of the Pamir Mountains, the
Taklamakan Desert, Tibet, the Silk Road and the Transhimalaya
(Gangdise today). He was the first to unearth the ruins of
ancient Buddhist cities in Chinese Central Asia and in 1901 he
discovered the ancient Chinese garrison town of Lou-lan in the
Taklamakan. The many manuscripts he found there are of huge
historical importance. His great goal – never realised – was to
reach the forbidden city of Lhasa. His books, which include
Through Asia, *Central Asia and Tibet*, *Overland to India*,
Transhimalaya, and *My Life as an Explorer* have been
excerpted, translated and published in dozens of languages
throughout the world.

The book is full of incident . . . an entertaining account with
picturesque descriptions and no less extraordinary personalities.
The Geographical Journal

Tauris Parke Paperbacks is an imprint of I.B.Tauris. It is dedicated to publishing books in accessible paperback editions for the serious general reader within a wide range of categories, including biography, history, travel and the ancient world. The list includes select, critically acclaimed works of top quality writing by distinguished authors that continue to challenge, to inform and to inspire. These are books that possess those subtle but intrinsic elements that mark them out as something exceptional.

The Colophon of Tauris Parke Paperbacks is a representation of the ancient Egyptian ibis, sacred to the god Thoth, who was himself often depicted in the form of this most elegant of birds. Thoth was credited in antiquity as the scribe of the ancient Egyptian gods and as the inventor of writing and was associated with many aspects of wisdom and learning.

THE SILK ROAD

Ten Thousand Miles through Central Asia

Sven Hedin

Foreword by John Hare

TPP

TAURIS PARKE
PAPERBACKS

Published in 2009 by Tauris Parke Paperbacks
an imprint of I.B.Tauris & Co Ltd
6 Salem Road, London W2 4BU
175 Fifth Avenue, New York NY 10010
www.ibtauris.com

Distributed in the United States and Canada Exclusively by
Palgrave Macmillan
175 Fifth Avenue, New York NY 10010

First published by Macmillan and Co. Ltd. in 1938
Copyright © 1938, 2009 The Sven Hedin Foundation, Stockholm
Copyright foreword © 2009 John Hare

Cover image: 'Northwestern Xinjiang' © Li Gang/Xinhua Press/Corbis

ISBN: 978 1 84511 898 3

A full CIP record for this book is available from the British Library
A full CIP record is available from the Library of Congress

Library of Congress Catalog Card Number: available

Printed and bound in India by Thomson Press India Ltd

CONTENTS

LIST OF ILLUSTRATIONS

FOREWORD

THIS IS the second book of a trilogy Sven Hedin wrote describing a formidable, 7,000 mile motorized journey he made in 1933 and 1935, pioneering his way through the Gobi desert on a highway reconnaissance mission at the behest of the Chinese Ministry of Railways.

His first book, *The Trail of War*, described how he was captured and his vehicles were impounded by the charismatic 23-year-old Chinese warlord, Ma Chung-ying (Big Horse). This book describes the tortuous and forbidding journey which took him over unmade roads and through wild terrain from Nanjing to Urumqi and beyond.

The expedition got off to a disastrous start. On the very point of departure, Dongora, a Mongolian team member was killed when an expedition vehicle failed to go through a level-crossing in time to avoid an oncoming train. Hedin's Swedish driver survived without a scratch, but Dongora, who had had a premonition the night before that catastrophe awaited him, spotted the approaching train and flung himself out of the truck, with fatal results.

It was an ill-omened start for an expedition which was to take Hedin, three lorries, two Ford cars and fifteen men thousands of miles along the track of the old camel highway which linked the then Chinese capital, Nanjing, in the east of China to the country's far north-west – a vast stretch of the ancient upper Silk Road.

Progress was tediously slow, with innumerable stops to dig immobilized vehicles out of soft sand, retrieve them from swollen rivers or deal with bent or broken axles and springs. Through the bitterly cold winter months the indomitable Swedish explorer ploughed on through the

Gobi sands in temperatures which plummeted to -30 degrees Celsius. At the very height of winter he encountered one of the last great camel caravans which for thousands of years had criss-crossed the harsh, forbidding deserts of the Gobi. Paradoxically, the caravans he so admired and the colourful crew of rogues and rascals who travelled with them would shortly, as a result of his survey, be consigned to history.

As Hedin's team moved slowly towards Xinjiang, they were well aware that the far-flung Chinese province was in a state of political turmoil and also knew that Ma Chung-ying was harassing the corrupt administration on many fronts. As a consequence, Hedin's team members were constantly forced to keep alert for possible attacks by bandits, outlaws and car rustlers. It seemed that they were wary of the intangible too; it is fascinating to learn that this dry, pragmatic and highly competent scientist and explorer could also be influenced by the amorphous and restless spirits of the Gobi:

'One sees dark spectres everywhere, and ghosts with twisted arms and legs. They stretch out their hands towards us to tear us to pieces; we hear stealthy steps approaching us from behind ... on still nights, mysterious sounds of lamentation reach our ears – are they the unquiet spirits of dead malefactors, or only wolves and wild cats?'

However, neither ghoul nor malefactor deterred Hedin. Whenever an intractable problem occurred, he responded immediately by summoning the senior members of his team and convening a 'council of war'.

'If we had got reliable news from Sinkiang [Xinjiang], should we have turned back?' he muses to himself. 'Certainly not. We had undertaken a task and set about it – we were determined to ride out all possible storms.'

And ride them they did. When his Ford car's front axle was severely bent in an encounter with an immovable object, it was laid on two blocks of wood to form an arched bridge. Then a fully loaded lorry was jacked up over the highest point of the arch and one of its wheels was gently lowered to straighten the bend. Such was the innovative nature of Hedin's 'bush' repairs and his unflinching determination to succeed against all odds.

When they arrived in Turpan, the town lay firmly under the control of Ma Chung-ying and the young warlord lost no time in commandeering the convoy of vehicles for his own use. Hedin was outraged, and narrowly escaped being executed. Following the seizure of the vehicles, dubbed 'the grey sows', the team members were twice imprisoned in the nearby city of Korla and only just managed to avoid being blown up by bombs dropped from the air by enemies of Ma. After Big Horse's eventual defeat, the freed convoy travelled to Urumqi, where Hedin encountered the Red Russians who had been aiding the Chinese administration in its struggle with warlord Ma. Shortly after his arrival, Hedin was invited to lecture to a group of 250 Russian Bolsheviks about his journey with camels across the Taklamakan in 1895. An extraordinary backdrop to this lecture was a large, red banner proclaiming in golden letters a message from Stalin. 'War is a curse and we [the Bolsheviks] want to live in peace with all the peoples of the earth.'

The political situation in Urumqi was extremely fluid and no sooner had the lecture finished than Hedin found himself once again detained, this time by the Xinjiang Governor-General, Sheng Tupan, who, ignoring the central government's instructions granting Hedin untrammelled passage through Xinjiang, told the Swedish explorer, 'We did not ask you to come here, so you must put up with having to wait.'

After numerous delays, frustrations and intrigues, Hedin was finally allowed to get his expedition underway and drove to Ansi, Dun Huang and from there into the hostile Desert of Lop which lies far to the south of Urumqi. Using other routes he eventually returned to Nanjing – all the while surveying and mapping new highways.

The major road Hedin pioneered across northern China is now, in many places, a double-lane highway linking Urumqi with Beijing. A journey which took him weeks can now be completed in hours. The robbers and the bandits have long disappeared and even the restless Gobi spirits have been pushed back by the constant ebb and flow of huge, heavily loaded trucks which now shatter the peace and stillness of the great desert – a peace which Hedin greatly prized and constantly longed for when detained against his will in Turpan, Korla and Urumqi.

The wild horses he observed have been hunted to extinction. The herds of wild Bactrian camels, the gazelles and the wild asses, which Hedin and his team saw in abundance, have all greatly diminished in numbers and retreated for survival into the heart of the desert. Today, even in these heartlands, the desert's tranquillity is disturbed by seekers of mineral wealth – gold, iron-ore and oil – materialistic men who see the desert only in terms of profit and loss.

Although man's machines can now venture into and conquer remote, forbidding desert spaces, they can never recapture the age-old magic, the charm and the mystery, the beauty and utter stillness of the desert. Fortunately, those disciplined and instructed by its austerity, those who are not dominated by and reliant on machines, can still discover remote and undesecrated places where the elusive spirit of the Gobi survives.

Hedin's prophecy that the great desert of Lop, which surrounds the ancient lake of Lop Nur in the south of Xinjiang, would soon be traversed by a major highway has not been fulfilled. He rhapsodized that the motorized traveller in the future would, 'see the oases on the edge of the Gobi, the mysterious deserts between Tun-hwang [Dun Huang] and Lou-lan [Lou Lan], the wild camels' desolate homeland. He will have seen a glimpse of the wandering lake [Lop Nur].'

But the erudite Swede could not foresee that the river which fed Lop Nur from the snowmelt of the Tien Shan mountains would be dammed forty years later, 400 miles to the west along the Tarim river to provide an irrigation system for farmers. The result – thousands of dead trees, a dry desert of Lop and a waterless Lop Nur lake – a desert of death, turned by the Chinese, not into a navigable area rich in wildlife, but into a highly secret, nuclear and missile weapon-testing site. But that's another story.

John Hare

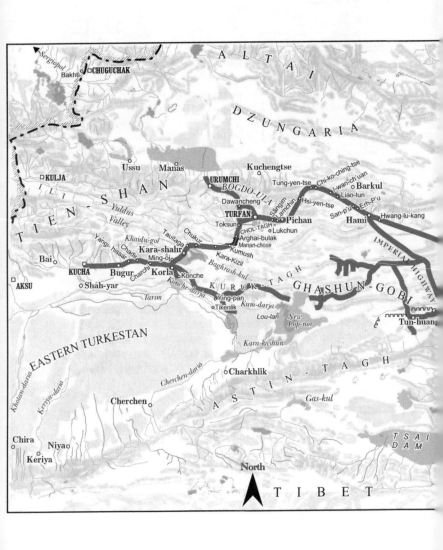

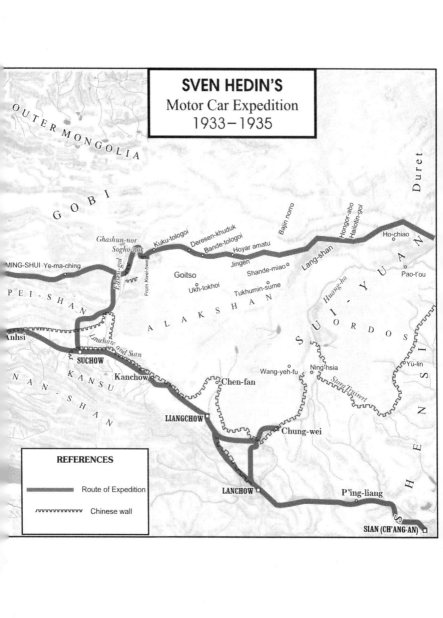

SVEN HEDIN'S
Motor Car Expedition
1933–1935

OUTER MONGOLIA

GOBI

Duret

Ghashun-nor
Sogho-nor
Kuku-tologoi
Deresen-khuduk
Bande-tologoi
Hoyar amatu
Bajin norro
Hongor-abo
Hailotin-gol
Ho-chiao

MING-SHUI Ye-ma-ching
From Kwei-hwa
Jingen
Goitso
Shande-miao
Lang-shan
Pao-t'ou

PEI-SHAN
Ukh-lokhoi
Tukhumin-sume
Edzin-gol
A L A K S H A N
Huang-ho
ORDOS
SUI-YUAN

Anhsi
Lanchow and Sian
Yü-lin

SUCHOW
Kanchow
Chen-fan
Wang-yeh-fu
Ning-hsia
Siang-tu-iret
SHENSI

NAN-SHAN
KANSU

LIANGCHOW
Chung-wei

LANCHOW
P'ing-liang

SIAN (CH'ANG-AN)

HENAN

REFERENCES

———————— Route of Expedition

∿∿∿∿∿∿∿∿∿ Chinese wall

THE SILK ROAD

INTRODUCTION

CHRISTMAS EVE at sea off San Francisco! New
Year's Eve at Honolulu! And January, 1933, on
the Pacific, which did not act up to its name, for the
President Garfield rolled gallantly over storm-lashed waves.

I landed at Tientsin on January 19 and went on at once
to Sweden House in Peking, where the great expedition
was to be wound up.

Peking seemed as little an abode of peace as the sea.
Japanese soldiers were manœuvring with machine-guns on
the glacis outside the Legation quarter as if they were
already masters of the famous old Imperial City. The
armies of Nippon were approaching the renowned temple
city of Jehol, which fell into their hands on March 4. It
was thought that Peking and the five provinces of Northern
China would be the next step.

The torches of rebellion blazed over Sinkiang, and the
revolts against Chinese dominion were spreading all through
the province like a steppe fire. The Tiger Prince, Yollbars
Khan, had seen the whole of his territory around Hami
devastated with fire and sword, and was brooding over his
vengeance in his fastnesses among the Celestial Mountains.
The Prince and grand lama of the Torguts at Kara-
shahr, Sin Chin Gegen, had refused to obey the order to
take the field against Yollbars; he had been summoned to
an audience of the governor-general Chin Shu-jen at
Urumchi, and there he and his staff had been treacherously
shot down.

On April 1, Chin telegraphed to Nanking that Eastern
Turkistan had broken away, and that he had called upon

the Tungans' strong man, Ma Pu-fang, in Kansu, to attack Ma Chung-yin, " Big Horsè ", who was then at Suchow with his troops. Nanking's reply was to rebuke him for having tried to stir up civil war instead of suppressing the rebellion and keeping his province in order.

Then this criminal's voice was silenced. On April 12 his *yamên* was surrounded by armed Russian *émigrés*; he himself succeeded in escaping through Siberia to Nanking, where he was sentenced to a term of imprisonment.

At this time it was generally believed in Peking that Big Horse would succeed in his attempt to conquer Sinkiang, and it was rumoured that Urumchi had fallen.

On February 2 Dr. Erik Norin turned up again in Peking after several years of fruitful research in the heart of Asia. He jumped out of the train looking well and sunburned, and his first words were: " Let me go back to Tibet again soon ! "

He had not had enough of the vast continent of Asia and its immense geological problems !

A week later we had Dr. Birger Bohlin and his caravan leader, the Dane Bent Friis-Johansen, back at Sweden House in good fettle. Bohlin brought with him a full load of valuable palæontological collections.

Thus the Swedish colony grew. Sweden House was the scene of great activity. Cases were filled with specimens ; fossils dug out of the mountains of Asia were unpacked, and the material distributed among the different persons who were to work on it. Our discussions often lasted far into the night, and we frequently took counsel with the president of our committee, Professor Lin Fu, and the head of the Chinese geological research department, Dr. Wong Wen-hao.

A room in Sweden House was turned into an art school, and there Norin, Bohlin and Bergman drew on three big tables a gigantic map of the whole field of our labours. It was 18 feet long and 6 feet 6 inches high, and embraced 2¾ million square miles, ten times the whole area of Sweden and a tenth part of Asia. The mountains were shown in a warm brown tone, woodland and cultivated land in green, the deserts in yellow, rivers and lakes in blue, and the winding routes we had travelled were a bright blood-red. It was a pleasure to contemplate this illusive picture of the enormous part of the surface of the earth to which we had devoted seven years of our life. In the spring it was sent to Chicago and exhibited in a hall next to the lama temple from Jehol.

Sad news reached us from Dr. Nils Hörner, who was still on the Etsin-gol with our Chinese astronomer, Parker C. Chen. The able and scholarly Balt Walter Beick had shot himself at Vajin-torei in a fit of depression and worry. Beick had been roaming about alone in Central Asia for fifteen years, and had made splendid collections, especially of birds and eggs, for the Berlin museum. He was buried among the remotest tamarisks of the desert, not far from where the Etsin-gol runs into the desert lakes. We thought of Walter Beick and his loyal work in our service with sorrow and gratitude, and subscribed whole-heartedly to the words he had written on a scrap of paper in his tent just before his desperate act: "As God lives, I have devoted all my strength to the making of some contribution to natural history research in Central Asia."

One day at the beginning of February some of us went to call on my old friend the Tashi Lama, who was living in the Ta Li Tang Palace, close to Nan Hai, or the Southern Sea, in the Forbidden City. We talked of the old days of 1907, when I was his guest at Tashi-lunpo for six weeks. He now hoped, after a visit to Inner Mongolia, soon to find the road open to his homeland Tibet. When he heard of Norin's and my longing to return to the land of the snows, he assured us of a welcome in his monastery city.

Our anxiety for Dr. Nils Ambolt, of whom nothing had been heard for several months, was increasing daily. As Captain Lutz, of the German-Chinese Eurasia aeroplane company, was just about to fly to Suchow, I asked him to take a letter to Gerhard Bexell and Manfred Bökenkamp, who were still at work in that region. I ordered them in the letter to try to get into touch with Ambolt. I had received the following telegram in January from the Swedish missionaries at Kashgar :

" Two men who arrived at Yarkend about Christmas-time report that Ambolt was at Cherchen on November 8 and proceeded to Kansu."

I asked them to try to get some fresh information about him.

We assumed that Big Horse had barred all the roads from Kansu to Sinkiang. We had heard that Ambolt had left all his valuable baggage by the wayside in Northern Tibet and had reached Cherchen in a destitute state.

My first thought was to make a lightning dash by car to this oasis, 1,680 miles away as the crow flies. But our resources were coming to an end, and we had to wait.

The situation in Peking was becoming more and more exciting. One fine day all the thousands of rickshaws in the city had disappeared—they had been requisitioned for the transport of ammunition ! On March 16 martial law was proclaimed, and one might not go into the streets after dark without a pass.

All the branches of the post office in and immediately outside Peking were ordered to send their day's takings to the central office every evening, as it was feared that marauding Chinese troops might at any moment overrun and plunder Peking. Such things had happened before ! On April 30 the Japanese troops were less than fifty miles from the town.

On the morning of May 11 a reconnoitring Japanese airman hovered over Peking. Machine-guns rattled here and there. We wondered what was going to happen. The valuable collections of Han manuscripts on wood, which Bergman had discovered on the Etsin-gol, were brought to Sweden House by Professor Lin Fu, because they were thought to be safer under the Swedish flag in the event of bombing from the air, invasion and looting.

A few days later leaflets were dropped from the air declaring that if the Nanking troops were not withdrawn bombing would begin.

On May 20 eleven airmen were buzzing over us. The Japanese advance troops were only nine miles from the city. Parties of fleeing Chinese soldiers crowded into Peking and forced people to give them billets.

On May 22 that excellent American author, Owen Lattimore, and his wife were dining with us. We were sitting at table when the German Embassy rang up and gave us the following instructions :

" If you hear two gun-shots, watch the American Embassy's wireless mast. If you see on it three white and three red lights, go at once to the Rockefeller Institute, whence army cars will take you to the American Embassy. There is reason to fear that Peking will be looted to-night."

But the night passed quietly, and no shots were heard. The city gates were kept shut during the day as well. All the trains were overflowing with fugitives, but now the railways were to be handed over entirely to the military authorities. We went for a drive through the northern quarters of the city to look at the barricades and other preparations for defence.

Our anxiety for Ambolt grew as time passed. Telegrams which I had sent via Peshawur to the mission at Kashgar brought us only the information from the first-named town that wireless communication with Kashgar was interrupted and that telegrams could only be sent to Misgar, whence they were taken on by mounted messengers in eleven days. So the Chinese wireless station had been destroyed by the Mohammedan rebels.

We heard too that a large number of the Swedish missionaries had gone home or crossed the Indian frontier for the time being.

On May 9 the missionary Roberntz telegraphed from Kashgar :

" No news from Ambolt since in October from Cherchen."

What had happened to him ? Was he alive, was he a prisoner, or had he been killed ? Eight months' silence was too long a time even for the heart of Asia. My order to Bexell to try to get into touch with Ambolt had been countermanded by Big Horse, who would have no foreign interference. He promised to look for the missing man himself. But later on he allowed us to take up the search, and on May 15 I sent Dr. Erik Norin on the hopeless quest of searching for Ambolt and, if possible, helping him.

Norin, when taking leave of me, asked me to lend him the gold ring I had received from the Tashi Lama in December, 1916, a signet bearing His Holiness' emblem and the sign of long life. Norin was strongly inclined to believe that the ring of a " living Buddha " must possess magical power, and that it would crown his search with success— perhaps, indeed, save both Ambolt's life and his own.

And so he went with the ring to Nanking. There, thanks to the friendly assistance of the Swedish Consul-General, Mr. Lindquist, and the counsellor of the German Embassy, Herr Fischer, he got his official pass in the twinkling of an eye and secured just as quickly a seat in the Eurasia aeroplane which took him to Suchow, where he was to start his operations.

We are most profoundly indebted to the German Air Force officers, Captains Lutz, Baumgart, Ratje, and others, for the readiness with which they conveyed our letters to and from the sections of the expedition which still had their headquarters at Suchow, and for the valuable information they gave us about the situation in the towns of Sinkiang and Kansu which were on their air route.

Captain Lutz went to Berlin early in the spring, intending to return to Peking by air, via Omsk, Urumchi, Hami and Suchow, with our old friend Herr Wilhelm Schmidt, the Luft Hansa representative in Peking.

This flight over the largest continent of the globe, a great achievement of its kind, was carried out to perfection under Lutz's guidance, and on June 25 he was back in Peking, unfortunately without Schmidt, who had an aeroplane accident in Germany.

On account of the news Lutz had obtained at Urumchi about the situation at Hami and Big Horse's operations, he had not landed at Hami on his eastward flight, but had flown direct to Suchow. There he had met General Hwang Mu-sung, who, with his staff, had been sent to Sinkiang by the Central Government in the middle of May to investigate the position and mediate between the combatants. It looks as if General Hwang had intended to seize the supreme power in Urumchi for himself. With this object he attempted a coup which cost three high officials their lives. The most powerful man in Urumchi was then the military governor-general, Sheng Shih-tsai, and it was he who frustrated General Hwang Mu-sung's plans and, as a mark of respect for the Central Government, allowed him to return in safety to Nanking by air. We were later to make this General Sheng Shih-tsai's acquaintance, an acquaintance of a rather curious and exciting nature.

On April 27, Dr. Bohlin went home to Sweden. Norin left us, as I have said, on May 15. But Sweden House had been recompensed on the 11th, for then Dr. Nils Hörner and Mr. Parker C. Chen returned from their desert solitudes ; their four years' wanderings on the Etsin-gol and Lop-nor, in the Pei-shan and Nan-shan had yielded splendid results. Among other things, they had made a great discovery—the new Lop-nor lake formed in 1921. Hörner has published a book, which will be found extraordinarily interesting, about his and Chen's experiences and adventures.

At the beginning of May we had transferred Sweden House to a perfectly fascinating Chinese establishment at the south-western corner of the Central Park. Each of us had his own little Chinese house and courtyard. Fru Bergman was hostess for the colony.

At the beginning of June the rain was pattering monotonously on our grey-tiled roofs, and violent thunder-claps were crashing over Peking. But on the night of June 7–8 my house was as silent as the grave, and I was lying naked on my bed reading. It was three o'clock in the morning. Then I heard the sound of the wooden garden door being cautiously opened. Soft steps were heard on the stones. My study door was opened almost inaudibly. Then all was quiet again. The door between the two rooms stood open.

" Who's that ? " I cried. Aha, no other than our own *kan-men-ti*, or watchman, entered and handed me a telegram.

It must be something important!—for otherwise the telegraph office did not deliver the messages till the morning.
I opened the telegram eagerly and read :

" Ambolt safe at Khotan—returning via India—Roberntz."

Thank God ! Now we could breathe freely again ! I
wrote telegrams at once to stop Norin and Bexell, and to
inform those at home—and also to Lindquist and Fischer.
I called for Hörner. He came in and executed an Indian
dance in my room. Then we sent a boy to fetch Bergman.
He appeared in pyjamas and sat down on a chair, half
asleep. When he heard the curt but momentous message,
he asked : " Is that all ? "

Ambolt got through Tibet to India without help and
thence home. He has told the story himself in his book
Caravan. Space forbids me to tell of Bexell's and Norin's
experiences in this book. The former was stopped before
he had got very far. The latter had already disappeared
into the mountains of north-eastern Tibet. His life was in
danger among East Turkis at Temirlik, who took him for
a spy. The Tajinär Mongols too, in Tsaidam, received
him with suspicious looks. But when they saw the Tashi
Lama's ring, they treated him with the most profound
reverence, and he was able to return eastward unmolested.

One Sunday at the beginning of June, when the rain was
splashing down on to the stones of my courtyard, a tall,
slim man enveloped in a grey ulster came striding up to
my door. He bore a famous name : it was General von
Seeckt, Mackensen's chief of staff in the Great War, and
a few years ago commander-in-chief of the Reichswehr.
General von Seeckt was one of my best war-time friends.
We had met daily during Mackensen's advance through
Galicia. Now, after a visit of some duration to Marshal
Chiang Kai-shek, he had come up to Peking to spend a
few weeks there.

The dinner which the German Ambassador Trautmann
gave in General von Seeckt's honour on June 28, 1933, was
to have a strange effect on my fortunes. It was raining in
torrents. The rooms of the German Embassy were blazing
with light. Among the guests were to be seen many dis-

tinguished Chinese—the War Minister, Ho Ying-chin, General Hwang Fu, Mr. Ho, who had been Prime Minister, Foreign Minister and Ambassador in Paris, and others. A tall Chinese with fine features, wearing white evening dress, attracted my attention, and I asked a member of the Embassy staff to introduce me to him. His name was Liu Chung-chieh, his title Assistant Foreign Minister, and he had been staying in Peking for some time to act as a connecting link between Nanking and the diplomatic corps, the greater part of which still resided in Peking.

We began to talk about conditions in Sinkiang. I had been there lately, and long before had spent several years in Eastern Turkistan. The Minister subjected me to a regular cross-examination about my experiences and my opinions, and I answered him frankly.

" In the semicircle of buffer States under Chinese authority, which the Emperor Chien Lung created round the Central Empire, only one link remains. Since the Republic was introduced you have lost Tibet, Outer Mongolia, Manchuria and Jehol, and Inner Mongolia too is seriously threatened. Sinkiang is still Chinese, but is split at the moment by Mohammedan revolt and civil war. If nothing is done to defend the province, it will be lost too."

" What do you think we ought to do ? " the Minister asked.

" I think the first step which ought to be and can be taken is to make and keep up first-class motor roads between China proper and Sinkiang. A railway line into the heart of Asia is the next step."

We had a long and detailed conversation, and Mr. Liu asked me to call upon him at his office next day. On this occasion we examined the problem still more thoroughly, and finally the Minister asked me to draw up a memorandum and mark on a map the roads I considered the most suitable.

In the middle of July I submitted my memorandum and map to Mr. Liu. The document was to be translated into Chinese, and Marshal Chiang Kai-shek, the Prime Minister Wang Ching-wei, and the Minister for Railways Ku Meng-yü, were each to receive a copy. I concentrated on the question of trade and communications. Russian trade had driven out the Chinese and was well on the way to killing the British trade from India. At Kashgar, Kulja, Chuguchak, and in the Altai, the Russians were much closer and had excellent roads, which were continually being improved, right up to the frontiers of Sinkiang. Chinese trade, on the contrary, had from ancient times been mainly conducted by camel caravans from Kwei-hwa-cheng through the Gobi desert to Hami, Kuchengtse and Urumchi, and the caravans took three months over the journey. If motor lorries were used instead the time would be reduced to ten or twelve days, and the Chinese could compete with some prospect of success. That things were developing on these lines was shown by the fact that the merchants at Kwei-hwa-cheng had already formed a company for motor-lorry traffic between their town and Hami. But the first lorries despatched had mostly been wrecked owing to the badness of the tracks. The first thing to be done, therefore, was to lay down one motor road across the Gobi desert and another along the southern Imperial Highway through Kansu.

During my conversations with the Assistant Foreign Minister Liu I never guessed what they would signify to me personally in the immediate future. Only Norin, Bexell and Bökenkamp were still in the field, and when they had returned to Peking, as they soon would, we should all go home and begin to work out the results of our large and long expedition.

But it was written otherwise in the stars ! Mr. Liu went to Nanking at the end of July and laid my memorandum before the Marshal and the Prime Minister. It awakened their interest, and on August 3 I received the following telegram :

" Mr. Wang Ching-wei, president of the Executive Yuan, wishes to meet you at Nanking as soon as possible. Please reply to Liu Chung-chieh."

Then I understood that my destiny was to take quite a new turn, and I dreamed already of the pleasure of being able to do the Chinese Government a service in return for all the hospitality I had received on Chinese soil ever since

1890. I certainly had some experience of Central Asia, and no one could wish more sincerely than I did that this might be of some practical advantage to China. If there was to be a new expedition, I should perhaps have an opportunity of seeing the part of the " Silk Road " I did not yet know, a road which led along the northern shore of the new Lake Lop-nor and the new course of the Tarim which had come into existence in 1921.

I left Peking on the evening of August 5. Summer was at the zenith of its beauty, and warm winds blew over the low country as the train, next day, rushed through the groves of ancient cemeteries to the capital of the republic.

In company with Mr. Liu I visited the Foreign Minister, Dr. Lo Wen-Kan, a man who recoiled from no difficulties and whose attitude towards life and its problems was bright, cheerful and unprejudiced. He told me that since General Hwang Mu-sung's mission had failed he had decided to go to Sinkiang himself to quell the unrest in the lacerated province and make peace between its fighting generals. Dr. Lo told me also that the Government meant to invite me to conduct a motor-car expedition to Sinkiang.

So my intuitions and desires were on the way to fulfilment !

An hour later I sat with the Prime Minister Wang, who confirmed all that I had heard already. To build railways into the interior would be too expensive, he said ; they must content themselves with motor roads to begin with, and these were necessary. But they must be connected with the termini of the already existing railway lines in Northern and Central China. A northern motor road ought to start from Kwei-hwa, a southern road from Sian. The work should begin without delay. The Government had not yet made up its mind, and he himself wished to discuss the matter with experts. I should have an answer in a few days.

Several more conferences were held, and I wrote five new memoranda on various details—routes, distances and other conditions. These were to be analysed by experts and then discussed in the council of Ministers. It soon became clear that I must arm myself with patience. But

I had nothing to complain of. I lived like a prince in C. T. Wang's villa. Mr. Liu often dined with me, and we sat in the garden in front of the villa in the warm night air and the brilliant moonshine, and concocted plans for the strengthening of the bonds between China proper and its largest and most westerly province.

The temperature stood at 102 degrees [1], and the air was sometimes cooled by torrents of rain. The new astronomical observatory on the summit of Purple Hill, 800 feet above the Lotus Lake, was approaching completion. A little farther down the slope Parker C. Chen lived in the magnetic observatory. I had put in a special request that Chen should be allowed to take part in the proposed motor journey through regions he had got to know so thoroughly in Dr. Nils Hörner's company.

In the middle of the month the Foreign Minister Lo informed me that the Government had come to a decision about the motor journey, and I heard from the Ministry of Railways that the following cardinal points had been fixed :

The expedition was to be entirely Chinese and was to be under the orders of the Minister for Railways, Dr. Ku Meng-yü ; the enterprise could not receive official sanction in accordance with the law until he returned from a visit to Peking.

I was to be the leader of the expedition, and was to receive the title of " adviser to the Ministry of Railways ". I had the right to take with me the Swedes I thought necessary, a doctor, a topographer and a couple of mechanics. The expedition might not take more than eight months. The outward journey was to be through the Gobi desert to Hami, the return journey along the ancient Imperial Highway, the so-called Silk Road. We had the right to carry out researches on the new course of the Lower Tarim and the Lop-nor lake that had been newly formed in 1921, and especially to examine the possibility of irrigation and colonization in the country round Lou-lan that had been colonized in ancient times. All the members were to receive personal passports, arms and motor-car passes, and were to be freed from *likin*, or internal customs duties.

[1] Fahrenheit, and in subsequent passages.

The Swedes' pay was to be covered from the subsidy, which was estimated at 50,000 Mexican dollars. The Chinese were to be paid directly by the Government. I was responsible for the purchase of the motor-cars and the rest of the equipment.

Then came a few more clauses. We were to observe complete neutrality in the internal quarrels of Sinkiang and have nothing whatever to do with politics. Even without this instruction we should have understood that interference, or taking sides, in political affairs would be a fatal blow to the whole enterprise. In my earlier book I described how we were compelled against our will apparently to side with Big Horse by the forcible seizure of all our cars, an adventure which all but cost us our lives.[1]

Another point in our instructions was that neither the leader, nor any member of, or employee in the expedition had the right to carry on archæological research in any form. This unfortunate provision, which, as I shall show later, came near ruining the whole enterprise, emanated from the Minister of Education at Nanking. The Government as a whole was absolutely innocent as regards this prohibition, the absurdity of which is best shown by the fact that the ancient Silk Road and the exploration of its course—especially between Tun-hwang and Korla—was archæology pure and simple. My proposal to revive the old Silk Road and turn it into a modern motor road had been approved by the Government. A member of the same Government had, as representative of science in China, forbidden us to pay the least attention to any relics from ancient times by which we could identify the old road, whose traces had been obliterated by the storms of 2,000 years. To achieve the object of the expedition, therefore, we were compelled to violate the archæological clause in some degree, and I took the responsibility for doing so without hesitation.

As the Minister for Railways did not return from Peking I went there and, thanks to his determination, got the whole thing definitely fixed up in an instant. Mr. Sheng Chang, head of the Peking–Suiyuan railway, was empowered to

[1] *The Flight of Big Horse*

pay over the whole subsidy and to discuss the final preparations with us. He informed us of a new supplementary instruction. With a view to future motor traffic, we were to examine one of the following three routes within the province : Urumchi–Kashgar, Urumchi–Kulja or Urumchi–Chuguchak. How this was to be done when the province was ablaze with civil war, rebellion and brigandage, we did not know. Disturbing news of bloody fighting and devastation was arriving from Sinkiang. The Foreign Minister, Lo Wen-kan, who had flown to Hami and gone on to Urumchi, had returned, after encountering great difficulties, via Chuguchak and Novo Sibirsk. Like General Hwang Mu-sung, he had failed as a " peace commissioner," and now it was our turn to penetrate the disturbed province—not to negotiate peace, but to mark out roads. Intelligent people in Peking thought we had one chance in a hundred of success, and that we were about to embark upon a mad enterprise. Some thought that Soviet Russia would look with anything but favour upon an undertaking which aimed at motorizing the old caravan routes between China proper and Sinkiang, and reviving China's dying trade with the province. They thought that the Russians would try to obstruct our expedition in one way or another. In the fullness of time these anxieties proved to be unjustified. The representatives of Russia in Sinkiang showed us the greatest kindness and helped us in many difficulties.

One fine day the engineer Irving C. Yew presented himself at our headquarters, and a little later his colleague, C. C. Kung, both selected by the Government to accompany us on the long journey. The first impression they made on us was good and agreeable, and they justified this promise down to the last day of our companionship. Then Mr. Parker C. Chen from Nanking, Dr. David Hummel from Jämtland, and Georg Söderbom, who came this time from Chicago, appeared at Sweden House, and when the Mongolian drivers and the Chinese servants had been engaged, the personnel of the expedition was complete.

One day we paid a visit to Big Horse's representative in

Peking, Mr. Pai, who gave us a letter to the general and assured us that, as we were in the service of Nanking, he would receive us with all due consideration.

On October 10 we drove to the station at Hsi-chih-men, the north-western gate of Peking. There stood our three lorries and our smart Tudor Sedan, all Fords, loaded on trucks forming part of the train which was to leave for Kwei-hwa-cheng at 3.30 p.m. Georg Söderbom, our trusty servant, the Mongolian driver Dongora, and another young Mongolian driver named Jomcha accompanied the cars, taking with them the petrol supply, provisions and all the rest of the equipment. A good deal of preliminary work was to be done at Kwei-hwa before the whole expedition assembled there.

On the last evening in Peking the Swedish missionaries, our old friends, Herr Joel Eriksson and Herr C. G. Söderbom, Georg's father, came to say good-bye to us and wish success to our journey.

And so another night fell over Peking. One chapter in our story had ended. Next morning a new one would begin, a time full of uncertainty and wild adventures among brutal Asiatics. We were all determined to fight like lions for our honour, and not to return till we had done our utmost to carry out an undertaking which most people considered impossible and hopeless.

A DISASTROUS START

ON the morning of October 21, 1933, Dr. Hummel and I drove between the yellowing trees of the avenues to the Hsi-chih-men station. The members of the motor expedition had assembled among friends who had come to say good-bye. There were Professors Lin Fu, Hsü, Ping-ch'ang and Paul Stevenson, Mr. Boshard, *The Times* correspondent Mr. McDonald, and many others. When the train rolled away to the north-west, most of them thought that they had seen us for the last time.

The city wall of Peking, with its imposing towers, disappeared behind us ; the open country lay around us, grey and dreary, and soon the train was taking us up through the Nankou pass, by the granite masses of the Great Wall, winding in generous curves over the hillside. At dusk we stopped for a short time at Kalgan, and at midnight we made up our fur beds in the unheated waggon which had been placed at our disposal.

I was awakened at six in the morning by eager voices talking Swedish. The door was flung open and a youth got in and shouted a four-fold hurrah, while an elderly lady handed me a cup of boiling hot coffee. The train had stopped at Feng-chen, where the Swedish mission had one of its stations. The fair, blue-eyed youth was Karl Efraim Hill, a missionary's son of twenty, who had received from American experts the highest testimonials as a motor mechanic, but had been prevented by other obligations from accompanying our party. The lady with the coffee cup was Fru Nyström, whom I had met in Ninghsia in 1897.

But the waggon began to jolt on ; our excellent country-men jumped out and began to sing " Du gamla, du fria " on the platform, running alongside the train.

The hours passed; the walls and towers of Kwei-hwa rose to the south-west; the train stopped and was met by a swarm of people, variegated and loud-voiced.

Georg Söderbom's gigantic form appeared outside our carriage window. Hummel hurried up to him, and Georg, in a half whisper, told him something which caused him to exclaim in astonishment: "What, is he dead?"

I had a fearful shock. Bexell and Bökenkamp were still in the field, and we had heard nothing at all from them for a long time. Georg must have had news of the missing men's fate. Had their caravan been destroyed, and one of them killed, the other carried off by robbers? Had some fearful drama been enacted in the desert, and had our great expedition, at the eleventh hour, been besmirched by a deed of blood? I called Georg to my window.

"What has happened?"

"I have to report a terrible accident."

"Bexell!" I thought again. But no, thank God, the fatality that was being reported to me had nothing to do with the earlier scientific expedition, though it cast a cloud over the first day of our new enterprise.

Georg told us what had happened. He knew we were to arrive on the morning of Sunday, October 22, but trains are often late, so he wanted to go to the station and find out what time ours would arrive. The Mongolian driver Dongora and the sheepdog Pao were to accompany him, and the small car was got ready. Dongora was depressed and gloomy, for he had dreamt in the night that he and Georg were driving at full speed towards a broken-down bridge over an abyss, and now he had a premonition that some catastrophe awaited him.

Georg had seated himself at the wheel, with Dongora on his left and the dog Pao in the back seat.

They were driving along a street which leads northward to the station. Where the street runs out into open country, a seldom-used railway track approaches it at right angles, only six feet from the last houses. No traffic constable stood at the end of the street to give a warning. The last house to the right obscures the view in that direction. Georg, therefore, did not notice an engine coming along the track, tender first. Both car and locomotive were going too fast to be able to use their brakes. It was a matter of a fraction of a second, and just in that fraction of a second the two machines crossed each other's tracks. Dongora gave a despairing cry of " Burkhan mini ! " (my God !), flung open the left door and jumped out, followed by Pao.

There was a terrific crash, a fearful blow ! the tender's coupling was driven into the side of the car, and the locomotive pushed the crushed vehicle along before it. The left wheels were forced diagonally across the sleepers, and the axles were bent like steel wires, but the coupling prevented the car from swinging round. Georg should have been crushed already, if guardian angels had not protected him. He sat, squeezed as though in a vice, between seat, wheel, lever and the forced-in door, quite unable to move. Meanwhile the crushed car jumped twenty-five yards over the sleepers before the locomotive stopped.

Tender and bruised, Georg managed to worm himself out of the wreckage. He found to his astonishment that he could walk and stand. He called to Dongora, but received no answer. He found the poor fellow thirteen yards from the point where the collision had taken place, fearfully mutilated and with his forehead crushed. Clearly he had not been able to get clear, but had fallen under the car.

The doctor from the Catholic Mission, who was summoned immediately, had only been able to certify that Dongora's death had been instantaneous. The police wanted to arrest the engine-driver, but when Georg explained that he himself was equally to blame, the law took no steps.

We visited the scene of the disaster, where our splendid driver lay covered with blood under a bass mat. The dead man was later laid in a coffin, which was placed in a temple. His relatives demanded compensation, and we supported their claim vigorously. The Ministry of Railways at Nanking granted us a new car, a Tudor Sedan like the one that had been destroyed.

The strangest part of it all was that Georg was alive.

He had been sitting screwed into the car with a railway engine on his lap. It was his good fortune that he *could* not move. If Dongora had kept calm, or failed to open the door, he would have escaped without a scratch.

We needed a new driver in place of Dongora; so we telegraphed to Hill, bought his release from the post he had already, and took him into our service, where he was a universal favourite from the first day. We never called him either Karl or Efraim, but simply Effe.

We made Georg's house our headquarters at Kwei-hwa. Here the " Suiyuan–Sinkiang motor road expedition " was to be finally organized. The yard was turned into a depot and workshop, where work went on unceasingly. Five white Mongolian tents were made there and lined with felt, and there sat eight Chinese tailors making us sheep-skin sleeping-bags and furs that reached to our feet, also of white sheepskin. In other words, we were equipping ourselves to meet a Central Asiatic winter, with snowstorms and bitter cold.

It was of great importance to send a petrol caravan in advance to the Etsin-gol, as we could not carry with us anything like all the petrol we needed. A supply of 1,260 gallons of petrol in forty-two solid iron plate cylinders was bought and was to be sent on to our first important halting-place, the Etsin-gol, on forty camels hired from the merchant Nogon Deli. The luggage was stacked in our yard so that things which were not needed till we reached the Etsin-gol could be taken on by the camels. All this was loaded on to the lorries and driven by Georg to the monas-tery town of Beli-miao, 100 miles north-west of Kwei-hwa, where Nogon Deli's camels were waiting.

We paid visits to the pleasant governor-general of Suiyuan, General Fu Tso-yi, the Swedish missionaries and the Catholic mission, as well as the Minister of the Interior Hwang Shao-hsiung. The Minister had come up from Nanking to go to Beli-miao, where the Mongol princes had assembled to discuss autonomy for Inner Mongolia.

Everywhere the countries and peoples were disturbed by political unrest. At Paotou lay the robber general Sun Tien-ying, of evil repute since, in 1928, he had plundered

the Eastern Emperors' tombs of treasures of enormous
value. He was now about to move off with his savage
hordes to the Ching-hai (Kuku-nor) region and colonize
the country round about. A little war threatened to break
out between him and the governor of the province of
Ninghsia, who refused to allow Sun's troops passage.
According to current reports marauding soldiers of Sun's
were now and again raiding as far north as the road along
which our convoy was to advance westward.

From Sinkiang too an echo of the current rumours
reached our ears. Young General Ma Chung-yin, called
Big Horse, who was master of Hami and Turfan, was still
engaged in a bloody war with Urumchi. General Fu telegraphed to Ma announcing our approach, and Ma replied
that we were welcome. Perhaps he calculated even then
that our cars might come in handy !

We received the following charming telegram from our
chief, the Minister for Railways Ku Meng-yü :

"Having learned that you are now embarked on your long
and great expedition, I send you my cordial best wishes for
this truly historic and gallant enterprise, and hope you will
fight to the uttermost and achieve a great and unforgettable
success."

He understood that the mission was difficult and dangerous, and that if we succeeded in marking out new motor
roads through the heart of Asia, the enterprise would be
sure of a place in the history of the mighty continent.

War and rebellion everywhere, robbers in every village,
an accident, a death the very first day ! This expedition
was not beginning under friendly stars or cheering auspices.
Georg took a gloomy view of the future, and thought that
Dongora's death was an omen of catastrophe for us all.

But no one hesitated ; and our Chinese comrades, Yew,
Kung and Chen, from the first day to the last, showed in
all crises a courage and resolution which excited our
admiration.

If October 22 had been a day of sorrow for us, the 31st
was a day of rejoicing of the first order. Bergman had come

up from Peking in the morning with the new car. We were sitting in my study in the twilight when Chen came in and said with his usual imperturbable calm :

" Bexell and Bökenkamp have arrived with Georg."

Georg had taken petrol and baggage to Beli-miao on our three lorries. On the return journey he had met the two long-missing men and their caravan, relieved their camels of their loads, which were stowed on board the empty returning lorries, and had hastened down from the mountains to Kwei-hwa with the expedition's lost and recovered sons.

We hurried out into the road outside the gate. There stood two of the lorries containing Bexell's collections, the result of four years' hard work in wild, perilous regions of darkest Asia.

The third car was just coming round the corner. Georg sat at the wheel. The other two jumped out. They looked like highway robbers—bearded, dusty, ragged, but healthy, weather-beaten and browned by the autumn sun of the Gobi desert. They brought with them an atmosphere of the wilderness life that awaited us, and the dust which clung to their soles came, in part at least, from regions where no white man had before set foot.

" Thank Heaven we've got you back alive ! "

They were escorted across the yard in a sort of triumphal procession and were subjected to a cross-fire of questions round the coffee table ! A wonderful meeting ! Such things hardly happen in novels. Our former expedition, which had lasted seven years, had now been woven together into one connected chain in the very town from which we were starting on a new journey, and almost on the eve of our departure. Our anxiety about the last field workers was removed, we need no longer worry about sending a search-party to rescue them ; the gates of innermost Asia stood wide open to give us passage, and the game could begin. On November 1, Norin returned from his search for Ambolt, after having, in Tsaidam, added several fine sheets to his wealth of maps.

I now had around me all the veterans from the spring of 1927 and all the members of the new expedition—once

more a real Swedish headquarters before our departure
on an endless journey.

The Mongol Serat, who had worn the Swedish gold
medal for several years for his loyalty and efficiency, now
re-entered our service to replace the dead Dongora.   On
the way from his home in Inner Mongolia he had been
attacked by robbers and had all his personal belongings
stolen.   He had made his way to Kalgan half-naked and
in an extremely destitute and enfeebled condition.

But time passed quickly, and we had to part again.
The bonds which for some days had linked the two expeditions together were loosed.   At the farewell dinner I
wished them all happiness, both those who were going to
Peking and Sweden and those who, with me, were steering
a course back to the heart of the desert.

On the evening of November 9 the three motor-lorries
stood ready in the road outside the gate.   For the last time
for a long time to come we went to bed in warm rooms.
Next morning we were to roll out along fog-bound roads
and sleep at night in our Mongol tents under the eternal
stars, with the old sad songs of the desert winds in our
ears.

II

THE ROAD TO BELI–MIAO

ON the morning of November 10, Georg, Effe and Serat took their seats in the drivers' cabins of the three heavily loaded trucks, while the small car, driven by Hummel with Yew, Kung and myself as passengers, went last in the convoy. One more handshake for Bexell, Bökenkamp and the good Swedish missionaries, and our cars rolled noisily through the old town, through a dry river-bed and out into the country with its little villages, grey huts of sun-dried brick and patches of field where peasants tilled the soil. We continually met travellers, mounted and on foot, strings of donkeys laden with coal, creaking ox-carts and camel caravans bringing wares from Suchow and the Etsin-gol.

The deep ruts made by the ox-carts spoiled the high road for the cars which ran between Kwei-hwa and Beli-miao (Pei-ling-miao) but as the drivers did not obey the order forbidding them to use it, long holes two feet deep had been made in the road, which the draught animals between the shafts could not get over. They were no obstacle to motor-cars, but Georg was unlucky enough to slip down into one of the holes with his left back wheel.

Off with the load, out with the jacks—two hours' work. The vehicle rose slowly and the hole was filled with stones and rubble. At last the lorry was on an even keel again and could be reloaded. No axle was broken! But we had still 10,000 miles to cover. Would a single one of our cars return intact after such a trial? Here was the village of Pakou-tse, inhabited by 200 families, 90 per cent of them named Kou. A custom-house, a plague to the caravans, did not trouble us. We plugged along in a river-bed, where one narrow channel trickled amid the gravel.

Now the road ran uphill through the pass, which grew ever narrower and steeper. There was a fence along the edge of the road. Here there was a hold-up of traffic, both from China and from Mongolia. A number of carts drawn by oxen or horses, and laden with wheat, were slowly and cautiously trying to creep past one another. Horns sounded ; horses, donkeys or oxen, harnessed in pairs, shied, reared and threatened to leap to their death down the slopes.

From the top of the pass we had a wonderful view over the variegated crowd, amid which the Chinese, with whips and sticks and piercing cries of exhortation, were urging their stubborn beasts onward. A party of mounted soldiers burst through the mob, and along the open road they had made we ran sharply down to the village of Pai-lou-kwan.

The road was horrible. Georg was within a hair's-breadth of overturning his lorry in the partly frozen bed of a stream. The gravel came to an end and the road wound between gently sloping red hills. It was nearly five when we reached the Kuku-irgen brook, where Effe's lorry stuck in the ice. Out and into the water with spades and picks ! Nothing could be done till the lorry had been unloaded. Another two hours lost !

The sun set ; it grew twilight, and then dark. The night came on ; what a pleasant night, the first on the Mongolian plateau !

At midnight we reached a little frozen stream. And now it was Serat's turn. His car went through the ice-crust and, after vain efforts to free himself, he was stuck as fast as in a vice. The rays of the headlights swept blinding white over the ice ; we cut, hacked and dug, the ice-floes were heaved aside, and the silence of the night was disturbed by the orders of our two Swedish mechanics given in Chinese and Mongolian. But the lorry was inexorable. After a trying wait the stillness of the night conquered. Our men had been up long before sunrise, and the first day in the field had been a hard one. They were dead tired, and one after another disappeared into a driver's cabin or on to the top of a load.

Suddenly I woke. The headlights had been extinguished, the blackness of night surrounded me on all sides ; there was dead silence. The reveille was sounded. The men set to work with renewed strength, and at last the car was got over. We went on through the night till 2 a.m., when Serat finally stuck fast in the little river Chao-ho, and we pitched our first camp. " Dinner " was served between four and five in 20 degrees of frost. There was a glimmer of dawn in the east before we began our first night in the tents and sleeping-bags—with a silent prayer that the winter nights to come might not be like this one.

We did not rise early next day ! In an indolent mood we inspected the Chiri-gegene-sume temple, an old fortification close to the camp, and a few Chinese patrols, whose duty it was to protect the caravans against robbers. We were only nine miles from Bagha-nor, where the Altai Torgut Arash had settled with his family and a brother who was a medicine man. When at last we started the sun was not far below the horizon, and a magnificent fiery-red reflection gilded the dreary steppe.

Arash had his *yurt* pitched inside a square wall, and there we were courteously received. We were invited to sit down on rough mats round the fire. Tea, cheese, cream cakes and sugar were served on low stools. The eternal Buddha sat over an altar by the wall and, shining like gold, dreamed in the dim firelight.

Meanwhile, our tents were being pitched outside the wall, and our cook, Chia Kwei, who had learned to make rissoles and fry pancakes at a Swedish missionary station, served our dinner in the tent which I shared with the doctor and Bergman.

We stayed with Arash three whole days. The loss of time did not trouble us, as we had heard that our petrol convoy, which was to go ahead of us to the Etsin-gol, had stopped 100 li (30 miles) from Beli-miao, because some of the petrol drums were leaking. The men dared not proceed, but sent a messenger to us and awaited orders.

While we were resting the whole of the baggage was rearranged and reloaded. Our intention was that only one lorry should be needed at each camping-ground and that the other two need not be touched. Our daily provisions, the kitchen, tents and beds were loaded on to the same lorry. One tent was scrapped when we found that we could get on with four. Our three Chinese comrades had one ; another was occupied by Georg, Effe, Serat and Jomcha, who were permanently responsible for looking after the cars ; a third by Chia Kwei with the kitchen, and the attendants San Wa-tse and Li ; and Hummel, Bergman and I had the fourth. We had our meals in this tent. So there were eight of us masters and five servants.

We had driven as far as Bagha-nor with single tyres, but during our rest double tyres were put on to the back wheels of the three lorries, which made travelling over soft ground much easier. Spare tyres and beds were wired on to the outside of the cars so as not to encroach upon our space, which was largely occupied by petrol drums and provision boxes.

The time passed quickly. Everyone was busy. The doctor put in plaster one of Georg's big toes, which had been crushed by a falling petrol drum, and Effe's right hand, which had been torn by a nail while he was loading up. Parker Chen took our bearings and carried out the meteorological observations. Bergman and the two engineers worked on the map of the new motor road. I read and made notes.

Bagha-nor is situated in the district of Shiret-shabi and is under Tumet and Turnet-gun. The most powerful man in the neighbourhood is one Erikchen Fu-kwan.

One evening after sunset, eleven of our camels, which Arash had been taking care of for some years, came into the camp. The dark silhouettes against the still light background in the west were a splendid sight. They had all been branded with an " H " on the left cheek while in our service ; but in the course of the six years the mark had disappeared in every case but one, in which it could still be faintly distinguished. This veteran had also been to Lop-nor with Hörner and Chen. He must have recognized us, for he left his comrades, strode up to us with majestic gait and head erect, and stretched out his beautiful rough head as in the old days, for bread. We understood what he wanted ; a big roll was tossed into his dribbling mouth. It was like meeting an old friend and comrade from a time rich in memories.

On the night of November 14–15 the temperature was minus 4 degrees. Winter was coming on. We were called and had breakfast early ; the fires were put out, the tents struck and rolled up, with the sleeping-bags. Everything was ready. We took leave of Arash and buzzed off across a gently undulating steppe past the little soda lake Ulan-nor. A herd of wild horses followed us for a time at full gallop, crossed the road with clattering hooves and were left behind. Now and again we met ox-carts and riders. Here was an opium caravan of, I suppose, a hundred camels, striding along to the rhythmic beat of its copper bells. Then another, twice as big. They were coming from Liangchow and were escorted by soldiers to protect the valuable smuggled goods.

We reached the frozen Targan-gol, and followed its course the whole way to Beli-miao. The cultivation by Chinese colonists ends here, and the wild undulating plains of Inner Mongolia extend to the mountains on the north-western horizon. Here was an old ruined wall some 6 feet high, but rounded and smoothed by time, with ruined towers every 500 yards.

In a depression in front of us we at last sighted the goal of our day's march, the end of the first stage of our journey, the great holy city of Beli-miao.

We drove on to the hard level space outside the temple gates, where the Tashi Lama's Tibetan, Mongolian and Chinese escort was being drilled. A swarm of people surrounded us as soon as we stopped. Among bare-headed lamas in red cloaks, officers and soldiers we saw a distinguished little group of Westerners—" Duke " Larson as conductor, Mr. and Mrs. Oliver (Reuter) and M. Bécherat (Agence Havas). They had come to Beli-miao to get news of the Mongolian princes' negotiations about Inner Mongolia's independence with the Chinese Minister of the Interior.

The Tashi Lama himself was now living in the holy city. His object was to work for a peaceful solution. Another

old friend of ours, Dilowa Gegen, a " living Buddha " from
Urga, turned up in the crowd.

We pitched our tents a mile or so from the monastery,
near the spot where we had encamped at the beginning of
November, 1929, and had said good-bye to Hörner and
Chen, Bergman, Bohlin and Bexell. In the evening we
had a splendid feast in my tent—pea soup, rissoles, coffee
and photographing for fourteen. Two of these were very
charming ladies—Mrs. Oliver, a Russian, and Miss Mary
Fordham, a Mongolian, from the Ghashatu mission station.

Next day, while Georg and Serat had gone to our caravan to repair the leaky petrol drums, Hummel, Bergman,
Larson and I drove to the holy city and filed into the temple
enclosure, where Barun Sunit Wang had pitched his large,
gaily coloured felt *yurt*. This potentate, whom the Chinese
call Teh Wang, was the Mongols' vigorous spokesman in
the independence question. He was a strongly built man
of distinguished appearance, and championed with force
and authority the independence, freedom and honour of
Genghis Khan's blue-blooded race.

We were conducted by an adjutant into the reception
yurt and sat down on the mats round the wooden curb of
the fireplace. In a moment Barun Sunit Wang entered,
dressed in a dark blue fur-trimmed robe and wearing a little
cap. He knew us well ; we had been his guests in his
stately palace at Sunit Wang ; and he stretched out his
hands to us in greeting.

After the usual questions about our journey, he spoke in
considerable detail of the Mongols' demand for independence, and tried to prove that such an arrangement would
be to the advantage both of China and of Mongolia.
Larson had been his and the other Mongolian princes'
adviser, and endeavoured to bring the negotiations to a
peaceful solution. The agreements and decisions which
were reached were short-lived. The Japanese were already
in Jehol and were threatening Chahar. A year and a half
later they were to bring Tientsin, Peking and Kalgan under
their control, and so the links that had joined Mongolia
and China for many centuries were broken, for who knows
how long ? But rather more than two years after our

meeting, at the end of January, 1936, we read a telegram from Peking saying that Sunit Wang had declared Inner Mongolia an independent state and was expected to have himself proclaimed emperor.

Sunit Wang asked us about our plans in Sinkiang and what routes we meant to take. He did not seem particularly interested in these questions. Possibly he thought that " as the shortest and best route to Hami starts from Kwei-hwa, and touches Beli-miao, we Mongols will in any case dictate the conditions on which trade is carried on ".

Later in the day we were received by the Tashi Lama in the finest of all the monasteries. We were met in an anteroom by a lama, who offered us tea and after a while led us to the audience chamber. His Holiness came towards us with his charming friendly smile and held out both hands to us. We were invited to sit down on rug-covered benches, and the conversation turned on Asiatic geography, the politics of Europe and its last remaining kings, Dr. Hummel's journey to Tebbu and mine to Tashi-lunpo twenty-six years before. He smiled when I showed him the golden ring he gave me in Peking in 1926, which would certainly bring the expedition luck on its new trip.

I had no other gifts to offer him but the Chinese editions of, *Åter till Asien* and *Mitt liv som upptäcktsresande*.[1] He presented us with three pretty little agate bottles of the kind which the Mongols use as snuff-boxes. Of greater value were his latest portrait, with a dedication in Chinese and the high priest's red stamp, and a letter to the ruler of the Kara-shahr Torguts.

About a month after our visit to the Tashi Lama the Dalai Lama died at Lhasa, after having on various occasions played an important part in Tibet's relations to China, Russia and British India. It was this dignitary's inexorable hostility that had compelled the Tashi Lama, in 1924, to flee from Tashi-lunpo to Peking and Inner Mongolia. After the Dalai Lama's death his prospects grew brighter, and the last we heard of him in Kansu, in 1935, was that he was at Alakshan, on the way to his and his gods' holy land.[2]

[1] *Back to Asia* and *My Life as an Explorer*.
[2] The Tashi Lama died at the beginning of December, 1937.

III

START FOR THE GOBI

THE last evening at Beli-miao, Barun Sunit Wang and
the wang from Jun Sunit honoured us with return
calls, and at a later hour we were the Tashi Lama's guests
in a circle of high lamas and Mongolian and Tibetan officers.

At night the sound of bells was heard, faint and hard to
distinguish in the distance. Slowly it grew clearer, and its
rhythm betrayed the measured step of camels. It came
nearer and nearer, and when the first bell passed our tent
its sound was loud and piercing. The others followed in
due order, and finally we heard the last sound produced by
the tongue of the last bell of the last camel in the caravan.
I listened, moved by these old familiar bells, the special
melody of the caravan routes for a thousand years past,
around which the whole desert life of traveller, driver,
merchant unfolds its varied and fascinating pictures. It
was long before the sound of the bells had died away and
faded into the night.

On the morning of November 18 the lorries stood ready,
loaded with forty-two drums of petrol each containing
thirty gallons. The start was delayed by Georg having
driven into the holy city to pay for our purchases of flour,
camels' dung and a more portable range than that which
Chia Kwei had brought from Kwei-hwa.

In the cold that prevailed the motors had to be warmed
by braziers placed under them. I was a little uneasy about
the danger of fire, but soon grew accustomed to the daily
procedure.

When all was ready, the three lorries went off first, at a
proper distance from one another on account of the dust.
I came last in the small car. My driver was Dr. Hummel,
my fellow-passengers Yew and Bergman. Bergman, with

the compass on its tripod, was taking bearings on the last lorry. When our map-makers had got into the routine, their work went fairly quickly. The objectives were marked by small red flags, which were stuck into the ground and pulled up again. Bergman worked with the two engineers and Chen.

Beli-miao disappeared behind us, and the desert began. We followed the edge of a precipitous ravine. Our road crossed several minor gullies almost like cañons. At one of them the brake of the small car refused to work and we plunged down into the gully, but luckily did not upset. The spades were at work for half an hour before we got up on to the road again.

Here and there we passed a well, by which caravans of nomads were encamped. At one of them a detachment of Mongolian soldiers was posted, and here we crossed the frontier, between Darkhan-bel and Mingan-jassak.

The grass formed yellow strips on the dark soil. Cairns crowned some of the more conspicuous hills. They are called *obos*. One of them is named Bayin-bogdo, or " the rich god ". Another, Khara-obo, or " black cairn ", stood on one of the sombre hills around our headquarters— camp no. 8—of the spring and summer of 1927. This region so rich in memories, Hujertu-gol, was visible some way off to the south.

Around us and ahead of us to westward lay the Mongolian high plateau, as boundless as the sea. The road was good and hard, the grass scanty ; large herds of antelopes bounded gracefully past.

The hours of the day passed quickly. Mapping the road itself, and the main features of the country on each side of it, took some time. Bergman took bearings now ahead, now to the rear, using the cars as a mark. The small car was as hot as a greenhouse, especially for the passenger on the sunny side. Now there was a puncture ! Effe had to change a tyre. Meanwhile, the twilight was spreading its wings over the silent land. We went on working with the help of headlights and electric torches.

When we approached the day's camping-ground, Ikhe-nor, " Great Lake ", Georg and Serat had got the tents up already. In my airy dwelling the stove was lighted, and a lamp illuminated the interior. We had no beds ; sleeping-bags were spread out on the ground, with only a piece of canvas between ; and we lay down with crossed legs in our respective sleeping-places. The cars were placed to windward on account of the danger of fire.

While we were sitting writing up our diaries and waiting for dinner, a small snowstorm blew over the plateau. The tent-cloth flapped and banged, the poles creaked, the lamp swung to and fro, and the whirling snowflakes pattered against the tent. Large tarpaulins were spread over the cars and wired fast. In the evening the whole countryside was white and winter-like.

The night was cold (— 13 degrees), but by morning the thin layer of snow had for the most part evaporated and the sun shone brilliantly from a flawless blue sky. We were approaching a district with a bad reputation. To southward, on the other side of the Lang-shan mountains, the robber general Sun had his army quartered in the country between Paotou and Wu-yüan, along the loop of the Hwang-ho, and the Mongols of Darkhan-bel and Min-gan had a painful experience of marauding bands. These savage customers were fond of accosting travellers in the Yang-chang-tse-kou valley, through which we were to pass in the course of the day. In China it is not always so easy to distinguish between soldiers and robbers. If the former are dissatisfied with the scanty pay they receive, they often prefer to desert with rifle, pistol and ammunition and live in luxury by robbery and plunder. And just as often whole robber bands take service with some enterprising general who is prosecuting his own ambitious aims.

The orders of the day for November 19, therefore, were that all firearms should be held in readiness, and cartridge-belts were dealt out to our marksmen.

When we reached Ikhe-nor we had covered a fifth of the whole distance to the Etsin-gol, which is rather more than 600 miles. So we ought to be at our old desert river about December 4. But several circumstances were against us. It took some time to get the formation of the convoy, and the daily routine, to run quite smoothly. The map-making work occupied much time; the roads were bad, and got worse and worse the farther westward we pushed forward. There were, moreover, the unforeseen hindrances and delays which upset all calculations. For the first four days everything had gone pretty well, but the fifth, which had looked so promising with its brilliant sunshine, crushed our hopes.

It took some time to thaw the oil in the motors, which had frozen as hard as stone during the night, and the sun was high when Georg and Serat rolled off from Ikhe-nor with their two motor-lorries. The map-making cars followed a little later.

The caravan road, hard and level, led us between scattered tufts of vegetation on earth mounds or low hillocks as far as Chendamen. Here Georg had surprised a flock of sheep and its shepherds; he had bought two sheep from the latter for five silver dollars and had already slaughtered them. The shepherds were allowed to keep the skins.

Old graves, marked by stones laid so as to form rectangles, probably date from the time of the Huns or Turks.

In the valley of the Honin-chaghan-chölla-gol there was a little stream, partly frozen, on whose banks we had encamped in 1927, and by which some Chinese settlers had now established themselves. From the westward came a caravan of 593 camels, striding with slow, dignified gait and bearing three flags, on which were the names of the trading firms to which the goods belonged. The camels were carrying bales of wool to Kwei-hwa and the coast.

We crossed yet another small river, the Liu-tao-kou. It curves to the westward towards the Hwang-ho, whose western watershed (5,200 feet) we had left behind us.

Crossing broken country, between small mountain ridges and boulders, we reached the Yang-chang-tse-kou valley and a stream frozen hard. We could see Georg's and Serat's lorries in front of us, black silhouettes against the setting sun. Georg reached the bank of the stream and went straight ahead. The front wheels were nearly over when the back wheels broke through the ice-crust and the lorry was stuck fast in the broken ice. We all jumped out and attacked the ice with picks and spades. The doctor tried another place, where the river was wider. He drove me across the ice at full speed in the small car and returned just as easily to the eastern bank, where Effe and Serat were waiting with their lorries.

Now the drivers held a council of war, and it was decided that Effe should cross the river at the place we had just tested, and then tow Georg's lorry out of the ice. Effe stepped on the gas for all he was worth ; but his car was too heavily loaded, the left back wheel cut through the ice and sank to the bed of the stream, while the left corner of the chassis struck the ice violently. So we had two cars in the river. Both were unloaded, and the baggage was carried to the left bank, where we were waiting. The twilight came creeping on, and the lamps were lit. The tents were pitched. Our hopes of getting past one of the most ill-famed robber districts during the night had been destroyed.

We were short of fuel. The doctor took the small car and went to a new Chinese settlement, Ulan-hutuk, where only a few poor families lived—sick, miserable and lonely. When he had bandaged up a few poor wretches he returned with three sacks of camels' dung, and the fires were lighted.

Meanwhile Georg's car had got free and towed out Effe's, which on closer investigation was found to be seriously damaged ; the back axle-box had been smashed. At dinner in my tent gloom and depression prevailed.

What was to be done ? Another council of war was held, till far into the night. Our first decision was that a night guard should be set, with reliefs every two hours. It was clear that we were tied fast in robberland, by the Yang-chang-tse-kou, for some time to come.

When the whole back part of the lorry had been dismantled, the unlucky car rested on a few large drums of petrol. The whole of the next day was spent in a thorough examination of the wreck, and the end of the story was that Georg, with Jomcha and the small car, was ordered to return to Peking and Tientsin, via Beli-miao and Kwei-hwa, to buy a new back axle-box and a new motor-lorry. Jomcha was to return from Kwei-hwa with the small car to the wreck, where we were remaining for the time being. Georg was to try to reach us as quickly as possible with the newly purchased motor-lorry and a quantity of other things. To shorten the time of separation, we would proceed slowly westward.

It was not the first time during this rash road-finding expedition that we had needed angelic patience, and, Heaven knows, not the last! Instead of being united at full strength in that dangerous region, we were split up right at the start. And we had to kick our heels for five days at that place of all others.

On the morning of November 21 Georg and Jomcha drove off eastward. The latter ought to have been back the same evening. But the whole day passed, and two days more, without anything being heard of him. He had a passport, of course, but such things are no help against robbers. We had reason to be anxious about the solitary Mongol. Serat tried to read his fate in the shoulder-blade of a sheep, which is put on the fire, dried, and breaks up into irregular cracks. A lengthways crack did not reach the neck of the shoulder-blade, so Jomcha had got no farther than Beli-miao! The oracle was wrong. Jomcha took three days, not two, as Serat had predicted. But at last he came, having left Georg at Kwei-hwa to go on by train to Tientsin. We could have started then if Bergman had not fallen ill, with a fairly high temperature, and been ordered a few days' rest. Yew was on the sick list too; he had broken his nose when Effe's car stuck in the ice, and the camp was transformed into a hospital.

The petrol caravan passed our tents the same day. Twenty-three camels were loaded with five-gallon tins, five on each side, hanging side by side and wired fast together. So we had 1,150 gallons *en route* for the Etsin-gol. Fourteen other camels carried the men's equipment and some of our provisions.

Not till November 25 did the doctor allow the two patients to start, and then the diminished column moved westward again. Jomcha and Chokdung, a Mongol whom we had engaged at Arash's, were left behind on the Yang-chang-tse-kou. They had a tent and provisions, and were to keep guard over twenty-six large drums containing 780

gallons of petrol. Our two lorries each carried six large
and twenty-five small petrol drums, or 610 gallons in all.

The road led down through " the winding valley ", and
we kept on crossing streams, now frozen, now open water.
The valley widened out between low hills, but its river
dried up in the sand before it could reach the Hwang-ho.
The country grew open ; on the undulating plain we drove
past a grave with high tombstones. The jagged ridge of
the Lang-shan stood out clearly to the south. Now and
then we saw the whitened skeleton of a dead camel.
Wolves are common in those parts. The ground was
black with lava. A lively herd of wild horses flew over
the gravel, trying to keep pace with us.

We were not yet in the real desert ; this region was
inhabited. We sighted a couple of small lama temples at
some distance. Sometimes we met mounted Mongols, on
camels or horses. We saw large herds of antelopes,
fascinating to watch.

After a time we drove past the petrol caravan. The
camels grew rather nervous, but did not lose their self-
control. Two vultures sat on a hill-top waiting for
camel's meat.

Our camp for that day was pitched on the left bank of
the Haileotai-gol, where the petrol caravan overtook us in
the evening and helped us carry over a large part of the
luggage, so as to make it easier for the lorries to cross the
river.

We had come to lower regions. Here we were only
5,000 feet above sea-level. The temperature had risen ;
at night it was only 13·8 degrees. We had porridge, pancakes and cocoa for breakfast. And when that was stowed
away, we got the small car and drove across the bed of the
river, some 200 yards wide and divided into three arms,
only one of which was not frozen. We proceeded along
a soft, rather uncomfortable road. Where camels' dung
was plentiful, Serat stopped and collected a few sacksful
for the camp-fires that evening.

We stopped for the night by the Hongorin-gol (" River
of Love ") where there is a large cairn. Just above our
camp numbers of gazelles (*Gazella subgutturosa*) came to the

river to drink. Bergman hit one of them, which disappeared among the scrubby grass of the steppe. It was not easy to follow the creature's flight in the thickening dusk. But our new Mongolian dog, Pelle, followed the gazelle up. When we reached it it was lying on the ground screaming with pain, but Effe's knife put an end to its sufferings.

IV

TIME OF WAITING

A NOTHER cold night; — 10·7 degrees. It was bitterly cold when we got up by lamplight an hour before sunrise on November 27, for our stock of camels' dung had run out. The sky was clear and dawn was breaking. To westward the shadow of the earth formed a dark blue crescent above the horizon. It sank and disappeared into infinity when the sun rose and gave the desert colour and outline. I opened the flaps in the tent-cloth so that the sun might shine in, but it gave no warmth. It is a chilly business, crawling out of a sleeping-bag and putting on one's clothes, when one has no crackling fire to dress by of a winter morning.

But the cars were in worse plight, with no fuel to warm up the frozen motors. One lorry got going at last, and towed the other till it could look after itself.

Pelle had fallen in love with a bitch belonging to a Mongolian camp close by, and had vanished with his lady-love. Just as we were ready to start, the bitch came to look for something eatable round the dying fire, and hard on her heels appeared he who had courted her by the " river of love ". But he was put on a lead and relegated to his place in the small car, and so there was an end to that love story.

A grassy plain lay round about us. We drove over a few frozen tributaries and a gully of alluvial deposit with a gravel and sand bottom. A number of caravan routes cross hereabouts. Several are local only, and run to small temples. Here and there, too, were Chinese merchants' shops, in felt *yurts* or tents. We saw nomad *yurts* very seldom; they existed, but mostly among the low hills to either side of the road.

At Ghashatu, where we encamped, were eight large canvas-covered piles of goods bound from Kwei-hwa to Hami, which had been dumped there hardly a year earlier, when the rebellions in Sinkiang made all trade impossible. We found in the place a Chinese trading house and three curious dwellings, half *yurts*, half stone walls. A Mongolian military post, in charge of Dondur-gun's interests, was quartered within four clay walls. A custom-house fleeced the caravans with *likin*, or inland dues. But immediately after us there arrived a supervisor sent from Nanking, whose duty was said to be to abolish the custom-houses at Ghashatu and other places.

We went on towards the interior of the continent along a bumpy, winding road. Here and there long grass grew, but soon the country grew broken and barren. We were fairly high up again, 5,660 feet. Antelopes grazed by the wayside, or displayed their slender silhouettes on the hill-tops. They had a curious inclination, when in flight, to cross the road just in front of the swiftly moving cars.

After crossing a shallow little pass with a cairn on the summit, we left to the south of our track the road we had followed in the summer of 1927 to the narrow Morguchik valley, whose dark hills were visible some way off to the southward. The same route, the so-called " winding road ", was taken in 1926 by Owen Lattimore, who has published an excellent description of his journey.[1] The road we were following was the same as that used by Sir Francis Younghusband in 1889. Another road, which runs rather far north, is never used nowadays, because it goes for part of the way through republican or Outer Mongolia.

The scenery was desolate and monotonous. Blue-grey clouds were piling themselves up in the west, and there was a fresh breeze. The wind swept through the scanty tufts of steppe vegetation, and miniature sand dunes were created on their lee side.

Our tents were pitched once more by the streamlet Unien-ussu, " Cow's Water ". Immediately after us a strange car arrived, carrying eleven men and one woman.

[1] *The Desert Road to Turkistan.*

They had neither tents nor provisions with them, and had no idea of the way to their destination, Ninghsia. They spent the nights with merchants or nomads and got along by asking their way. They had started from Kwei-hwa and were to travel via Wang-ye-fu, in Alakshan. The car had been bought at Tientsin for Ma Hung-p'ing, who was in charge of the defence against Sun and his troops, while his cousin, Ma Hung-kwei, was civil governor of the province of Ninghsia. He was the adopted son of the well-known Ma Fu-hsiang. At present Ma Pu-fang is governor of the province of Ching-hai or Kuku-nor, with his seat of government at Sining. The Mas belong to the same family. They are Tungans and followers of Islam. Ma means Mohammed, but also horse. "The five Big Horses" is a current phrase. We were to become pretty intimately acquainted, a few months later, with yet another Ma of the same family—Big Horse.

A caravan arrived at the Unien-ussu the same evening as ourselves. It consisted of 32 camels, and was carrying skins and hides from the Etsin-gol to Paotou. At the Haileotai-gol the caravan was to meet a man from Paotou, who would say whether there was any possibility of travelling to that place, where General Sun lay with his army of robbers. If there was none, the caravan was to proceed to Kwei-hwa, sell its load and buy cooking-pots, saucepans, cans, and other iron and bronze goods, and then return to the Etsin-gol. The owners of the caravan were two merchants, who made this journey twice a year. They cheered us with the information that seven days' marches west of the Etsin-gol the region began where robber bands from Outer Mongolia lay in wait for travellers, and that these occurred the whole way to Hami.

We decided that a day of rest was necessary. Bergman felt ill again, one or two of our servants had headaches and temperatures, and the cars had to be greased and examined.

The temperature was rising again—13·1 degrees on the night of November 29. Charles XII's Day was overcast in the morning, but cleared up later.

I began to work up my notes. Hummel had turned the small car into a pleasant study, sunny, warm and comfortable. In front of me I could see our tents, behind me our petrol convoy with its cargo ready for unloading. We hoisted our flags on Charles XII's Day.

On December 1 there was a brilliant turquoise sky; 21·2 degrees at night was an abnormally high temperature for the time of year. Bergman was confined to his sleeping-bag—jaundice can be a long business. We had come up against pretty serious difficulties right at the start, but patience! things would improve with time.

The four caravan men who were to have carried our petrol to the Etsin-gol in twenty days were ordered to encamp at Wayin-torei and await our arrival there. We were sure we should not see them again till we reached the Etsin-gol.

A party of Torgut pilgrims we had met at Beli-miao arrived at our camp on their 53 camels. There were twenty of them—men in blue and red fur coats, a picturesque sight in their gaily coloured dresses. A lively, weather-browned lad who was with them came up to the car in which I sat writing, got in with perfect assurance, sat down on the front seat and remained there till his father came and called him to start. And so that party too disappeared over the hills to westward.

The doctor borrowed a large felt *yurt* from our neighbours, a couple of Chinese merchants, and this was fixed up as a hospital for Bergman.

On the night of December 2 the temperature was as high as 23·2 degrees. We wondered and guessed what Georg was doing. Where was he now, and when would he come back? The full moon shone gloriously over the silent steppe. Not a sound was heard, no caravans passed, no news came from east and west. The first Sunday in Advent dawned bright and clear, with only light white clouds hovering above the horizon.

Effe drove Chen to our old road of 1927, to the southward, to connect up with Norin's triangulations. The car was soon back, but Chen preferred to walk and sketch.

Serat consulted a sheep's shoulder-blade and prophesied that Georg would return on December 16. It was a fortnight now since he had left us. A prolonged period of waiting and uncertainty generally has a demoralizing effect, but no disagreeable symptoms were to be noticed in our party. This was to be attributed in no small degree to the unruffled placidity in all weathers of our three Chinese friends, Chen, Yew and Kung. They were philosophers and optimists, and found it quite natural that a motor-trip into the heart of Asia should have troubles of different kinds at the outset.

Effe bought and slaughtered three sheep, and he and Serat shot the same number of antelopes. We had thus plenty of meat, and were independent of nomads for our journey westward.

One day was spent in turning out our tents. The sleeping-bags were taken out, hung on ropes drawn from lorry to lorry, and thoroughly beaten, likewise the blankets and pillows. We reoccupied our dwellings with a sensation of comfort after the airing they had had.

On the evening of the 4th, in a dead calm, white snow-flakes were dancing round the tents. Were we to be snowed-up, and would Georg be caught in drifts? We had made no use of the fine days of early winter and the clear moonlight nights. And now the winter snow was coming too. Patience! We *must* get on. It was a point of honour that we should make a good job, for the Chinese Government's sake, of what we had undertaken.

All night the snowflakes fell against the tent-cloths like little parachutes, and their sound was hardly discernible— a faint uninterrupted hissing. The cloth was gradually weighed down by the snow; all holes by which air could enter were stopped, and it grew warmer than usual inside. It was still snowing next morning, but towards midday the sun broke through, and the snow that covered everything swiftly diminished.

The doctor, who was also an extremely accomplished cook, prepared a dish of ribs for dinner. When we left Peking we had forgotten to bring playing-cards with us, but Yew's skilful hands made a couple of packs from my visiting-cards, originally intended for quite other purposes. In China one must leave cards on every custom-house, every military post—not to speak of more exalted people in Sinkiang. But luckily I had a considerable supply ; and I therefore gladly sacrificed my cards to the bridge-lovers in our party. They began the fight at once, and went on till 1.30 a.m. in Bergman's warm *yurt*.

Late that night I was awakened by a violent south-westerly storm, which threatened to blow the tents over. The men were mobilized, and all the tent-pegs were driven more firmly into the frozen ground with hammers. Petrol drums were rolled along to weigh down all the folds and make our airy dwellings more capable of resisting the storm. The wind howled and whined, tore and tugged ; tent-cloths banged and flapped, animated talk and exhortations were heard. But soon things grew quiet again, and only the wind's lament disturbed the silence of the night.

In the morning the weather was cold and unpleasant, overcast and dark, and we were reluctant to creep out of our warm sleeping-bags. I called Effe and told him to move the cars to windward, or else the sparks from our morning fires might set the petrol alight.

When that had been done we could light our fires with an easy mind, get up, dress and go to breakfast in the "hospital". When the doctor was making my bed in the evening, a jerboa sprang out of it. These pretty little rodents, which had been disturbed in their winter sleep, appeared in the other tents too, and in the *yurt*. Presumably the warmth from our fires had made them think it was spring again, and that this winter had been unusually short.

At daybreak on the 7th Effe and Serat drove with one empty lorry to the camp by the Yang-chang-tse-kou, where Jomcha and Chokdung were waiting for Georg by the wrecked car. They had orders to stay with their comrades for three days and then return to us with a full load of petrol. The idea was simply to make Georg's load lighter for a few days.

A caravan of twelve camels came marching up from the Etsin-gol, bound for Paotou. We entrusted our letters to its Chinese drivers, to be handed over to the post office at Paotou. Our Christmas letters had gone earlier to reach home in time. There, in the boundless deserts of the interior, eastward-bound caravans were the only possibility one had of conveying news to the outside world.

On the evening of the 11th a car's headlights gleamed through the darkness like a wild beast's eyes—Effe and Serat, returning with sixteen large petrol drums. They had found the two Mongols by the wrecked car, rather depressed and impatient after their long wait.

The same evening a cheerful, melodious sound of bells from the westward heralded the arrival of a new caravan. Kung had been appointed postmaster, and urged everyone to have his letters ready in time, as the caravan would continue its march to Paotou next morning.

It consisted of 169 camels, laden with wool, twenty-five men, and a merchant, who had his wife and children with him. They had started from Anhsi two months earlier and taken a desert track by the southern foot of the Pei-shan to Bayin-bogdo on the Etsin-gol. They had found that river unfrozen and running in one channel, three or four feet deep and hard for camels to cross. They had marched on to Mao-mu, followed the Etsin-gol and crossed the deserts to the Unien-ussu. At two places they had had to pay 1,300 silver dollars in inland customs duties, and they had another of these blood-sucking stations to pass before they reached Paotou. They could buy wool in Anhsi for 4 dollars per 100 gin and sell it at Paotou for 21 dollars. This trip was done twice a year, and would have been highly profitable but for the crushing customs duties.

The melodious caravan had a cook, who, after they had pitched camp, made excellent macaroni soup with minced meat for the whole party. According to old caravan custom, he enjoyed certain privileges in his travelling company ; the right, for example, to have his personal belongings and all his stores and water-pots carried by the first string of camels, so that he could prepare meals while the others were unloading the camels and pitching their tents. He was also allowed to keep the skins of all the sheep that were slaughtered on the journey.

The merchants told us that all was quiet in Anhsi, an oasis which was under the control of General Ma Pu-fang, like Suchow and Kanchow on the " Imperial Highway " or " Silk Road ".   Ma Pu-fang had now blocked the roads from Kansu to Sinkiang.

The invader, General Ma Chung-yin—Big Horse—had, they heard, established his headquarters at Turfan and had still 3,000 men at his disposal.   He had a small garrison at Hami.   They strongly dissuaded us from going to Hami if we had not unimpeachable passports from Ma Chung-yin himself.   They warned us, too, against the mountainous regions west of the Etsin-gol, which were infested with Turki and Kirgisian robber bands.   But perhaps the robbers would not dare to attack us.

We discussed the possibility of taking the road via Mao-mu.   But it was still too early to take any decision. We were sure to get more reliable information farther on. The news that interested us most was that of a desert road from Anhsi to Mao-mu along the southern foot of the Pei-shan.

But now we had had more than enough of the Unien-ussu !   In spite of the spring-like breezes which blew over our tents by day, Serat assured us that the Unien-ussu had a bad reputation for cold in winter and its quantities of snow, in which respect it surpassed all other districts on the caravan routes through this part of Mongolia.   This was confirmed by Bergman, who had twice before seen heavy falls of snow in those parts.

Bergman was now so far recovered as to be able to stand a journey by car to the Etsin-gol, and on December 13 orders were given that everything should be ready for a start next morning.   Then a new stage of our journey would begin, and a fresh step would be taken towards the frontier of the great province of Sinkiang, the land of our dreams, where an unknown fate awaited us.

V

GEORG'S RETURN

THE shadow of the earth raised its dark blue crescent in the west, with a reflection of the sunrise on its upper edge and above this the sky, pale blue and crystal clear, when we emerged from our tents on December 14.

We had a light breakfast while the tents and their contents were being packed and stowed away on top of the loads. We went aboard, and the convoy rolled off in a south-south-westerly direction from the northern road to the southern, the continuation of our road from Morguchik. It was only 9½ miles to the southern road.

We drove between low granite hills. To the right we saw a row of some thirty stones, 50 yards long. Bergman connected them with a story he had heard, which came from one of the old travellers who had visited the court of the Great Khan, that the Turks erected such rows of stones to indicate how many enemies had been killed in a battle. They are not uncommon in Eastern Mongolia.

The road was tiring on account of the knolls and tussocks over which the cars bumped. A herd of wild horses were grazing peacefully among the antelopes, but made off as quickly as the latter when the cars came buzzing along. The mountains to southward were a part of the Lang-shan. Dried-up watercourses run from them in a north-westerly direction. The beds of these are soft and sandy, and probably more difficult to cross in summer. It often took us nearly an hour to cover three miles.

When we had reached the southern road we met two pilgrims of the Khalkha tribe, a man and a woman, resting by the wayside. They had neither draught animals nor mounts, but were going on foot, and we were astonished

46

at the loads they bore. A baby, well wrapped in furs, lay swathed in a kind of bag, while other bundles contained a tiny tent, clothes and provisions. They carried travellers' staves in their hands.

We had now made our way to Lao-hu-kou, the "Tiger Valley", the bottom of which is so filled with boulders that not even a high-wheeled cart can get along. The road we were following led into a valley between naked, much weather-worn mountains.

When Bergman travelled through this region on December 20, 1929, he had snow a foot deep and a temperature of — 22 degrees. Our last night there the thermometer had risen to 3·7.

In the Serebon valley a trading caravan from Liang-chow, bound eastward, was resting. After difficult and unpleasant experiences in this deep-cut valley, the haunt of magpies and pigeons, we came out into open country again with a sigh of relief. Long grass grew in places, and in one of these we met yet another wool caravan from Liangchow, led by Chinese riders in gaily coloured cos-tumes, sitting comfortably on their tall camels.

We drove past Dal-ulan-obo, where Bergman, Bohlin, Hörner and Bexell had celebrated the Christmas of 1929 together before separating to pursue their researches in different regions. Awkward places, erosion terraces and soft ground delayed our progress.

We drove past a large caravan laden with cloth, candles, tea, Hatamen cigarettes, etc. It was going via the Etsin-gol to Suchow, and a party of riders on horses and donkeys was travelling in the same direction. And here stood a couple of *yurts*, inhabited by a Chinese merchant. He sold milk and other things to passing caravans. A large caravan came from Ninghsia, evidently smuggling opium in small boxes wrapped up and hidden in bales of wool.

On the horizon to our left rose the Lang-shan, and nearer to us the little dark table-topped mountain Tebch. Our earlier expedition had found there rich fossil beds, including the gigantosaurus, a giant lizard which lived in marshes or lakes. It was half-past five when we halted at

Khara-tologoi, " Black Head ", a name derived from the
dark hill which rises hard by.

The cold by night increased to — 2·4 degrees. The
sun rose above the horizon like a sparkling diamond. As
early as nine o'clock it was warm in the car, but in the open
air it was bitterly cold, especially for those who had to
handle metal. The country here lay in low, undulating
waves, and the view over them was sharp and clear. Now
we crossed a huge channel which carried water only after
the summer rains, now we bumped along between low
hills or passed encamped caravans and grazing antelopes,
which displayed their clear-cut, graceful silhouettes on the
hill-tops before vanishing westward.

Eastward we could see for an enormous distance, as
though over an open sea. From the point where we were
it is only two days' journey to Shande-miao, the great
monastery city where we spent a quiet time in 1927.

We found two tents by the wayside, and there we rested
to wait for Serat, who had had a puncture. A caravan
was resting there too ; it had started from Suchow a
month earlier with over a hundred camels and twelve men,
and was bound for Kwei-hwa with medicinal herbs and
roots. The price of the goods was stated to be as high as
20 dollars for 100 gin. Two Chinese owned the camels,
while two others, who were merchants, had hired them to
carry their wares. They invited us into a large smoke-
blackened tent, in which two cooking-pots were boiling on
tolok, or iron rings over the fire. Tea was served in china
cups and soup with flour and meat. It is always pleasant
to enter one of these Chinese caravan tents, however sooty
and smoky it may be, for one feels that one is welcome and
that one's hosts consider the visit an honour to themselves.
Life on the endless Chinese caravan routes, and in the
merchants' and drivers' tents, is as picturesque and variegated as it is agreeable and stimulating to the imagination.
These born salesmen have lived and worked thus for
centuries past, and life was just the same in the caravans
which marched with bells ringing through the wide spaces
of Asia in legendary times, long before the dates mentioned
in the oldest records preserved. The conditions were

the same then as now; men and camels, country and climate—none has undergone any change worth mentioning. The Chinese caravan people are a caste apart, a brotherhood with laws and regulations, traditions and customs of the greatest antiquity, against which none can offend without losing his reputation for ever.

A common trait which distinguishes every Chinese caravan driver is an inextinguishable good humour. His life is hard and wearisome, and yet he is always cheerful and content. One wonders how he can be content with a monthly wage of less than two shillings and the plainest food! He walks for countless miles, singing as he leads his string of camels. His patience is never exhausted. In winter, too, part of the marches are done by night, because the camels need the daylight to find the hard, dry, spiky tufts of grass which serve as their food.

At last the next well is reached. The strings of camels are led forward in long lines, and in the twinkling of an eye the loads are lifted from the lying beasts' pack-saddles. The camels are led out to graze at daybreak and thence to the well, where the water is hauled up in wicker baskets and poured into basins or troughs. Gradually the men assemble in the tents, where the cooking-pots are boiling and the tea-kettles spitting. The long pipes, with their white metal heads, are produced, and life is found worth living. There is no singing now; the men eat, drink and smoke, tell stories and talk of everyday things. One after another spreads out his fur coat on the ground in the tent and falls asleep, while the lice feast on the sleepers' blood.

When the sun is on the western horizon the signal for departure is given. Drowsy, unkempt and permanently unwashed, the travellers spring to their feet, collect the camels from the pasture-ground, drive them skilfully and swiftly to their loads, and, by a jerk of the head-rope, make them fall on their knees and lie down in such a way that two men can lift the load on to the pack-saddle with a couple of heaves and make it lie secure and steady with two loops and a peg.

To a stranger from the West the rapidity with which a

caravan of several hundred camels is made ready for departure has the effect of a conjuring trick.   In a few minutes
the tents are struck, rolled up and flung on to the backs of
those camels which carry all the camp equipment.   One
string after another moves off, the bells begin to ring, and
the long winding procession marches silently on through
the desolate weather-worn hills.

Our road led us to a broad river-bed, now dry—the
Tsaghan-gol, " White River ", which runs in a northerly
and north-westerly direction.   A broad plain followed.
The road wound among clumps of vegetation, the ground
became awkward, and we crossed three troublesome deep
ravines.   We left a black offshoot of the Lang-shan on our
left.   Far to northward pale blue mountains came in sight,
and above them a loftier peak, probably within the territory
of the Mongolian Republic, raised its head.   After crossing
more dangerous ravines we arrived at camp no. 11, in the
Tsondol region, where a Chinese *maj-maj*, or merchant,
was selling mutton.   But we had enough of that for three
weeks, and obtained for ourselves instead a good stock of
dry wood, which was fetched from some way off.

The next day greeted us with a dark and sullen countenance, but the weather cleared up again about midday.
Our neighbour the merchant told us that at that time the
year before snow had been lying 3 feet deep.   So far we had
had good luck, and the first third of the winter had been
kind to us.   Certainly we had had cases of sickness, and
the cars had given us trouble.   But brittle vessels are like
that, and a car which can be relied upon in Mongolian
conditions has not yet been constructed.

A party of twenty Mongols, with women and children,
passed us, coming home from a pilgrimage.

At four in the afternoon the sound of motor-cars was
heard from the westward, and three motor-lorries came
leaping and swaying wildly over the uneven ground.   In
a short time they rattled up to our tents in clouds of dust.
They belonged to the omnibus company at Kwei-hwa, had
been detained for two months at Hami and had not obtained
permission to go on to Urumchi.   When General Ma
Chung-yin had at last released them, their drivers had

stepped on the gas all they knew and covered the distance from Hami to Tsondol in eight days, from the Etsin-gol in three.

They had not much luggage, but nineteen passengers, including Mr. Mo, one of the directors of the omnibus company. We asked him and one or two of the others to stop for a little while and have a cup of tea, but they were inexorable in their determination to race off eastward again at the same breakneck speed. We did not, therefore, succeed in getting much out of them. After leaving Hami they had driven south of the Pei-shan without meeting any robbers. Mo had gone in one of his cars to Turfan, where General Ma Chung-yin then was. The General had been friendly and obliging, and interested in the establishment of the omnibus route. We had certainly nothing to fear from him, Mo said. Sinkiang was peaceful; all military movements had come to an end, but General Sheng Shih-tsai was guarding the frontier north of the Tien-shan and Ma Chung-yin south of the same mountain range. On the whole we received good and reassuring news from Mr. Mo, and thought that all would go swimmingly. Unfortunately Mr. Mo was lying, for reasons which are easy to perceive.

Then they jumped up into their vehicles, thundered off, rolling like boats in a choppy sea, and in a few minutes had disappeared among the ravines.

On the morning of the 17th we were awakened at four-thirty. But it was an eternity before the frozen motors could be warmed up by the red-hot coals placed under them in iron braziers. So we had plenty of time to crawl out of our lairs, dress and have breakfast. When I was ready, and the tent had been struck, I preferred my usual place in the small car to the officious attentions of the chilly morning breeze.

Just as we were starting, a party of well-to-do Mongolian pilgrims came along, in their picturesque blue fur coats and imposing fur caps. They had been at Lombotchi, south of Shande-miao, at the foot of the Lang-shan mountains, and were now on their way home. Their caravan con-sisted of ten riding- and ten draught-camels, noble, handsome beasts with prominent thick humps. The men lit their pipes and had a good look at us.

We took our places and rolled on westward along the tracks made by the omnibuses of the day before, through sand and gravel, between gullies and tussocks. One gully ran between sharply defined beach-like terraces and had a conspicuous cairn on one side. We drove now in top gear, sometimes in second or lowest, according to the nature of the ground we were covering—we were changing gear all the time.

Antelopes were so common that we ceased to pay attention to them. A couple of small well-defined peaks rose ahead of us—Bayin-untur, " the rich and lofty ". We had to go round a horrid ravine with cañon-like offshoots. South of the low hills we saw to our left the holy city Shande-miao. We left the Bayin-untur behind us on the same side ; to our right was one solitary tree.

We passed through a belt of low hills and again had an endless plain ahead of us. The ground was sandy and soft, and we could not increase our speed beyond 3 miles an hour. Occasionally we passed a *jagh* or saksaul bush. Bare dunes of shifting sand stood out against the northern horizon at some distance.

The sun set a burning golden red, and it was nearly dark when we pitched camp at Gung-hutuk, " Deep Well ".

When we woke next morning after a temperature of 7·7 during the night, the sky was heavily over-clouded and a few snowflakes were falling through the still morning air. There was no need for us to be cold where we were, for quantities of scrub grew in the pronounced gully in which we had pitched camp. We had seen no real desert as yet. All the way to the Etsin-gol we were meeting travellers, and at the wells we usually found Chinese merchants' tents and Mongols in *yurts*, near which splendid camels and spirited horses were grazing.

We found stretches of hard gravel, but these were interrupted here and there by belts of soft soil. To our right the dunes raised their pretty yellow curves, like dolphins' backs. We had not got far before a strong northerly wind set in and a snow blizzard with it. The whole landscape was blotted out. A mountain to the north-west, which had been our sole landmark, disappeared. The ground was getting lower; we had descended a thousand feet the day before. In a depression, tamarisks were growing in such abundance that Serat, who was now ahead, stopped and picked a few armfuls, for no one could know if we should get any fuel for the evening otherwise. Now and again we passed older car tracks—those of the missionaries Hunter and Fischbacher in 1932, Gösta Montell and Georg Söderbom in 1930, and others.[1]

Now the whole country was white, and a few solitary elms raised their naked trunks out of the snow. The road was excellent. It now ran along the foot of the mountains to the right. At Tsaghan-hutuk, " White Well ", a number of trees grew, and there was a trough cut out of a tree-trunk at which camels and horses might drink. A river-bed cut between solid mountain walls afforded an excellent road. Many trees grew in it—delightful to see in that almost treeless desert.

At Hoyer-amatu we were out in open country again. There we found a whole village, consisting of some ten *yurts* and a few merchants living in tents, and the omnibus company had a petrol dump there. Soon after we drove across a stretch of *gobi*, absolutely barren desert. We still had the belt of sand dunes to our right, but the yellow dolphins were now white with snow. Bushes grew on fairly high but isolated mounds. The Saglarin-gol was a river-bed which ran down to Abder. A few small groves of trees delighted our eyes. We had only covered about 50 miles when we pitched camp no. 13 in the desert.

On the morning of December 19, the night temperature having touched − 4·7, the atmosphere was so wonderfully clear that even the mountains on the far western horizon stood out sharply defined. We followed a track which had been worn and torn by camels' pads, on ground as hard and firm as the finest concrete, on which for short stretches we could drive over 30 miles an hour. The country was barren for a time, but then pleasant tufts of

[1] *Våra vänner på stäppen*, by Georg Montell.

vegetation reappeared. If the road to Sinkiang was like this all the way there would be no need for any road-making.

Abder, "the Box", raised its broken pyramid over the surrounding country, and in the range farther south a hill with twin peaks stood out, like a two-humped camel. There was a fresh water well there. The place was well known to us from our great expedition, and several of its members had collected there tools from the later Stone Age.

The road led through a giant ravine with red terraces, wrought into fantastic shapes by erosion and the wind. Weather-worn stones were abundant. Not a blade of grass grew there; the landscape was impressive in its desolate grandeur. We lost ourselves in a labyrinth of red and black terraced hills, emerged by degrees from their curiously winding corridors, and were back in the hard, level gravel desert, with a belt of sand dunes to the southward. We had just crossed the frontier of the republic of Outer Mongolia. The Yingen well, the goal of our day's journey, lay in its territory. Serat, who was particularly good at finding the way, led the convoy towards an isolated peak. His lorry and the small car got safely across a silted-up river-bed, in which Effe stuck fast. Then the long, foot-wide canvas mats were brought and stretched out on the sand to act as rollers, and the lorry began to move again.

This episode was repeated a little farther on, but this time it took a more complicated and time-wasting form. The scene was again a broad depression in whose sandy bottom saksauls grew. As nothing was seen or heard of Effe, we turned back to see what had happened. Yes, indeed, there he was, stuck fast among the bushes. He had followed our wet wheel-tracks in the sand. The canvas mats were no use now. The men laid down bridges of dry wood across the track, but the wood snapped like glass. Serat tried to tow the unlucky car, but the ropes broke like thread. Very well then, we must unload the baggage. With Serat towing, Effe's engine working, and everyone pushing we got the car up on to solid ground again, and the loading recommenced. While this was being done one or two of us collected dry wood for the evening fire.

And the cars rolled on. It was breathlessly still. The

sky was blue and cloudless. Not a soul was to be seen, not a sound to be heard; this was the Gobi, the desert, the home of dead silence. On the west-north-westerly horizon the low jagged mountains hovered in mirage like a row of black pearls without contact with the earth.

We pitched our tents on sandy soil by the Yingen, or "She-Camel", wells. The northern well is in Outer, the southern in Inner Mongolia. We had driven a short distance over the republic's soil, but here the frontier ran right between the wells.

The ground was very sandy, and sand always gives a feeling of cleanness. There were plenty of saksauls, and when it was growing dark jolly young Effe lighted a bonfire —it might have been a challenge to all the Mongolian frontier horsemen under Soviet Russian orders who might happen to be roaming about in the neighbourhood of the wells. Travellers may fare badly if they fall into the hands of a large enough body of mounted frontier guards. They are compelled to accompany their captors to Ulan-batur-khoto, "the City of the Red Warrior", as Urga is called nowadays under the Red Flag, and at Urga they are examined and run the risk of being detained for an indefinite time.

But we saw no horsemen—indeed, not a human being. We went so far in challenging fate that we decided to stop at Yingen for a day. For Chen was to take bearings there, and Yew and Kung, with Serat as driver, were to try to find a more southerly route, for it would have been rather rash of us to propose to make a Chinese motor road over even the smallest snippet of Outer Mongolian territory.

After supper the silence of the grave descended upon She-Camel wells, and the smoke from Effe's dying bonfire rose in blue-grey rings to the stars.

On the night of December 20 the thermometer fell to — 7·8 degrees. Our day of rest was used for work of various kinds; the mechanics mended the motor tyres, the engineers found suitable routes to the southward, and Bergman collected a quantity of neolithic objects.

The following night we had — 9·9 degrees; mid-winter was approaching. Effe had lighted a crackling fire, and

by it we could have whatever temperature we pleased. I
sat with my back to the sun, which had just peeped over
the dunes like a gigantic diamond, and my face to the fire,
and saw the last trace of the earth's shadow disappear in
the west. The fire sank, the embers collapsed; the
shadows of the saksauls grew shorter. Our hope of getting
away early was frustrated. One of the motors short-
circuited. Bergman found the trouble; the generator had
shaken loose and rubbed against an electric connexion,
which could easily be mended. At last the cars were hum-
ming again. We left the sand belt and reached hard
ground. To the southward was a patch of low ground, a
pale yellowish grey, which extends to quite near the Etsin-
gol. On its farther edge we descried three dark parallel
lines, possibly old river terraces.

Utterly barren red hills, cairns, and occasional skeletons
of camels marked the road. Sometimes a summit was
adorned by a cairn bearing a camel's skull. Two blocks of
slate set up askew were like monumental stones. There
was no sign of life—absolute desert.

At Yingen we had been in a depression, only 2,100 feet
up. We were now climbing slowly, and 12½ miles on we
were at a height of 2,300 feet. A small caravan was resting
at the Horun-bosuk well. Then followed a labyrinth of
small hills, with an excellent road through them. Cairns
marked the tracks leading to the wells, which all have
names and are well known to the caravan people, but are
difficult to find in a snow blizzard or sandstorm. We passed
through a fresh labyrinth of little black ridges and heavily
weathered dark green slate. Then the ground became
level again.

We rested for a short time at Bante-tologoi, " Bald Pate ",
where there were fourteen *yurts* and a modest house belonging to a merchant. His goods—tea, hides, wool, etc.—
lay piled upon wooden scaffoldings a little way above the
ground for protection against drifting sand. We bent off
sharply southward round a belt of sand, with an abundance
of dry wood and whole trunks of dead trees. Our camp-
ing-place for the night was determined by Serat, who got
stuck in a patch of sand where quantities of saksauls grew.

Another big fire was lighted. We had water with us as usual. Dinner was to be plain—soup, tongue and tea—for the merchant at Bante-tologoi had treated us to some first-rate *pilmé*, a kind of small rissole, mince-meat in a covering of dough. Our cook, Chia Kwei, was also a master in the preparation of this tasty Asiatic dish.

A motor-drive across the Gobi, over that endless desert with its scraggy little ridges, its low hills where cairns sit enthroned like fossilized wizards, its vast plains crossed by countless shallow dried-up watercourses, and its dunes with their waves of drifting sand, formed by the wind on a regular system—may to a certain degree be monotonous, but has also an indescribable fascination. You pitch camp every evening by a spring or in a place where there is fuel ; you have lovely dreams in your sleeping-bag on the ground, you breathe fresh air day and night, live simply and have only two meals a day. And between the camping-grounds the desert or steppe unfolds day after day this flat, desolate scenery. And one never gets tired of it. One can never have enough of it. One always longs to get back to the desert. The boundless space alone fascinates by its majestic grandeur as the sea does.

The mountains that grow blue in the distance offer magnificent scenery, and the low undulations of the ground follow one another like the ocean swell. One must be very tired even to go to sleep in the car. And if one does, one is woken in a few minutes by a jolt, an uneven place caused by erosion, a tussock, or the sound of bells from an approaching caravan. The objects of our attention changed continually—lightly bounding antelopes, an eagle, a hare, sometimes a wolf. The only test of our patience was the road-mapping, but that was necessary, and we were soon reconciled to the delay it caused us.

Events of any kind, an intermezzo to break the day's monotony, were pretty rare. Interruptions through punctures, or the cars getting stuck fast in the sand, were unfortunately all too common. We grew accustomed to these little misadventures too, and took them philosophically.

But on the morning of December 22 an episode of unusual dimensions occurred. At eight o'clock we were very nearly ready ; only the rolled-up tents and their poles had to be hoisted up on to one of the two motor-lorries and made fast with wire. Bergman and I stood chatting by the pleasant morning fire. Suddenly Bergman turned his head and seemed to be listening attentively to some sound to the eastward in that noiseless desert.

" What is it ? " I asked.

" I thought I heard a car . . . wait, I can hear it plainly - now ! "

" Yes, certainly, quite distinctly."

A few seconds later the top of the driver's cabin of a motor-lorry appeared over the nearest terrace to eastward.

" It's Georg ! " Bergman cried.

" Has he got only *one* car ? "

" No, there comes another ! "

They swung round in our tracks and stopped next moment quite close to our camp-fire. All our fellows had hurried out to welcome the comrades they had missed so long. Since Georg and Jomcha had left us on the morning of November 21 we had waited and waited in vain. Jomcha, indeed, had come back pretty soon, but Georg remained absent, and at last we " cut him out " and no longer speculated as to the mysterious cause of his all-too-long delay. It was no use talking about him. He might have been taken ill in Peking or Tientsin, he might have been captured by robbers on his way back ; anyhow, he could not tell us what had happened to him.

And now, on December 22, he turned up out of the silent desert, quite suddenly and unexpectedly. He brought with him two lorries, so that he had obeyed my order to buy another. But now he had stopped and jumped out.

He was greeted with shouts of welcome.

" What's happened ? Why have you been so long ? "

We sat down by the fire, and Georg began to tell his story. He had hastened from Kwei-hwa to Tientsin, when he had obtained all he needed. He had there learned from Ford's agents that after we had started from Kwei-hwa a telegram had arrived from Edsel Ford, addressed to me, in which he offered to present me with an eight-cylinder motor-lorry, 1933 model, as a contribution to the road-making expedition. I need not say how full of gratitude we all were for this great kindness.

" Have you got any letters ? "

" Rather, a whole bundle, and newspapers too."

Georg gave a short outline of his journey—we could hear the details later. He and Jomcha had arrived at Kwei-hwa on the evening of November 21, and the latter had returned thence to our camp. Georg was at Tientsin on the 24th, spoke to Ford's agent, and heard of Edsel Ford's gift. But it was not ready ; the driver's cabin and roof still had to be built, and meanwhile Georg had to wait. On December 4 he drove the new lorry to Peking loaded with 500 gallons of petrol, some in big drums, some in square tin cans. He stayed four days at Peking and at last obtained a goods truck on which the lorry could be carried by train.

He arrived at Kwei-hwa on the 10th with the whole new outfit of spare parts, ropes, spades, hydraulic jack, etc. He started on the 12th with his fully loaded car and drove over the pass, taking our old Mongol Naidang with him to give him a hand. On the 14th he was with Jomcha and Chokdung, who declared that they had gone half mad from sitting and waiting so long. The first day was spent in building a dam round the wreck of the car, for the river was rising, and the car could not be touched until it was repaired. Georg and the three Mongols put their backs into the work and had everything ready for a start early on the morning of the 17th. They were at Tsondol on the 19th, and reached Hoyer-amatu late on the night of the 20th. On December 21 they started before sunrise, drove hard all day and pitched camp at Bante-tologoi after dark. There they heard that we had gone through the day before. This encouraged them ; they started before dawn, followed our wheel-tracks, and reached us at eight on the morning of the 22nd.

Georg had only a bare hour in which to talk. Our delight was indescribable. We were all in high spirits. Our convoy had been strengthened ; we had now four lorries, one small car and fifteen men. We were still 132 miles from the Etsin-gol. All the same, perhaps we should reach our old desert river by Christmas Eve! So when we had read our letters and made sure that all was well at home, we took our places and drove on westward.

VI

CHRISTMAS EVE ON THE ETSIN-GOL

THE convoy presented an imposing appearance with its five cars in single file, and the ground was troublesome—it was all little undulations which made us roll and compelled us to drive slowly. And then we went down into dry shallow sand-filled gullies, where tufts of herbage grew. Georg was leading the column; but he stuck fast in the sand and we swept past him. The road was fairly deep cut, and we could distinguish the tracks of the cars which had been our predecessors.

Khara-muck-shandai is a well in an absolutely desolate region. On our left, to southward, rose a terrace, and beyond that the long stretch of low ground reappeared which we had seen on the previous day. Flat surfaces were spread between dark hills. Vultures were making a good meal off a camel not long dead. We passed among knolls and mounds and over black lava beds, and drove up a steep slope. On the top of a low ridge we waited anxiously for the others. Serat came thumping noisily along, and after him Jomcha and Effe. Georg was well behind with his new car, which we called "Edsel".

On the other side of the ridge lay a broad plain. Then we crossed a large river-bed, as dry as a bone and with a gravel bottom; it ran in the direction of the long depression to the southward. Not a plant was to be seen. The road was marked by cairns, always erected on small hillocks. Sometimes they were crowned by camels' skulls.

Nogo-orobok is a well in a belt of sand, and there we saw scrub again, growing on mounds. The plain we were crossing extended to the foot of a chain of mountains in sight to the northward, called the Tsaghan-ul or "White Mountain". We obtained water for the night at the Bil-

cher well.   The road went in among low black ridges and
sharp slate rocks.   Often they rose in picturesque pyramids,
jet-black, but their feet covered with yellow sand.   The
day was waning, and the shadows spreading over this
dreary moon landscape.

At Derisin-hutuk stood one of the omnibus company's
buses, shabby and abandoned.   There were also dumps of
hides from Sinkiang and petrol from Kwei-hwa.   A
merchant ruled over three *yurts*, and a few Khalkha Mongols
had found their way there to make their purchases.   The sun
sank, a glowing red like molten gold.   The Tsaghan-ul
raised its crest to the northward in pale violet hues.

We had covered just 62½ miles when we camped for the
night in the dark.   It seemed absurd that we could not do
more in a whole day.   And that day's journey, on the
shortest day of the year, was the longest we had done so far.
But just try the roads of Central Asia !   And on top of
that there was the map-making which took up so much
time.

The tents were scarcely pitched before all our travellers
took out the letters they had received from their homes.
It was quiet that evening in our airy dwellings ; everyone
was reading letters.   But when Chia Kwei had dinner
ready, there was an interlude.   We were in rattling good
spirits ; we had all had good news from home, and there
was no holding us.

December 23 opened with a brilliant clear sky ; not a
cloud, not a breath of wind.   The temperature had been
— 4·5.   Mongols of the Orot tribe used to live in the
Tsaghan-ul region.   In 1928 the Khalkha Mongols came
down and said to the Orots :

" You must submit to Ulan-batur-khoto ! " (Urga.)

The Orots' chieftains and lamas replied :

" Then we shall go away from here and send our soldiers
to fetch our families and lamas, our camels and our
belongings."

The Orots migrated to the southward, and Khalkha
Mongols came in their place.   But when they found that
the country was sheer desert, where only camels could find
nourishment, they shifted the Khalkha frontier from 30 to

70 miles northward. Hardly had this happened before the Orots returned to their old dwelling-places. Their chief was a very rich and aristocratic lama at the Tsaghan-ul temple named Niemi Gessi-kwei, who guarded his tribesmen's interests with strength and authority. The only advantage the Khalkha Mongols obtained was that the Chinese traders visited them *sub rosa*—trade between them being forbidden in the existing political conditions.

Ahead of us the mountain Yaggan-khärkhan raised its sacred peaks. In Mongolia it is unlucky to utter the name of a holy mountain, and brings misfortune on one's head. One can say *khärkhan*, " the holy mountain ", but not the name itself. If one does, one loses camels or horses, loses one's way, gets a headache or meets with stormy weather.

At the foot of the mountain grows a bush called *kharaburgas*, from whose twigs the Mongols and Chinese cut the nose-pins which are stuck through the camels' nose-rings. Caravans stop there to obtain a supply. A spring at the mountain foot is called Yaggan-ussu.

Sometimes the road was firm, sometimes it ran through sand and gravel. At the next spring a caravan was resting ; it was carrying tobacco, tea, flour and other things to the Etsin-gol.

A little farther on we were checked by a small black ridge which sloped steeply to a pass deep in sand. On the farther side of it extended a broad plain, among whose saksauls we collected a supply of wood for the evening's campfires. We encamped for the night at Kuku-tologoi.

On the morning of Christmas Eve we were roused earlier than usual by the doctor, who was hurrying on ahead with the small car and Serat's lorry to choose a pleasant, inviting spot for our Christmas camp. After breakfast with Georg and Effe I seated myself in the former's driving cabin, where the heating apparatus was turned on and it was warm and comfortable.

The sun rose, and shifting shades of dark grey and yellow passed over the desert. Our camp had given life to that realm of silence and death just for one night. Now we were going on, silence would descend upon the scene once more, and the tracks of our cars would be erased by the winds and storms of time.

All went well to begin with, but the soil became softer, and each of our four lorries carried at least 2½ tons. One or two of them stuck in sandy ground, and the rope mats had to be produced. Naidang was useful on such occasions ; he knew every track. He guided us up out of the soft belt on to firmer ground, where he soon found the old well-worn camel road again. Sand was the most serious obstacle to a motor road to the Etsin-gol, and it would have to be dealt with drastically if it was not to be a permanent hindrance to traffic.

Moon landscape ; black ridges, sharp rocks with paler heaps of gravel. Between the hills spread dark gravel plains, over which the caravan track wound like a yellowish grey ribbon. In the Bagha-hongorchi region we crossed a bright level stretch of gravel between black mounds and pyramids, on which not a scrap of vegetation grew. The ridges were seldom more than from 30 to 60 feet high, and the space between them scarcely a hundred yards.

Just after midday we crossed the frontier between Alakshan and Etsin-gol, the country of the Torgut Mongols. This important spot was marked by a cairn. Here and there heavily weathered quartzite rocks stood out con-spicuously against the black and red ridges. White lime-stone occurred there too, which the Torguts use as a kind of cement for building their temples. We drove through a labyrinth of low hills, and descried between the farthest of them the wood by the Etsin-gol—a glorious and refreshing sight, the best Christmas present we could have had !

We steered direct for Wayin-torei. There was Serat with his lorry waiting for us. The small car was not to be seen. It was evidently out exploring. We came into typical Etsin-gol scenery ; a very sandy soil, sand dunes, naked or clothed with tamarisks, and small poplar groves. But it was pleasant to see trees and bushes again, and to pitch our tents under living green. As usual, the luggage we required was unloaded outside the tents, after which the cars were driven away and parked in a row, at a safe distance from all danger of fire.

Mongolian *yurt* pitched in the courtyard of a temple at Beli-miao

[Photo by Montell]

The prince of Barun Sunit and his mother

[Photo by Bergman

Camp No. 5 at Yang-chang-tse-kou

Scene of the accident at Yang-chang-tse-kou

[*Photo by Bergman*]

"Road" across sandy scrub-covered steppe between Bayin-untur and Hoyer-amatu

[*Photo by Bergman*]

Camp fire at Yingen well

[*Photo by Bergman*

Our base camp at Baller, on the Etsin-gol

The author and Bergman in our mess tent on the Etsin-gol

[Photo by Hummel

The prince of the Etsin-gol Torguts   [Photo by Montell

Mail-carriers Liang and Chakter on their return from Suchow

[*Photo by Bergman*]

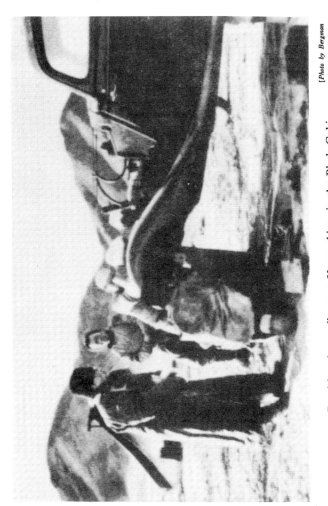

Repairing the small car at Ye-ma-ching, in the Black Gobi

[Photo by Bergman]

Georg in his open-air workshop at Ye-ma-ching

[*Photo by Bergman*

The Dambin Lama's robber castle

[*Photo by Hummel*]

[Photo by Montell

Chinese trade caravan in the Gobi desert

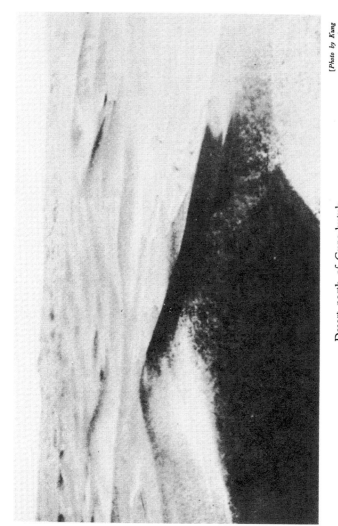

Desert north of Gung-hutuk

We were in a hurry now. One could hear and see everything being put in order and preparations being made for a worthy celebration of Christmas. Georg drove off in the small car to fetch water and came back with a few drums full and a couple of pheasants besides. Meanwhile I sat and wrote in the driver's cabin of " Edsel ".

Our petrol convoy had gone from Wayin-torei to Nogon Deli's camp. We held a council of war, and decided to remain where we were for a few days and then go round the Sogho-nor to the Oboen-gol, which we must cross before the melted snow had come down. We had also thought of sending Georg to Suchow with a lorry to fetch our mails. But now it was Christmas Eve, and the plans must wait for the present. We had driven 630 miles from Kwei-hwa, and our camp at Wayin-torei was no. 18.

As it was getting too dark to work, I went to Yew's tent, where Georg and Effe too had established themselves, and we had a pleasant chat by the open fire while waiting for the surprises Hummel and Bergman were preparing for us.

Not till nine o'clock were we summoned to the Christmas tent. We marched off with a lantern before us. A guard of honour was drawn up at the entrance to the tent. The Swedes shouted " God jul! ",[1] and cheered. Inside the tent the gramophone was playing a lively march. Our inventive doctor had joined two tents together to make one, and along it ran a long board, consisting of the rough wide planks Georg had taken with him for use as bridges in crossing hollows or soft ground. These rested on petrol drums. The interior was magnificently decorated with Swedish and Chinese flags.

In the middle of the table was a wonderful Christmas tree, and in its topmost branches a little card bearing the words in Swedish " Behold, I bring you glad tidings of great joy," written in ornamental script by my father many years before and brought with us as a greeting from home and a reminder of old-time Christmasses. The boughs of the tree—which was not the customary fir, but a tamarisk— were decorated with silver paper, and gnomes and tinsel hung in them in the light of little red wax candles. Our

[1] " Happy Christmas ! "

family photographs were placed under the tree. The whole cloth was decorated with a table-runner, on which paper gnomes, children and pigs paraded. On entering this wonderful room one was blinded by a sea of light, gleaming silver and many colours. Piles of sweets, chocolate and cakes lay on small paper plates.

The doctor had also acted as cook, and the menu was excellent and abundant : antelope soup—just as at the Sebisteis spring at Christmas, 1927—fish-cakes and sardines, ham from Stockholm with peas and other vegetables, rissoles with pea-pods and beans, preserved fruit, apricots, peaches and plums, and finally spiced bread, butter and cheese. Drinks were served—liqueurs, lemonade and coffee—what more could one want in the Gobi desert? But it was Christmas Eve, and that day shall be held in honour. Speeches were made, with reference to our dear ones at home, and we all sent heartfelt greetings to our relations in Sweden, China and Mongolia.

Then the Mongolian drivers and Chinese servants were called in and asked to sit down along one side of the table. A special speech was made to them, translated into Chinese by Yew and into Mongolian by Georg. Serat made an excellent reply on behalf of himself and his comrades. He said that they all understood the importance of our expedition and assured us that they were proud to be able to take part in it. We could be sure that every one of them would do his duty.

Then Effe and Chia Kwei sang Christian hymns in Chinese, touching in their very simplicity. The gramophone played " Hail, fair morning hour [1] ", Beethoven's " Song of Praise ", Händel's " Largo ", and so on, and then cheerful mundane pieces. Our servants were given tea with cake, sweets and cigarettes. All our men and Naidang were there, a really jolly, happy party in a genuine Christmas spirit, without a thought of any dangers that might threaten us farther west.

The red candles burnt themselves out on the tree, and white candles were put on the table. That very day, Christmas Eve, we had completed the first stage of our

[1] " Var hälsad, sköna morgonstund," a favourite Swedish hymn.

journey to our old river the Etsin-gol, and hoped that the following days would go equally well. We had left Kwei-hwa with four cars and had arrived at the Etsin-gol with five, a strange record.

Yew, Kung and Chen withdrew at midnight, and the servants had already disappeared. We five Swedes remained seated at the table, reading poetry and listening to the gramophone. And at last we too, now that the Christmas Eve jollifications were over, vanished into our sleeping-quarters.

VII

DAYS OF REST ON THE ETSIN-GOL

AFTER a temperature of − 5·8 during the night, we awoke on Christmas morning to find a south-easterly storm raging. The air was full of flying dust, a vague semi-darkness surrounded us; trees, bushes, dunes, tents and cars loomed through the mist like weird spectres. I read newspapers in the cabin of " Edsel ", for Georg had driven with the small car to Arbdang's mother, who had come to our camp every day in the autumn of 1927 with a can of milk for me.

It was the first real dust-storm we had had since we left Kwei-hwa. It did not blow hard, but the darkness was gloomy and oppressive. A party of Torguts appeared through the haze, mounted on splendid camels, and visited us in our tents.

We read in a *Peking Chronicle* which Georg had brought with him that General Ma Chung-yin had captured Urum-chi, and wondered whether this event would be to our advantage or not.

While the storm howled and whined in the branches of the poplars, we were invited to dip in the pot, and were then regaled with ham, sweet cakes and coffee.

Our camp no. 18 was pitched by the river Ontsein-gol, in which there was no water till late in the spring. On the morning of Boxing Day Georg had a talk with some Chinese caravan men who were camping in our neigh-bourhood with their camels. It was arranged that they should transport nearly all our baggage, amounting to nearly 10 tons, the 22 miles as the crow flies to the arm of the Oboen-gol delta, where camp no. 19 was to be pitched. Some of our men were to accompany the baggage. We, with the almost empty cars, would make the detour round the Sogho-nor; that route was 53 miles long and led over soft ground, impossible for loaded cars.

The move was begun without delay. The convoy at once left the belt of vegetation and the more or less firm dunes and rolled out over soft level sand, with deep light yellow wheel tracks on a dark grey ground. We drove northward. We passed the spot where Hörner, Haude and Chen had had their camp at Christmas, 1931, and where one of the Eurasia aeroplanes had landed.

To the left we saw a fair-sized belt of barren dunes. The river disappeared here, but soon turned up again. We left the ruins of the famous city of Khara-khoto behind us, 20 miles away to the south-south-west. Our route crossed a few isolated dunes, off-shoots of a good-sized belt to the left. They were regularly constructed, and shaped like half-moons or shields. It was there that Hörner and Chen, the year before, had studied in detail the formation of the dunes and the laws by which they changed their shape when a strong wind blew over them. In one place we saw how a couple of isolated dunes had covered up a fairly old motor track, probably made by the two lorries of the missionaries Hunter and Fischbacher, who had travelled in these parts a year before us.

Our former expedition (1927–33) had several times been visited by the angel of death. During those years he mowed down seven men, and the strange thing was that six of them died close to the Etsin-gol. Stranger still, two members of the expedition died by their own hand in wooded regions which lay quite near one another.

The young Chinese student Ma, in a fit of depression and melancholia, took the life of his own Chinese servant, and then bled to death from wounds inflicted on himself with an axe. The other was the Balt Beick, whose grave we were now passing at some distance.

One Chinese servant died of sickness, while another, a caravan man, missed the place on the bank of the Etsin-gol where the camels used to be watered, got out of his depth and was drowned.

The last was Josef Söderbom, a brother to Georg, who had been employed in our service only temporarily, for a convoy from Suchow to our camp by the river. He had been ill for a long time, but kept going. On the way downstream he grew worse, and one evening he felt that he was going to die during the night. He called his servants and said to them :

" I'm going to die to-night. Don't trouble about my body. Don't take me home or bury me, just throw me into the river."

He died and was buried—provisionally—by his servants.

It is not so unusual, of course, for those who wander over the earth to die on their travels. But how can one explain two able, educated men taking their own lives, and that in the same region ? A strange coincidence ? But in the eyes of the superstitious Mongols and Chinese it was no coincidence when, a year after Ma's unhappy end, a young Torgut girl fell down dead just as she was passing the place where he had pitched his tent for the last time and killed his servant and himself.

We ourselves, who took a cooler and more sober view of such tragic occurrences, could not help feeling curiously affected by these mysterious deaths. But our imagination did not take refuge in the animistic doctrine of the natives. For as long as they could remember men had died on the lower Etsin-gol, and demons and spirits haunted the places where they had died. There spirits unable to find peace stole about and played their pranks in the twilight and darkness, and might beguile the living into the commission of desperate acts.

On two different occasions, in 1927 and 1934, I have spent several weeks on the lower Etsin-gol, and I have never been able to find this region anything but wonderful and delightful, an earthly paradise after the long journey through the eastern Gobi ; one is fascinated at the sight of the ancient poplars, enjoys the shade of the foliage in summer, and in winter listens with delight to the rustling of the wind in their leafless tops. The sand dunes stretch their curved banks like giant dolphins, now quite naked and shifting before the wind, now covered with vegetation and held fast by tamarisks, whose handsome violet sprays blossom in spring, and whose impenetrable thickets afford a refuge to the shy, graceful pheasants. And amid this curious, genuinely Central Asiatic scenery the river cleaves its course sword-like through the Gobi, the world's greatest desert.

When, after resting awhile, one quits this region and its inexhaustible store of water, pasture and fuel, and fares westward through the fearful desolation of the Black Gobi, one feels as if one were on board a ship leaving a luxuriant South Pacific isle, and steering out to sea again over the endless water spaces.

And yet I understand the Asiatics' belief in spirits and demons among the trees, the brushwood and the dunes, and I confess that I should not care to walk through those woods alone on a moonlight night, and still less during a sandstorm. One sees dark spectres everywhere, and ghosts with twisted arms and legs. They stretch out their hands towards us to tear us to pieces ; we hear stealthy steps approaching us from behind ; we hasten our steps and run straight into the arms of a monster whose vague outlines loom up out of the flying dust. On still nights mysterious sounds of lamentation reach our ears—are they the unquiet spirits of dead malefactors, or only wolves and wild cats ?

Walter Beick preferred to die rather than return to the vast, silent majesty of the desert. Others thought that what horrified him more than anything was the thought of returning to the roaring life of the coast after fifteen years' solitude in the interior of Asia. He preferred his lonely grave on the verge of the desert to accompanying our party to Peking.

On a level, slightly undulating stretch covered with black gravel the wheels sank in and the engines worked hard. To the north-west the lake Sogho-nor was visible in its entirety. It looks rather insignificant and is $6\frac{1}{4}$ miles long. I had navigated its clear salt water in the autumn of 1929 with Henning Haslund, in a canoe made by Larson.

At 1.30 the lake was due west of us, and we saw Boro-obo to the west-north-west, with the cairn crowning its terraced summit.

We crossed a hollow full of dead saksauls. At times the ground looked level and solid, but it was horribly treacherous from its softness, and was continually forcing us to take capriciously winding detours. In the next hollow saksauls grew. All the way we kept outside the ancient boundaries of the lake as delimited by Hörner and Chen, and so had no signs of the former extension of the lake to our right. To our left were the mountains with Boro-obo. We made our way towards them, rising gently over fine sand and dust, slabs and flakes of black or dark green sharp-edged slate.

At last we got stuck in the small car, and walked up to Boro-obo. From the edge of its terraced ridge we had a splendid view over the whole lake Sogho-nor, which looked much more insignificant in a bird's-eye view than it had seemed from the surface of the water, when we rowed and sailed from end to end of it. But it was pretty, and there was a blue-green shimmer on the ice. Not a soul was to be seen, not a tent, no flocks. But to eastward we caught sight of the four motor-lorries in single file. They were moving slowly forward, and soon disappeared behind a terrace.

So we said good-bye to Boro-obo and its view and went back to the small car; we freed it by our combined efforts and proceeded westward. The sun set. The lake was no longer to be seen. Our route crossed a belt of tamarisks, scrub and dry wood in soft sand. Several others followed, separated from one another by strips of level barren earth. More unpleasant ground could hardly be imagined.

We stopped for a bit and waited. Then we heard the sound of cars behind us. The four motor-lorries' headlights shone out like wolves' eyes in the darkness.

But now things grew worse. We had halted in a sandy gully. The four lorries stopped. Now one, now another moved forward a little, but stopped again. We drove up to them. Now three cars were stuck fast in the sand. Out with rope mats, jacks and spades! One after another was dug out, and its engine hummed a little till the car got stuck again. It took an eternity. At last we saw that all efforts were fruitless. Despite the moonlight it was too dark to be able to judge the situation. I ordered the men to pitch camp. Georg and Serat went off in the small car to look for water. It was only a short way to the Oboen-gol, where we were to encamp for a time.

The tents were put up, and soon dinner was served, without drink. We were all tired and thirsty, especially the men in the lorries, who had got stuck about fifty times in the course of the day. We had just finished the meal when the searchers returned with three petrol tins full of fresh water. Then tea was served. We did not go to bed till midnight, and then the camp became silent. We had learned that a motor-road ought not to be made north of the Sogho-nor, but rather across the arms of the delta by means of bridges.

There was no early rising next morning. We were still tired. At noon Jomcha was ready to start with his lorry, and stuck in the sand after fifty yards. Once more the blessed but heavy mats were unrolled on the sand. Georg, Serat and Effe, with their cars, followed, and each in turn stuck fast. It was a couple of hours before all were freed, and the convoy was bumping up and down between clumps of tamarisk and scrub-clad dunes, through sand and dust which whirled up in impenetrable clouds.

We were swathed in these suffocating clouds, out of which only the nearest car loomed up like a phantom. We swayed and jolted along till we reached the river and followed its right bank. The Oboen-gol does not contain a drop of water at this time of year. The track we were following ran along the outermost edge of the erosion terrace. Soon it grew too narrow, and there was a danger of someone falling over the edge and ending up wheels in air in the dry river-bed. We halted, and all our spades set to work again. We dug away obstructing hummocks and made the road wider. The first lorry just got through.

At last the convoy was on a wider road. The track left the river-bank and wound in among thick tamarisk bushes. It would have taken a good deal less to make some people seasick ; we were flung this way and that and had to hold on tight, while the whole landscape disappeared in clouds

of dust. But at last we came out into open ground and
drove up on to the firm, hard, barren plateau.

We steered for the Torgut prince's *yamên* and stopped in
the courtyard outside it. The prince was not there, but
his Minister of Justice received us and invited us into a
large *yurt* which was erected in the middle of the inner
courtyard.

Here we sat down and were regaled with tea, *tsamba*,
butter, cream cakes and sugar. In the centre, just in front
of the entrance, was a sort of low throne ; on this the
prince sits when dispensing justice to his people—his people
which is hardly a hundred *yurts* strong. We told the
Minister why we had come. He nodded approvingly, and
assured us that we were welcome in his master's kingdom.
In reality it was doubtful whether the Torgut prince could
welcome the construction of a motor road to Sinkiang, for
a new and freely used traffic artery through his province
might have an injurious effect on his people and in several
respects restrict his freedom and autonomy.

In the meantime we took our leave, got into the cars,
and drove on till Effe got stuck and caused a delay. Evening was coming on, and the sun was sinking. Now came
an adventurous drive in the dark through copses and brushwood, over ravines and dunes. Dry branches cracked
under our wheels. One after another stuck fast. The
moon went behind clouds, and we could see little of the
fantastic landscape. It took us several hours to cover a
very few miles ; but at last we regained the dry bed of the
Oboen-gol. It was nine o'clock when we reached the
Baller woods, where we were to encamp for some time.

All of us slept soundly after the tiring day. The new
camp looked inviting by daylight, and the tents were
picturesquely placed under a group of tall poplars, with
a background of tamarisk-clad dunes. We were encamped
on the left bank of the dry Oboen-gol. There was said to
be water and ice-floes six miles upstream, and a winter
flood was expected at Baller in a month's time. The
doctor made arrangements with our nearest Torgut neighbours for us to hire a large, roomy *yurt*, which was erected
under the trees in the evening. It was to be our mess,

where we were to have lunch and dinner, read and write
letters. The same solid oak planks which had served as
our Christmas table now became our dinner-table and
writing-table, and benches were ranged along them. An
iron-plated stove kept the *yurt* warm. After our first dinner
in this attractive resort we held a council of war to the
sound of gramophone music.

A number of Torguts came to visit us and tethered their
magnificent riding-camels to our poplars. One or two of
our guests told us that the authorities at Suchow, some
time ago, had sent policemen here to forbid the Torgut
prince to let any motor-cars pass through his territory
bound for Sinkiang. We had originally intended to send
Georg with a lorry to Suchow to send off and fetch letters,
but perhaps the car would be confiscated in that city, and
it might perhaps be safer to make use of Torgut couriers
on swift camels. One of our visitors undertook to ride
there in six days. So it was clear that we must wait at
least a fortnight, or till the courier returned. Meanwhile,
Yew and Kung were to make a reconnaissance in the delta
to find out the most suitable places for the construction of
bridges over the arms of the river and a motor road to
connect them.

Everyone was so delighted with the mess tent that
Hummel and Bergman hired another to live in, and our
Chinese friends Yew, Kung and Chen hired a third. The
mess tent had also to serve as a reception-room. The first
days were spent in letter-writing. Long letters to our
families at home were composed. I had also to write
reports to our immediate chief, the Minister for Railways
Ku Meng-yü, and to the Prime Minister Wang Ching-wei.

On the night of December 29 the temperature fell to
— 18·4, and at 2 p.m. on the 30th it was still 14 degrees.
Georg, Effe, Serat, Jomcha and Chokdung, with two of our
Chinese servants, moved to a place a mile and a half from
Baller where they could repair the cars more conveniently.
The ground by their camp was level and hard, and they
dug a rectangular pit in which they could easily get at the
cars from underneath. Our two mechanics usually had
their meals in their own camp, the mechanical workshops,

but they were often our guests, not least in order to rejoice their hearts with gramophone music.

On the evening of the 30th our post was ready and sewn up in its bag. The Mongolian courier, Chakter, was one of our old friends from earlier years. A young Chinese, Liang, was to ride with him. They had two wonderful camels, trained from youth to cover distances quickly. Lean and sinewy, they strained their steely muscles as night came on, and disappeared southward with their hardy riders.

It grew colder as the New Year approached. On the night of December 30 we had — 23·25 degrees. On New Year's Eve there was a grand banquet—soup, veal cutlets, pheasant, asparagus, sweet cakes, brandy and coffee. Two three-armed candlesticks stood on the red table-runner. Again a short speech was made, giving thanks for the time we had spent on our new expedition. Georg and Effe were welcome guests. With the servants' help they had dragged a dozen dead and dried poplar-trunks to the open space between the tents and the *yurts*, set them up like " piled arms " and filled the space between with boughs, twigs and rubbish. Just before twelve o'clock we all filed out, each man carrying a candle. The stroke of twelve was announced by a gun-shot, whereupon we all advanced to the bonfire and lit it with the flames of the burning candles.

Then we sat down round the blinding fire which illuminated the leafless poplars close by. Whole clusters of sparks sprang into the night sky ; the glowing embers crackled and spat till they fell to the ground one by one and produced new comets' tails of sparks. The temperature was below — 4, but we could have roasted ourselves if we had liked. We had nothing to fear from the winter cold ; the whole wood was full of dry timber. The minimum temperature on the last night of the year was — 22·5. When I got up or went to bed in my sleeping-bag, my stove, formerly a petrol drum, was heated red-hot, and there was a smell of burning where the pipe went out through a metal plate in the tent-cloth. I continued to live in my tent, but spent whole days in the mess tent. A fourth *yurt* was hired for the kitchen staff.

The thick undergrowth of tamarisk which grew on the dunes on the other bank of the Oboen-gol, right opposite our camp, swarmed with pheasants. The followers of Buddha do not kill them ; the birds know that they are immune, and so they came right up to the tents. But these particular birds made a mistake ; our guns were no Buddhists, and during our stay on the Etsin-gol we had pheasant at every meal. However, I forbade pheasant-shooting in the neighbourhood of the camp, for I myself could sit for hours watching the beautiful, dignified birds as they strutted towards the kitchen tent on the edge of the steeply sloping six-foot bank. There, in the bed of the river, was a dug well, around which fragments of ice always lay strewn. The well was the first objective of each new pheasant patrol. Ahead strode a scouting cock, which approached the well with slow steps and on a zig-zag course, gazing intently ahead. After him came a few more cocks, and when this knightly bodyguard in their brilliant variegated plumage had carried out their reconnaissance, the hens ventured forward, tripping coquettishly in the cocks' wake and in a garb of greyish-yellow which exactly matched the sandy soil. Then they would assemble round the well, perhaps a score of them, to peck and nibble on the ice.

Kung, who was an open ally of the pheasants, regaled them with rice and breadcrumbs, a diet which they fully appreciated. They were not in the least discomposed by our servants chopping wood a few yards away. When San Wa-tse went down to the well to draw water they retired a short distance, but hurred back when he had gone. The cocks were not very kind to the hens. When the latter came and pecked among the rice they were driven away.

The pheasants were fine, well-shaped birds and graceful in their movements, but credulous and incautious. After a few days they were firmly impressed with the idea that we were comparatively decent people who wished them no harm. If they had had any notion that we had treacherously killed and eaten a number of citizens of their pheasant sanctuary-state, they might have had a different opinion of us. But they suspected no evil, and did not understand that the savoury fumes which came from the kitchen tent emanated from their relations, sizzling in our saucepans.

Some seventy families of Khalkha Mongols, refugees from Outer Mongolia, lived on the Etsin-gol. Their *märin* or chief was said to be in secret communication with the Khalkha Mongols who were believed to live in the Ma tsung-shan mountains, on the way from the Etsin-gol to Hami. Their chief was called Naravaching Gegen. The prince of the Torguts allowed the Khalkhas to settle by his river only if they had sufficient means to guarantee their own and their families' upkeep—otherwise they might not stay, but had to go somewhere else. Later we visited their chief, Changerup Märin, who had been in prison at Urga for many years and fled when the Soviet regime entered the City of the Red Warrior.

New Year's Day passed peacefully and quietly. There was not a breath of air ; one could have sat out of doors with a candle alight. The sky arched its blue dome over the silent wood and our *yurts* as grey as trees, bushes and sand. The sunset was often magnificent. The poplars and tamarisks stood out as sharp black silhouettes against a blazing red-gold background, while the vegetation-clad dunes of the eastern bank, and their gracefully curving slopes, were lit up by an afterglow which was long in fading.

Georg and Effe had brought us their New Year good wishes the night before, and did not put in an appearance on the first day of the year. They were working at top speed, cleaning every single screw on the five cars. In their open-air mechanical workshop, where they had one *yurt* and one tent, they daily received guests, all of them our friends from the great expedition. Torgut women visited them too, and helped them to cook and wash their clothes.

1934, a year of uncertainty, had begun. What would the coming days bring us ? We knew nothing about the situation in Sinkiang. News items which had appeared in the Peking papers were only rumours, and not consistent. No caravans, no travellers or messengers from the mysterious great province passed by the Etsin-gol. What visitors we had were from Suchow, Anhsi or Liangchow. If we had got reliable news from Sinkiang, should we have turned back? Certainly not. We had undertaken a task and set about it—we were determined to ride out all possible storms.

At sunrise San Wa-tse used to come and light my stove. I woke for a moment then, but fell into a deep sleep again as if under a narcotic. It was as if I had need of all the sleep I could get after the hard struggle of the previous autumn, before the new expedition became a reality. Or perhaps it is quite natural for us, like animals and plants, to sleep long and deeply during the continental winter cold. This deep sleep is clearly beneficial, and perhaps times may come when it is a good thing to have had one's fill of sleep.

Magpies, sparrows, crows, ravens, partridges and pheasants kept us company.

The pheasants were an inexhaustible source of pleasure and interesting observation throughout our stay at Baller. It was comic to see our regular customers going slowly home after they had eaten their fill. They never flew. First one cock would cross the river-bed, accompanied by his harem; then another party followed, and soon the well was a centre of emptiness and desolation. They disappeared without a trace under the thick undergrowth of the tamarisks, where they presumably gave themselves up to love and dreams after their New Year's Day banquet.

The first sun of the New Year was setting. A Chinese strode past across the bed of the river leading ten camels without loads. The sun tinted them red, and their shadows fell long and black on the sand.

Our mechanics reckoned up our supply of petrol, consisting of 263 five-gallon and 38 thirty-gallon drums. There were 27 gallons more in the tanks of the five cars. We had consumed 760 gallons, and had covered an average distance of 4·2 miles per gallon. It was calculated that we should require 450 gallons to get to Hami, and would then have 2,030 gallons left. With this supply we ought to be able to cover the necessary length of road. We hoped, too, to be able to buy Russian petrol at Urumchi.

The wind rustled and whined in the leafless tree-tops

above us. It sounded like the voice of the desert itself, mournful and solemn, warning us against continuing our journey westward, and advising us to remain in the Etsin-gol woods or return to safer regions farther east.

One day I drove to see the mechanics' workshop at Yamen-tsaghan, where our Mongols also lived. The Swedish flag fluttered from a tall mast in front of their tent. The finer detailed work on the parts of the dismantled cars was done in the tent, while a temporarily employed carpenter made boxes and packing-cases in the open air. They had their own woodcutter; he supplied them with fuel and also had a fire continually burning under one of the large petrol drums, the water in which was kept permanently warm.

We thought of making a reconnoitring trip to Hami, the nearest town in Sinkiang, with the small car and one of the lorries. Only Yew, Hummel, Georg and Serat were to accompany me. We considered this tempting plan for a long time, and it appealed to everyone. But when we had slept on it and considered it afresh, we decided to wait till the couriers had come back from Suchow. They might bring us important instructions and news.

On the evening of January 5 Chen picked up a broadcast from Nanking which told us that between 2,000 and 4,000 Turkis at Hami had rebelled against General Ma Chung-yin and forced him to retire to Turfan. This news compelled us to await the return of Chakter and Liang from Suchow.

On January 6 reassuring news reached us from Hami. A report which Changerup Märin had somehow received, either from refugees or from spies, that all was quiet at Hami, did not seem particularly reliable. But what was more important, Chen again picked up the Nanking wireless, which said: "All quiet at Hami. The Nanking Government is sending a commission there to negotiate."

One day Georg came in "Edsel" and took us to call on the Torgut prince, whose village of tents was 6 miles north of Baller. The road there was phenomenal. If any-one accustomed to European or American roads could see it, he would swear that it was impracticable for cars. But Georg drove through sand, over scrub-clad dunes, gullies and reed-beds, through brushwood, loose stones and fallen trees. On a trip like that, one is so knocked about by the time one arrives that one can hardly stand.

After this bumpy journey we arrived at half a dozen large grey *yurts*, well concealed among tamarisk bushes and sand dunes. By some of them wood was stacked up in large piles for winter fuel. Two of the prince's men bade us welcome and invited us into the reception *yurt*, where the usual refreshments were served on a low table.

We were kept waiting a good half-hour before his Eminence deigned to enter and receive our *haddiks* or long pale blue scarves of honour, as well as a supply of preserved meat. He gave me in return a field-glass which he had received some time before from one of the members of our previous expedition. The expedition was touched on in conversation, and the prince asked what had become of the other gentlemen who had been his guests in previous years. Nothing whatever had been heard from Hami. As lately as two years ago the caravans had come and gone undisturbed, but since then silence had reigned, as though an insurmountable wall had been raised between Sinkiang and the Etsin-gol.

Our homeward journey was great. We were assured that there was a much better way than the one we had come. But presumably Georg misunderstood the description he had been given, for he had not been driving long before he stuck so effectually that it took a couple of hours to get the car out again.

On the evening of January 9, Hummel and I were sitting in the mess tent writing letters home. The night was quiet and still. About twelve o'clock the doctor started and called out, " I can hear a car ! " We hurried out. In a few minutes the lights became visible, and Georg drove up with the couriers Chakter and Liang as passengers. Georg jumped out and said curtly : " No letters for us, only for the Chinese ! "

The mail-bags were opened in the mess tent. All the envelopes were addressed in Chinese ; nothing for us but a number of wrappers containing the *Peking Chronicle*. The official letters from the Ministry of Railways were read and translated by Kung, who had woken up when the car drove in among the tents. One communication informed us that 2,000 dollars had been sent to the post office at Suchow for us. Another stated that the governors of Suchow and Ninghsia had been instructed to give us such protection and help as we might need, and that they had replied that they would do so. From the Minister for War we received permits for all the members of the expedition to carry arms during the year 1934. The head of the Eurasia told us in confidence that according to information he had received there were a thousand Turki soldiers at Hami and Ma Chung-yin was at Turfan. Less reassuring were the words : " Hami is not quite safe, new disturbances are expected."

That we Swedes had received no letters from home was quite natural, for Georg, when he left Peking on December 9, had taken with him all the mail which had then arrived, and letters which had got to Peking later had not yet reached Suchow. Chakter and Liang had also heard that no aeroplane had arrived at Suchow for two months, and that the mail despatched via the Imperial Highway needed twelve days to get from Lanchow to Suchow. It was clear, therefore, that we could *not* have had any letters beyond those we had already received.

What our two couriers had achieved was beyond all praise. The distance from Baller to Suchow is 240 miles, so that they had 480 miles to cover, there and back, and had been away ten days. But they had been detained for a day at Suchow, and one day had been lost by Chakter's camel going through the ice in crossing a river ; it had taken a whole day to get him out. So they had ridden 480 miles in eight days, or 60 miles a day. They had been stopped by sentries at the gate of Suchow, but when they had shown the postmaster a paper written by Yew and stamped with our red stamp, that official had guaranteed that their business was above board, and they had obtained complete freedom of movement. At Bayin-bogdo the two camels, which had been tethered at night, had for some reason taken fright, broken their head-ropes and bolted for the nearest mountains. This misadventure too had lost some time.

The men were in splendid condition and had not suffered the least harm from their fast ride. They received a dollar a day each, and 4 dollars extra for their board and lodging. They had actually not spent more than 2 dollars 45 on the whole journey. But what did the camels get for their trouble, they who after all had toiled the hardest? They had had to fast and not drink one drop of water the whole way. They stood there patient and silent, casting at us haughty, indifferent looks. Now they were to rest and graze before they were in form again and ready for another journey.

When we had got the mail from Suchow we had nothing more to wait for. We therefore decided to start as soon as possible, the whole convoy at once, and make straight for Hami. The way we had chosen went by Ming-shui— that is, to southward of my route taken in the winter of 1927–8, but the same as that taken by Haude, Haslund and Yuan. It is an advantage to travel at full strength when robber districts have to be traversed.

On the night of January 10 the temperature fell to − 19·2. At this time Chen made a trip to Derisun-hutuk to take bearings, and Kung went to the Tsondol area to study the building of a bridge that was needed. The river there was 125 yards wide.

On January 14 we left Baller for the mechanical workshop at Yamen-tsaghan, where we were all together again. Our neighbours came to say good-bye, but the pheasants did not show themselves amid the noise of the cars. It was really sad to leave a place where we had spent so peaceful an eighteen days. We sighted the new camp at sundown, and there stood the four lorries, full of petrol drums and boxes.

After − 27·8 degrees on the night of January 14, the lowest temperature we had had on the whole trip, we prepared for a real start next day, Meanwhile, letters were written ; our last chance of sending letters for a long time was by Naidang, who was now to return to Kwei-hwa. Yew wrote to the postmaster at Suchow asking him to keep until further notice any letters that might arrive for us.

We were called on the 16th at a few minutes past five.

The cold, — 25·6 degrees, cut us to the bone ; but we had a big open fire. The final packing and loading took longer than usual, and it was ten o'clock before everything was ready.

We followed the left bank of the Oboen-gol to the south-east and south. The general direction of the river is north-north-east, but there are sharp bends. The road was horrible to start with, but soon grew better. Pheasants were seen everywhere among the bushes. They drew back when the convoy came thundering along amid thick clouds of dust, but stayed under the bushes and peered out after us.

Dash-obo was sighted on the top of a firm dune to the left of our route. In passing we paid a half-hour's visit to Baychen, where Changerup Märin's headquarters were. He and his staff of twenty-four lamas had eight *yurts*. Two of the tents stood inside a wall and attracted our attention. One was a temple *yurt*, whose enormous cupola was supported by eight red-painted wooden columns; its interior was arranged like an ordinary temple, and the lamas sat there on cushions saying their prayers. One of two of us went in to listen for a time to the curious service, at once melodious and mystical. The other *yurt* was Märin's reception-room, in which we were given tea and cakes.

A mile and a quarter away to the left we saw a few clumps of poplars and high sand dunes covered with tamarisks. Tsondol lay there, our headquarters in the autumn of 1927 and the place where we had a meteorological station for two years.

We reached the left bank of the Etsin-gol at Manin-tsaghan and took a short rest. The river here runs in one single channel, 150 yards wide and then covered with a 20-inch layer of ice, on which was a sanded track for camels. On our bank poplars grew in small copses, on the other side were firm vegetation-clad dunes. This was a place where a bridge should be built.

We went on west-south-west over hard *gobi* of fine gravel, where not a blade of grass grew. Three of the motor-lorries were far ahead. The mirage made them hover a little above the horizon, so that they looked like aeroplanes which had just taken off. To the right an old ruined fort appeared, with the remains of yellow-brown walls of sun-dried brick. Its name is Mu-durbeljin, or "the bad square", and it is one of a cluster of fortifications which at this point form a *limes* 2,000 years old.

White-tailed antelopes dashed past us. To the west and south-west wide shining surfaces extended, resembling lakes or snow-fields ; but they too were a trick of the mirage. Here the great caravan road to Hami ran through sheer *gobi*, which afforded the most splendid surface. We passed a dry river-bed called the Narin-köll. We drove swiftly ahead over the hard level ground, and it was amusing to watch the three cars in front of us. They formed three triangles, point downwards and base uppermost. But they were continually changing shape and position—now they floated together, now they were separated ; now they were dark, now they grew light and rose above the surface of the earth.

Soon the eastern arm of the river Möruin-gol came in sight, a river which branches off from the Etsin-gol at various points, then combines and later separates again into two arms. We had soon reached the first arm, which Kung examined. The arm of the delta was 173 yards wide, but the ice-covered stream only 127 yards. The greatest depth was only 4 feet, of which 2 feet 7 inches were solid ice. We could see that this ice had been formed by new water flowing down over the older ice, layer above layer.

The second, or western arm is rather more than 2 miles away, and is rather larger than the eastern. Its bed was 203 yards, its ice-crust 175 yards wide. The maximum depth was 4 feet 3 inches. The Etsin-gol and its delta had previously been mapped by Bergman and Hörner and the Möruin-gol by Chen.

Camp no. 22 was pitched on the bank of the left arm, and here we had two good reasons for acceding to Georg's request for a day's break. For in the first place, our trusty Naidang was to return to Kwei-hwa, taking with him our letters ; in the second place, certain preparations had to be made for the long journey to Hami. Not the least-impor-tant task to be carried out during our day of rest was to break up ice in the river with axes and picks and fill nine bags with it—our water supply for the crossing of the Black Gobi.

Opposite us on the left bank was a custom-house with twenty or thirty sneaking rascals representing different firms on the Etsin-gol, but not armed. The customs is a public nuisance in China. Both Kansu and Ninghsia had their sharks on the Etsin-gol, who robbed and plundered traders and caravans. The right of exacting duties is farmed out to the highest bidder, and he takes what he can get, pays his principal, and keeps the surplus for himself.

Six miles away to the south, on the river, is the monastery of Etsin-lamain-sume, commonly called the Western Temple.

Everyone was busy on the last evening we spent in the Etsin-gol river complex. For in the morning we were to entrust our letters to Naidang. It was not without a certain feeling of solemnity that we enclosed the bundles of letters in their oilcloth and sacking, for no one could know whether this would not be the last chance we should have of sending news to our homes.

We had successfully completed the first great stage, the route through Inner Mongolia and the eastern Gobi to the Etsin-gol. A fresh stage, veiled in darkness and mystery, now confronted us. Next morning we were to burn our boats and defy that desolate wilderness which we knew well from our previous expedition, but only from a time when peace reigned in the heart of Asia. Now we had been warned that robber bands from the country of the Khalkha Mongols lay scattered about the desert, and we had heard a rumour that fresh revolts had broken out in Sinkiang.

When we shut the flaps of the tent-doors and put out the lights, we wondered if that night of January 17, 1934, our last by the Etsin-gol, would also be our last night of peace and quiet. The silence of the grave descended upon the camp, and the stars' pale blue shimmer trembled once more over our city on the march.

VIII

TO THE DAMBIN LAMA'S ROBBER CASTLE

ALTHOUGH the thermometer did not fall below 3·7 degrees, it felt bitterly cold in the strong south-west wind when we took our places in the convoy on the morning of January 18. My chauffeur, our noble doctor, need have no apprehensions about the ice on the Möruin-gol. It bore. It was at least 20 inches thick. On the left bank we drove up to the custom-house, where four of the trade-stranglers stepped out and showed us the way. No doubt they would have liked to levy dues on our baggage, but they dared not say a word.

We had hardly left this vipers' nest when we were up on barren *gobi* and drove past a large wooden cairn, set up to mark the road for caravans in sandstorms or snow blizzards. The road was excellent, and stood out like a pale stripe on a dark background.

A solitary foot-passenger came along leading a white camel. The desert was utterly desolate. This was the "Black Desert", called by the Mongols Khara Gobi. There was not a trace of vegetation except, very rarely, a few withered tussocks on low mounds. The country was level, and we only noticed the undulations of the ground when, now and again, the cars which were ahead disappeared from view. In places the caravan route was like a bundle of narrow foot-tracks. This is the great road which old Marshal Yang opened to traffic when he took up his post in the first years of the Republic.

The three motor-lorries, which were ahead, stopped to collect fuel for the evening's camp-fires. All the signposts were composed of dry saksaul stems, fastened together in small bundles. They stood along the route like branches set up in the sea to mark a fairway along the coast.

87

Ahead, a little to the right, low hills appeared, whose summits seemed to hover trembling above the horizon— the mirage and its deception tricks again.

In a short time we reached a curious place. Saksauls and a few poplars grew there among high dunes, and there was a branch custom-house and a temple called Kwan-yü-miao, built four years earlier on a slight elevation, whence there was a marvellous view to the west. When the custom-house was built, wood was stolen from a cairn close to the temple, and one of the thieves fell seriously ill in consequence. Kwan Yü was a still famous general of the time of the Three Empires, admired for his loyalty to his Emperor.

Close to the temple lay Lu-tsao-ching, " Reed Well ", around which reeds grew fairly thickly. When we left the temple, it was like putting out again into a desolate sea.

For miles and miles there was no change in the scenery. Only at rare intervals did we pass a belt of tussocks on dunes, and even more rarely tamarisks. Here was an old dried-up river-bed, with clearly marked erosion terraces, showing that water did sometimes find its way down the gully.

The hills we had just sighted were quite low ; yellow and black ridges, between which the road wound. Little shallow gullies, dark gravel, no vegetation. Porphyry with white veins of quartz ; small ledges and passes. We were in a labyrinth of little hills, where it was not difficult to drive in broad daylight ; but now the sun was sinking and throwing its blinding rays right in our eyes. The three lorries were ahead of us, and we followed in their tracks. But when the sun had sunk below the horizon, and the short twilight had given place to darkness, it was a hard enough job to see the little red flags set in the ground by the map-makers. This work is made much more difficult in such ground as I am describing by the fact that a hawk's eye is needed to detect the flags, and by the continual wind-ing of the route, which makes the bearings very short. In more open ground we took bearings on the cars' lamps after sunset. But at last we saw a fire far away under the little crescent moon, and reached our camp, which was ready to receive us.

After — 9·4 degrees during the night we proceeded along the clearly marked caravan track. Here, from time to time, we passed old camping-grounds, which betrayed themselves by heaps of camels' dung or the presence of holes for the caravan drivers' fires and cooking-pots.

The soil was for the most part absolutely barren. It was excellent for motor traffic, hard and level; road-makers could not improve on it. Sometimes we passed surfaces of hardened dry mud which had been carried down by rain-water into shallow depressions and had formed the finest parquet floor, as smooth as an asphalt road. Low hills rose at a distance to right and left of our route.

Everything went well till we had put behind us the first 6 miles of the day. Then the last car, Serat's, signalled to us to turn back. When the cars had assembled Serat told us that " Edsel ", the only one which was missing, had had a misadventure right in the camp, no. 23. Soon after we had left the place, and the motor-lorries were almost ready to leave, Georg, unable to get " Edsel's " frozen engine to start, had asked for a tow from Jomcha's car. " Edsel " stuck fast on a quite low but sharp ledge in a water-course while Jomcha was going at some pace. The jerk which followed bent " Edsel's " front axle somewhat, and put the lorry out of action. Georg sent us a message that he required at least two days to repair the damage.

We held a council of war. We should have to halt for a few days at the next well in any case to give Chen an opportunity of taking bearings. It was therefore decided that Jomcha and Effe should return to camp no. 23 with their cars and help Georg, while Serat with his lorry was to accompany us to the next camp.

So we proceeded westward. The ground now became rather worse, crossed as it was by a multitude of shallow little water-courses at only a few yards' distance from one another. This caused a rocking movement of the cars and materially checked our speed. The ground rose very slowly, with fairly gentle undulations.

Looking southward, the scenery was most impressive.

We saw, hardly 5 miles away, a very low dark ridge, resembling a sharply defined sea coast. Beyond and above it were visible three more ridges or elevations, coloured pale blue, and progressively paler as they grew more distant. This part of the desolate surface of the earth was quite confusingly like the sea and its mighty rolling swell. We could not take our eyes off the superb scenery; but we listened in vain for the roar of the surge against the cliffs. All was quiet and still, but for the west wind which howled and shrieked in the face of the cars. And the waves of stone were dry; there was not a drop of water.

The road crossed low narrow slate ledges. Three stone cairns stood on a ridge. Sometimes just one fair-sized stone, placed on end, was used to mark the road. To the right was a black mountain chain, 2 or 3 miles away; and from it, countless narrow gullies ran southward.

A little farther on, Serat halted to receive orders about pitching camp. He knew there were saksauls in a hollow a short distance to the left of the road, and that we had ample fuel there. We made our way towards it. Camp was pitched quickly and fuel-collecting began. In the meantime, Jomcha had arrived in his lorry with Kung as passenger. Kung told us that the situation at camp no. 23 looked rather serious. Georg had made his plans. " Edsel " was to be unloaded; the bent front axle was to be laid with its ends supported on two blocks of wood, but otherwise hanging free, like an arched bridge. Then a fully loaded lorry was to be placed with one of its back wheels leaning against the bent axle at the top of the curve. With the help of jacks, the wheel was to be lowered gently and gracefully, and the car's weight would force the axle back into its old shape. Heat and a blow-lamp were to be used to prevent the cold steel from snapping. Could so difficult an operation be successfully carried out in the middle of the desert? I was sceptical, and was quite prepared to lose " Edsel ".

On all sides, except to eastward, we were surrounded by hills and ridges, and jolted up and down over small gullies that crossed our road. We saw a kind of wagtail—a glimmer of life in that land of dead silence. We drove over hard, yellowish-red, slowly rising ground towards the foot of the hills that lay ahead of us. Then the scenery assumed a rather peculiar form. We crossed a small ridge, and went down its western side into a valley shaped like an arena. There was a scanty growth of ephedra bushes in the valley. Up again to another ridge, and down again into an arena-shaped valley. A whole string of these followed one another. The hills continually changed colour —grey, black, red and yellow. The earth too was yellowish-red. The road wound along—excellent, hard and sandless. Sometimes we saw skulls and whitened bones of dead camels. It must have been several years ago that they had fallen by the wayside, for trade had been paralysed during the war.

After crossing another little ridge we came into a labyrinth of low hills, valleys and dry beds of streams. Another ridge, and we saw before us a fairly wide open plain. We proceeded across it and found a well, the name of which we later ascertained to be Hung-liu-ka-ta-ching, " Tamarisk Root Well ". Camels' dung still lay there, left by caravans which had rested there a couple of years before. But the water had an unpleasant salt taste.

When we had waited vainly for the others for some time, we began to think that something had happened to them, and turned back. On the last ridge we found a red flag indicating a course to the northward ; and here, too, we came upon the tracks of our two motor-lorries. A little side valley led to Ye-ma-ching, " Wild Horse Well ", absolutely impossible to find except for one who, like Serat, had been there before. Here camp no. 25 was pitched, in a hole like a sack, with rather strongly marked hills on all sides.

In the new camp I put on my thinking-cap. Kung and Jomcha had brought reports of " Edsel's " condition which sounded rather serious ; they told me that Georg himself had thought it might possibly be necessary to send Effe with the front axle to the Etsin-gol, where he ought to catch Naidang before he started. Naidang would then take the axle with him to Peking to get it properly repaired.

In the circumstances I regarded it as my absolute duty

to find out for myself what the situation was, and to prevent Georg from taking any over-hasty decision on his own account—with the best intentions in the world—in order to save " Edsel " at all costs. The distance was only 60 miles, but even this was a long way in a waterless desert, where, according to the information we had received, we might expect to be attacked by robbers at any moment. The distance could easily be covered in the small car in three hours and a half, as we had no map-making to delay us.

I started just before noon with Yew as travelling companion and Jomcha as driver. Now, when we had the sun to one side and behind us, the desert looked if possible more beautiful than ever. The illusion of a boundless ocean was stronger than before. The wilderness lay spread out around us, silent and utterly lifeless. But no, completely lifeless that day the desert was not. Yew detected a black spot far away to the eastward.

" Is that one of Georg's cars ? " he wondered.

Out with the glasses ! In a little while we could make out that it was a camel, moving along slowly by the roadside. A few minutes more and we saw that it had no driver and carried no saddle. It was a wild camel, evidently one of those unlucky defeated rivals in the herd, who had too clearly betrayed his passion for the young she-camels and had been chastized by an older member of the herd. In such cases the victim is expelled and forced to live a solitary life till the mating season is past.

The beast had caught sight of us, and was presumably wondering why that clumsy black camel was in such a hurry. But he scented mischief, accelerated his speed, and vanished as swift as the wind among the hills to the southward.

Against the background of the hills by camp no. 23 we could see a tent and two motor-lorries. Good ! So Effe had not been sent to Naidang with the bent axle. Jomcha drove up to the tent, outside which Georg sat filing a screw, while the other three were putting on the wheel. They had not seen us, nor heard the noise of the engine until we were quite close to the camp.

" Well, how goes it ? " I asked.

" Why, everything's going A 1."

" Is the axle usable ? "

" Yes, perfectly ; we've straightened it out cold and didn't need to use heat."

" When will you be ready ? "

" At six to-morrow evening."

" We must start at dawn. Hurry up ! "

" What will you have for dinner, chief ? "

" *Pilmé* and tea."

Chokdung, who was an excellent cook, began to knead the dough at once.

Then Yew and I watched Effe, Georg and Jomcha putting the axle back into its grooves and screwing it tight.

Dinner was ready ! All seven of us, Swedes, Chinese and Mongols, sat down round the fire which burned in the tent *tollok*, and Chokdung served his *chef d'œuvre*, which tasted excellent. Bread and butter and strawberry jam completed this marvellous feast in the heart of the desert.

The tyres were put on by the light of electric torches and lanterns. We chatted round the fire till eleven o'clock, and then crept to bed, seven of us in the little tent. Yew and I had been placed side by side at the head of the chancel, just like Karl Knutsson and Magnus Ladulås in the Riddarholmskyrka in Stockholm. The others packed themselves in like sardines in a tin. The subjugation of " Edsel " had exhausted them, and their weariness was audible ; there was a regular orchestra of snorers, playing the weirdest tunes in every possible key. It sometimes sounded as if they were on the point of suffocation, or were making desperate efforts to swallow wild camels. The tent door was shut ; there was no breeze, only the fumes of returning *pilmé* and the combined perspirations of three nationalities. But at long last I fell asleep, and found life in the desert wonderful.

I was wakened next morning by the refreshing sound of " Edsel's " engine ; the lorry was doing a trial trip round and round the camp with its crew. The circles grew larger and larger ; " Edsel " was saved ! But the small car was a casualty instead. The cross-bar, which supported the

whole chassis, was cracked and must, I was told, be temporarily strengthened if I was not to have a spill. These
repairs would also take two days.

"No thanks, not now ; load up the cars and get ready
at once."

At two o'clock everything was ready. We drove slowly
to spare the small car. Twilight came, and then darkness.
At eight o'clock we were at the signal flag on the pass, where
the road turns off northward to " Wild Horse Well ".
The small car was ahead, doing not more than 12 miles
an hour. From time to time Yew and I made sure that
the headlights of the two lorries were shining behind us.
They gleamed like cats' eyes in the darkness. Sometimes
we could see only a reflection, and not the actual lights.

It took us only seven minutes from the flag to Ye-ma-
ching, where everyone hurried out of the tents on hearing
the noise of the engines. No one had thought that we
should be home again so soon, with " Edsel " saved and
in perfect working order. They had passed the time wandering about the neighbourhood, and Bergman, from one
of the higher summits, had taken a complete panoramic
photograph which gave a vivid impression of that labyrinth
of low, severely weathered ranges of hills, ridges and
valleys, and its fearful desolation. Not a sign of life in
any form had been visible, not even traces of wild animals.
The well did not justify its name, for no " wild horses "
or wild asses had put in an appearance.

In the evening Chen picked up the Nanking broadcast,
which gave us important news from China proper, but
none from Sinkiang.

We had to sacrifice one day at Ye-ma-ching. The cross-
bar must be strengthened before the small car was regarded as fit for service. Once more the camp resembled
an open-air mechanical workshop and a colony of settlers
in the wilds.

In the night of January 24 we had a temperature of
— 14·8, but the morning was still and clear, and it did not
feel at all cold. It took some time to start the cars, but
at last we were able to get clear away and drive out on to
the great caravan route. We left on our right the highest

point in the district, which is 4,940 feet above the sea. The doctor and Kung had built a cairn on its summit. The Ye-ma-ching camp was 4,680 feet up.

Crossing numerous erosion gullies, which showed that it really could rain hard in that arid region, we returned to Hung-liu-ka-ta-ching, near which there were small vegetation-clad cones. Fresh mountains rose ahead of us. At their foot we crossed a deep-cut water-course. We doubled the first black promontory which sprang out of the mountain like a cape. Then fresh gullies emerged from the mountain, and we passed another cape. The road ran right along the base of the mountains, and grew worse and worse. We went up and down and in and out over ravines, gullies and hills ; everywhere the ground was covered with rough, black, sharp-edged gravel. To find a better surface we went down a nasty, black-gravel off-shoot of the mountains and got into a steeply descending gully which was too narrow for the motor-lorries. We signalled to them, and they found a practicable way through. Then we clung faithfully to the base of the mountains, always through the same tyre-destroying gravel. In places the lorries took on so severe a list that one expected to see them turn over at any moment. The small car crept forward slowly and cautiously ; the four lorries followed. New black offshoots projected from the mountains to the right. More than once we had to wait for the lorries, wondering if one of them had been wrecked and would have to be dismantled. A road would have to be made here for the traffic of the future.

The road grew better later ; it was level, though the soil was loose, in the winding valley into which we now drove between black mountains, higher than those we had seen till now.

A flock of small birds rose and disappeared. What did they live on, and where did they get water ? It was as desolate there as in the moon.

To southward a valley ran parallel to us from east to west ; it probably formed a basin from which water could not escape.

Our valley grew narrower, and at last there was hardly

room for a draught camel to get through. So we had to back, turn round and look for another route. In a wider part of the valley the soil was very sandy, and two of the lorries got stuck. While we were trying to free them, the sun sank; so we pitched camp and lighted a fire. We had water with us always, for our store of ice was not yet exhausted. Saksauls grew there, and a bush which the Mongols call the *khara-burgas*. A fox's track was printed on the sand; what can Reynard have been seeking in so wretched a hunting-ground?

From the camp it was only a short distance to a pass, from which there was a superb view over an endless landscape to westward. On the other side there was a rather sharp descent through deep sand, which rose in clouds and whirled behind the spinning wheels.

We came to flat sandy ground with living and dead saksauls. A range of medium height rose to the southward; we steered south-west and soon reached harder ground with small and scanty tufts of vegetation. In one place the saksauls were regular trees. The road ran along a shallow gully between red, rounded terraces; then we were surrounded by low red hillocks with shallow gullies between them. We sometimes saw a cairn marking that lifeless caravan route. In sheltered places lay small patches of snow, left by a probably local snowfall. We ascended into a valley between savage grey cliffs; from its bottom rose the point of a rock, or possibly a detached block. During a rest, Effe seated himself in a niche-like crevice in the rock, and was photographed.

The valley grew narrower and narrower, and more and more picturesque; a savage piece of sculpture, with grey pyramid-shaped summits, and tamarisks and saksauls growing on mounds of sand. More and more snow lay in shady spots. We drove on through a regular scrub, between wild rocks. The dunes climbed up the slopes of the mountains on both sides. A little farther on, the mountains stopped and open country again lay before us. On the other side the ground sloped away very slowly to the north-west. This plain seemed to have no limit; only to north and south were mountains visible.

Serat, Jomcha and Georg were driving a little way in front of us side by side, the lorries looking like three grey elephants. They stopped and waited for us, but only to have a chat. Then they jumped into their cabins again and drove on over the desert that was as grey as themselves. They disappeared into a hollow, but soon reappeared on the farther side of it and seemed to stand motionless, sharply silhouetted, on the crest of an undulation that would otherwise have escaped notice. Round hillocks, only 10 feet or so high, stood about singly or in rows, resembling ancient barrows. The desert was entirely barren, but nevertheless we saw a few antelopes. To southward, a chain of hills ran away from us in a pretty subdued shade of blue. It may sound paradoxical, but it is true to say that the skeletons of dead camels were the only sign of life to be seen in that kingdom of death. We were often deceived as to the distance of objects. Sometimes a mountain seemed to be fairly near, but it took hours to reach it ; another time, we would take a hill close by for a distant mountain.

We passed a few scanty belts of vegetation and rolled up to a new ridge, about 5,000 feet high ; on the farther side the plain recommenced. Thence it was not far to the camp which had been pitched by the crews of the three elephants.

Next day the tufts of vegetation were rather more frequent than before. We passed a few old caravan camps and camels' skeletons. Around us lay a wide depression, whose sediment of yellow clay showed that it had once been the bottom of a lake. The mountains to southward are called the Ma-tsung-shan, " Horse's Mane Mountains ", and we understood that this name was applied to the whole district.

A curiously chiselled flat country, red-hued ; shallow depressions full of sand and tussocks separated from one another by plateau-like elevations with a hard gravel surface, *gobi* or sheer desert. To the south, quite close to us, we had a lowish black chain of hills ; and south of this again a higher grey-violet range, from which streaks of snow hung in a way that might have suggested a horse's

mane. Two herds of antelopes—five and eight strong—
were surprised grazing in a depression and fled over the
desert plateaux, bounding like balls.

Our route expert Serat declared that the Ho-shao-ching
well, "Cake Well", could not be far off; he recognized
the little clay mounds and higher tamarisk-clad cones which
betrayed its proximity. The well was not easy to find, for
tracks from old caravan camps converged there from several
directions. But at last we found the well. It seemed not
to have been in use for a long time, for it was full of dust
and sand, scraps of wool and other rubbish.

It was as hard a job to find the way back from the well
to the high road. At last we found it, through a depression
full of tall, handsome saksauls. Just beyond the well we
were 5,260 feet up, and so were ascending westward. And
the farther westward we moved, the larger were the snow-
fields which crowned the Ma-tsung-shan.

It was eleven o'clock when we halted at the Kung-pao-
chüan spring, which has its birth in a hollowed bed. Water-
weeds grew there, in which little crustaceans were running
about. Below the spring fair-sized ice-floes extended, like
a miniature frozen lake.

When we had eaten a simple lunch on the bank of this
attractive spring, we went on to the Dambin Lama's old
castle among the rounded foot-hills of the southern mountains. Here grey walls of stone and sun-baked brick surrounded a little courtyard. All the ceilings, which were
made of tamarisk-stems and other timber, had disappeared,
so that the castle made the impression of a ruin. The
various rooms were joined by confined passages and corridors, narrow staircases and doorways without doors. A
square watch-tower rose on one side of the courtyard.
Stone benches, fastened to the floor, stood round the walls
of the justice-room. Another room had been the audience
chamber. The Dambin Lama's private rooms, no larger
than cupboards, were reached by a steep and narrow flight
of stairs. From their peep-holes there was a wide view
over the desert. There was also a kitchen with a stone
range and place for a cooking-pot, as well as an opening
to let out the smoke.

The Dambin Lama, "the false lama", established himself in this strong castle and exacted dues from the caravans. Ten years ago before our visit he had been attacked by Khalkha Mongols and killed. Now the tracks showed that only foxes and birds were masters of the romantic fortress, a place that gave free rein to the imagination.[1]

[1] Lattimore, in his book *The Desert Road to Turkistan*, has described the Central Asiatic adventurer's life in some detail, and Roerich deals with the same subject in *Trails to Inmost Asia*.

IX

THROUGH THE BLACK GOBI

AFTER our short visit to what had been the " false
lama's " nest of robbers we had to cross an unpleasant stretch of vegetation-clad hillocks, lumps of clay
covered with scrub and grass, which are good for camels
but bad for cars. Serat stopped to examine the ice of a
frozen water-course, which was only 6 feet 6 inches wide
and obviously came from a spring. The ice bore.

A little farther on he halted again at a bad place, on which
he and two of the other men got to work with picks and
spades. It was up and down all the way through deep
gullies and scrub-clad mounds one after the other. The
soil was an almost white loose clay with an admixture of
soda.

Tiao-hu, " Leaping Lake ", was a typical reedy marsh
with several shimmering green ice-floes partly covered with
a thin layer of snow. Antelopes went there to drink. At
this point there were wide fields of the tall hard yellow
grass which the Mongols call *tsaghan-derisun*.

Once again Serat got caught in a horrid trap. He and
his men jumped out and began, with picks and axes, to
attack some nasty knolls, tough and obstinate because of
the roots which ran through and through them. Meanwhile the doctor tried to get past in the small car. Yew,
Chen and I jumped out to lighten it. But even with the
car empty he got stuck, with the bottom of the car inexorably caught up on a hillock. There he sat philoso-
phizing. Serat was more fortunate, and went on across
that disgusting field of loose clay and mounds, with their
framework of grass roots and scrub. He swayed and
bumped from right to left, up and down like a boat in a
heavy sea, and several times he was on the point of over-

turning. It seemed to me a miracle that both axles and springs did not break.

When he had driven out on to better ground, he came walking back to us. And now spades and picks were set to work on the scrub-clad hillock on which we had stuck. At the same time Georg, Effe and Jomcha drove ahead with their lorries. They had a rather easier task, since we had prepared the way for them. When the obstructing hillock had been well smashed up we all shoved, and the small car was freed.

After all this loss of time and hard work we went on, bumping and swaying, till we reached the end of that horrible area. I preferred to walk. Soon it was reported that the front spring of the small car had broken. Its longest blade was off and must be replaced by a new one. We could not obtain any fuel except roots.

To the south, the Ma-tsung-shan was looking more and more magnificent; for now the range was higher and covered with snow from summit to foot. Blue shadows emphasized its rugged contours as the sun approached the horizon. We were here about 5,500 feet up.

On January 28 we had a completely overcast sky, after — 4·5 degrees in the night. The whole morning was spent in putting in the new spring. It was nearly twelve before we got off. Effe's motor-lorry, in which Bergman was seated, accompanied us. Whenever he wanted to take a bearing he had to jump out, place the compass on its stand, and take the bearing. The three " elephants " were ahead, rolling on over the barren, undulating desert. In an hour and a half we came to a double well, which our Chinese thought to be situated exactly on the border between the provinces of Ninghsia and Kansu. We were not far from the boundary of Sinkiang, if it was true that it ran 20 li, or 6 miles, west of Ming-shui.

We took a small supply of water from the well, which was 6 feet 6 inches deep. Here too we saw the traces of caravans which had rested at the spot. Farther on we drove through a sort of gateway, 50 yards wide, between two conspicuous hills, and directly afterwards through another. Here we were 5,915 feet above sea-level.

To south of the road stood a herd of wild asses, with ears pricked, nostrils distended, and their eyes steadily fixed on us. They were reddish-yellow or tawny yellow in colour, with white chests and bellies, and they were as regally proud in their bearing, as supple and graceful as the Tibetan *kiang* or the *kula* of Tsaidam. When they had made quite certain that we were not of their kind, they swung about as though struck by an electric shock, and fled southward at a swift gallop.

Our road followed the bed of a river in among low hills, where bushes grew in abundance and the patches of snow became larger and more frequent. We were climbing all the time ; we were now 6,080 feet up and our course was north-west. We were evidently approaching a pass, a watershed. A winding valley led to it, and the highest point was 6,435 feet above sea-level.

On the other side lay a plain, spotted white with snow-flakes. Our direction was roughly west. We pitched camp no. 29 at a height of 6,800 feet.

The distance to Ming-shui could not now be more than 9 miles. On a brilliantly clear and still morning, after a night temperature of − 11·7, we proceeded towards this place. There we ought to be 162 miles from Hami, the town where our fate would be decided. Fairly high snow-mountains rose to the southward. A splendid argali head with great twisted horns shone as white as the patch of snow on which it lay. A couple of antelopes dashed away southward. The snow formed an arrow-head on the eastern side of each tussock—there had been a snowstorm from the west quite lately.

We crossed a low ridge between two mountains. An imperceptibly declining plain stretched to the westward, with scanty tussocks and soil in various shades of red and yellow, in places covered with snow. At several points we crossed the tracks of wild asses in the snow. The mountains to north and south, snow-clad from crown to foot, were like vast monuments of blinding white marble ; the scenery became beautiful in the grand manner, im-pressively majestic.

It was still early in the afternoon when we halted by the

ruins of the 2,000-year-old fort and the watch-towers, which still mark the great Han emperors' outermost defences to the north-west against the threatening empire of the Huns.

We jumped out and, while the tents were being pitched, inspected the blocks, still solid and defiant in their decay. A few gaping holes under them seemed to betray subterranean rooms, to which foxes' tracks in the snow led. Effe crept in with a gun, and the dog Pao was sent down on a reconnaissance. But all remained silent ; there was no one at home.

We were to stop for a few nights at Ming-shui, " Clear Water ", to give Chen an opportunity of establishing a second astronomical point between the Etsin-gol and Hami.

On the ridge we had just left behind us, where we had ascertained the height to be 6,920 feet, we had passed what was, according to our altimeter readings, the highest point on the whole of the northern motor route to Sinkiang.

On approaching Ming-shui, we wondered if any Khalkha Mongols or robber bands would receive us at this place, where water, grazing and fuel were all to be had. Perhaps General Ma Chung-yin had patrols or frontier horsemen there to guard the entrance to the province he intended to conquer. But nothing living was visible, not a trace of men or horses ! Antelopes were grazing on the plain ; but we could discover no other sign of life.

These fortifications of sun-dried brick had stood for 2,000 years in the midst of the arena-shaped valley, defying countless sandstorms and snow blizzards, and time had not yet been able to obliterate them. Seven solid blocks still remained, and it would certainly require further centuries to level them with the ground and extinguish their last traces. A day would come when the archæologists would no longer be able to identify the place, and the foxes would have to dig their earths elsewhere.

It was said that there was no longer any water in the Ming-shui well. It had probably silted up since the caravan traffic stopped. So it was lucky for us that a snowstorm had raged over the district only, perhaps, a

week before. We had thus an abundance of water just
outside our tents. In the gullies and depressions the drifts
were a foot deep. Curiously enough, camels' dung still
lay there in long lines, showing how the beasts had been
tethered at night. Two years' sun, cold, wind and rain
had not been able to destroy it.

We woke on January 30 to find an insignificant little
north-wester in progress. It was not blowing really hard,
only about 23 feet a second, and the thermometer had not
been below 0·9. But nevertheless it was cold and unpleasant, the whole sky was overclouded, it was half dark
and gloomy. We were reluctant to get up, and lamented
that the day looked so unpromising for Chen's observations. Now there had come a break in the long series
of beautiful clear, light days we had so far enjoyed since the
winter had begun.

It began to snow at 6 p.m. and was still snowing at
10 p.m., when all the ground was as white as a dead man's
shroud. It snowed sharply and silently. This snowstorm
need only continue for a few days for us to be snowed
up—so near our goal! But if we were snowed up and
detained at Ming-shui for weeks, there would certainly
be some higher meaning and significance in it, and it would
be to our own advantage. A bloody revolt would be over
before we arrived, or a ruthless general would withdraw
before he could get his claws into us. I therefore listened
with perfect peace of mind to the sound of the snowflakes
slithering down the tent-cloth.

Chen and his wireless afforded us a little distraction.
The evening before he had picked up the message, "All
quiet in China—Sun Fo has told a reporter that no news
has been received from Sinkiang." And on the 30th the
Nanking broadcast announced: "Hwang Mu-sung is being
sent to Tibet to mediate. Sheng Shih-tsai has informed
Nanking that southern Sinkiang has not, as has been
declared, separated itself from the province."

These two messages really told us nothing. "Nothing
new from the western front" most probably meant that
the borders of the theatre of war were so hermetically
sealed that no news got through. The assertion that

southern Sinkiang, or Eastern Turkistan, had cut itself
off from the province was, as we were soon to discover,
considerably nearer the truth on January 30 than the denial
that such a thing had happened. The two messages were
anything but encouraging for our prospects of getting
across the boundary of Sinkiang. This ought to have increased our anxiety, but we took the news pretty quietly
and coolly considered the future. The decisive day, on
which our questions would be answered, was only a week
off.

On January 31 the minimum thermometer showed
— 15·7. The ground was white everywhere, and we were
surrounded by a real winter landscape in all its desolate,
silent magnificence. Thick clouds covered the sky, but
in the afternoon the sun broke through. Bergman drew
a plan of the ruins, and the rest of us wrote in our diaries.
It was blowing from the north-west. Clouds piled themselves up round the sun as it approached the horizon.

We could tell by the state of the ruins that the north-
westerly winds had been stronger than the south-easterly
during the past 2,000 years, for the south-eastern sides,
and the blocks which stood there, were fairly straight, while
those which faced north-west were rounded and severely
weathered by the winds.

On the night of January 31 the cold increased to — 21
degrees. The sky was as hopelessly overclouded as before.
The sun sank into a bed of clouds, but the western horizon
was aflame with glowing red, dying away into pale violet
hues among clouds and cloudlets. Late in the evening
the sky cleared and Chen had a view of his stars. But he
needed another night, so we had to arm ourselves with
patience.

On the morning of February 2, we heard that Chen had
worked all night till 7.20 a.m., and that in a temperature
which fell to 58½ degrees of frost (— 26·5 degrees). Yew,
Hummel and Kung helped him till 2 a.m. by keeping up a
fire in the tent, so that he could sometimes warm his
hands. They also gave him tea and food to keep body
and soul together. After that San Wa-tse had to help him.

The morning was brilliant ; only on the horizon were

light clouds visible. Now a good deal of the fresh snow would no doubt disappear and do us no further injury.

Bergman had found that the old Han fort had formed an inner square 80 feet each way. Outside this seven or eight massive towers had been built, 20 feet high and measuring 17 feet across the base. On the north side the structure was protected by a wall, now resembling rather a low wide rampart 49 feet wide across the base. On the south side a natural ravine formed a trench. Bronze arrowheads of the usual Han type, and of different sizes according to the calibre of the bows, were found round the foot.

The night of February 2 was also cold, — 24 degrees being registered. Early in the morning a milk-white mist, like spilt cream, was floating across the plain, driven by a light south-easterly breeze. Over our heads the sky was blue. The mountains were hidden by the mist, but their summits rose above it. Grasses and scrub, packing-cases and petrol cans were covered with a thick hoar-frost and looked as if they were carved in alabaster. The ruins peered ghost-like out of the floating mist. The landscape was fantastically beautiful in a raiment which cannot be described in words.

So we drove away from the Han emperors' fort, left behind us on our right a detached tower on an offshoot of the mountain, passed close to one of the Ming-shui wells and steered north-west. Soon we were among mountains, and crossed the course of a brook where the snow lay fairly thickly heaped. We had to make a short detour to north-ward because of the snow. Regarded as a road, this course was horrible, a labyrinth of lumps and knolls, tussocks and terraces, gullies and ravines, all treacherously concealed by the drifts. We could not see or judge how deep the holes were, so that we often sank unpleasantly far into the snow.

The second well is situated in the valley, among the ruins of a couple of modern houses and granite rocks scooped out and made shapeless by the wind.

Here and there the ground was soft with sand, and it was slow work for our convoy. Now one of the motor-lorries stuck fast and had to be dug out, now another. Several times we had to stop and wait while the crew shovelled away the snow out of a ravine.

We were ascending gently towards a new pass. The mist did not rise so high, and the air was quite clear, but if one looked back one saw that the white veil still filled the bottom of the broad valley about Ming-shui. We reached the pass, only 120 feet higher than Ming-shui.

The drop from the top of the pass was rather steep, and all our brakes were put on. We descended into a fresh arena-shaped valley between slate rocks. We could make out in the distance the faint outlines of the Tien-shan. There was more snow lying west of the pass.

We had not seen the tracks of a human being for the past 300 miles; so that we were all interested when we saw in the fresh snow the tracks of a man walking in a southerly direction, leading a camel and a horse. We never found out who this traveller was.

All round us rose dark hills of medium height. Belts of country were thickly covered with scrub, and saksauls reappeared. The road, some 6 or 7 feet wide, wound over a broad plain. We were descending imperceptibly, but were already 1,140 feet below the last pass. The undulating ground was fairly hard, but was crossed by innumerable gullies full of snow. Serat stuck in one of these and had to be dug out.

Camp no. 31 was prepared 1,300 feet below Ming-shui in the middle of the open plain, which was framed by mountains and crossed by snow-filled gullies. One of these was deeper than those we had previously encountered; and a road had to be dug next morning right through the drifts. The first low pass we had crossed, east of Ming-shui, is the watershed between small local streams on the east side and a fair-sized collecting trough farther west, south of Hami. The other pass, north-west of Ming-shui, is of secondary importance. The deep gully close to Ming-shui runs to the collecting-basin south of Hami and unites with other local water-courses. The mountains to the south were part of the highest ridge of the Pei-shan.

The morning of February 4 opened clear and still, but

the sky looked threatening round Karlik-tagh, " the Snow-Mountains " [1], to the west-north-west. Gloomy blue-black masses of cloud gathered round the mountain-tops; they seemed to rise towards the zenith and approach us like a gigantic tidal wave rolling eastward. The nearest mountains to the south, with their strips of snow, were still visible, and in the east a patch of blue sky shone out, but it was soon beclouded and disappeared. In short, the sky over Hami was dark and gloomy, perhaps an omen of the events that awaited us there.

The quantity of snow decreased. We followed the camel route, which was well marked, because snow still lay on the track, sunk below the surface of the ground by constant trampling, so that it shone like a white ribbon. But here and there the snow was continuous and hid the track altogether, and we had to steer by instinct. Once we lost the way completely and had to halt and reconnoitre. Then we got stuck in a ditch again, and five of our fellows had to get out and ply their spades. At times the surface was treacherous. It would bear the small car for a little way, but then it would break, and there we were with a few feet of snow piled up under us. Then the car had literally to be dug out.

It began to snow lightly. Now the whole sky was wrapped in clouds. During the first two hours' travelling we stuck in the snow twenty times. Each lorry had two spades at its disposal, the small car only one.

Later the ground became more favourable; the gullies were now smaller and the road excellent. Tussocks and bushes grew on transverse belts of ground. An unusually large cairn was constructed of dry tamarisk stems and camels' skeletons, with a skull right on the top as a reminder of the way all flesh must go and the dangers that lie in wait for the desert traveller. The snow grew thinner; a little later patches of snow became rare, and those we did see were covered with drift-sand and dust.

The threatening clouds to northward had grown lighter, and the spurs and foot-hills of the Tien-shan became visible in faint outline.

[1] Karlik-tagh is a designation rather than a real name.

We rolled down a new sloping terrace, like several others we had passed. We seemed to be approaching lower and lower ground, as though descending stairs. On the steep slopes of the staircase drift-sand lay in heaps. A solitary poplar appeared in a little valley that crossed our route. There was no trace of snow now ; the last fall had obviously occurred only on the higher ground.

Late in the afternoon we reached Wu-tung-wo-tse, " Poplar Hollow ",—an ice-covered strip of water 15 yards wide and 100 yards long, supplied by an underground spring. Georg collected two sackfuls of ice. Then we went on, along the top of a terrace, where the grey soil was absolutely barren. It cleared up a little, but the Karlik-tagh was still hidden in clouds. At the last river-bed we had passed our lowest point—about 3,360 feet ; so that we had descended by more than 3,250 feet since Ming-shui.

The plain lay before us, seemingly endless. The clouds dissolved, and the evening sun peeped out. But it sank, and bearings were taken by lamplight. We encamped in the middle of the plain after a day's journey of nearly 60 miles.

During the night the temperature was nil. The Karlik-tagh was a magnificent sight in the early morning hours, with its blue shimmering snow-fields among the mighty contours of the mountains. But they were soon hidden in the same threatening cloud-wreaths as on the previous days. To westward the sky was clear. Now and again the shadows of clouds passed over the desert like black cloths.

On we went across the barren desert. We seldom passed a cairn, and just as seldom a skeleton. Now and then we saw the traces of old caravan camps. From Ming-shui we had been following a north-westerly course, but now were going west.

Five cairns crowned a small rise. Farther on we recognized the small flattish hills among which Miao-erh-kou, the most easterly village in Sinkiang, is situated. Miao-erh-kou was the first properly inhabited place we had reached on January 19, 1928, after our former trip through the Gobi. The doctor could even make out the white cupola-crowned *mazar* or saint's tomb, which stands on a dominating hillock.

In 1928 a few Turki families still lived in Miao-erh-kou.
If these decent people were still there in their simple houses
of sun-dried brick, we should meet old friends and find out
how the land lay, and if the war between Ma Chung-yin
and Sheng Shih-tsai was still raging, or if peace had been
concluded. It was, therefore, not without an understandable excitement that we searched the hills to westward
with our glasses.

Half an hour later the *mazar* was clearly visible. We
approached the little frozen brook of the oasis, with its
reed-beds and wild rose bushes. Now we had reached the
mountains which rose to the right of our track. To the
left, at the foot of a projecting cliff, we had seen six years
before a Chinese temple in a grove of tall trees. This
temple had now disappeared. The road wound between
the low hills up to the top of the plateaux. A herd of
antelopes fled from us—antelopes here, right on top of a
village !

It was one o'clock when we reached the village itself.
We could see at once that the tide of war had swept over
this little outpost. None of the houses had roofs, and the
clay walls were left standing bare. During a quarter of an
hour's rest we went in and looked round. Not a sign of
life was visible. No dogs had met us with their barking,
no chickens were pecking about among the houses. And
another herd of antelopes fled ; they had been right up to
the cottages. The village was devastated and abandoned,
and there was nothing of the smallest value in the houses.
But Ma or Sheng, whichever was lord over Miao-erh-kou,
ought to have left a picket in the place, the province of
Sinkiang's last outpost towards a trade route which not
long ago was one of the greatest in China, and towards
Kansu and Ninghsia. The whole business seemed to us
more than mysterious, and we left the silent village with
serious premonitions.

We rolled out into the level desert through the gateway
in the rocks we remembered so well. A herd of grazing
antelopes crossed the road just in front of the first car and
disappeared to the southward. We left on the right a
watch-tower and a solitary clay house.

We passed the I-kung spring on its terrace. The country was barren. At rare intervals we saw a cairn. They were no longer *obos*; we were now in Mohammedan country, where the cairns are simply called, in Turki, *nischan* or " marks ".

The sea, the sea! Once more the endless plain lay spread before us; its horizon seemed beyond our reach. The road was good, and the three " elephants " rushed westward in clouds of dust as though hunted by furies. Here stood a lonely little clay house, with the tracks of a cart running up to it. But it might have driven up long ago. Huge reed-beds! Tracks of cart wheels, sunk as much as a foot into the ground, and between them a shallower depression trampled by the draught animals' hooves, bore witness to busy traffic in the past. But now—not a soul, no fresh traces of men, animals or carts. We were in a forsaken country, as desolate as the desert itself, a land where only the silence of death reigned.

Almost suffocated in the clouds of dust stirred up by the cars' wheels, we could not see exactly where the others were. Serat was ahead of us; Jomcha had a flat tyre. Where was Georg? why, he was ahead too. We put on speed to overtake him. I gave orders for camp to be pitched; it was late, and it would not be desirable to drive right up to Hami in the dark. Georg drove on. Now the whole convoy was split up. It would have been better to keep together just then. The doctor and Chen ascended clay mounds by the roadside and gave the signal " about turn " with red flags. They could see Georg overtaking Serat, and both turning with great difficulty on that road, with its deep ruts and the impenetrable reed-beds on each side.

Gradually they all collected where we were, and we pitched camp by a solitary poplar. This camp, no. 33, lay 1,270 feet lower than the previous one. We had, in fact, been descending ever since we left Ming-shui. Here there was an open fresh-water spring. We did not know the name of the place, but we were only 2 or 3 miles from the village of Hwang-lu-kang, " Yellow Reeds Ridge ".

The four tents were pitched and the fires lighted. As

usual, we had tea with cakes and jam, served in my tent, and then had to wait a couple of hours till Chia Kwei had the pea soup and rissoles ready. Eighteen days had passed since we last saw a human being. Now we were quite close to the first outlying village of the Hami oasis.

But not a soul was to be seen, no patrols were out, no camels, horses or oxen grazed on the luxuriant yellow grass, and no dogs barked.

What had happened? Was the country totally devastated and depopulated? Who ruled over this abandoned region? In the robber districts to the eastward we had set a night-watch. But here no measures of precaution were necessary. We were in high spirits. There was talking and laughter in my tent, and we sat up longer than usual.

We would not give up till we had found all entrances and exits shut. If we were expelled from Hami we meant to make a bend to the south-east along the road to Anhsi and, about half-way to that town, swing westward and try to reach Altmish-bulak and Korla through the Pei-shan. We should, in a word, leave nothing unattempted before beginning the retreat to Nanking.

Under blazing stars, by paling camp-fires, we slept peacefully that last night before the die was cast and we crossed our Rubicon.

X

WE ARE ATTACKED, ROBBED OF OUR CARS AND IMPRISONED [1]

WHEN, on the morning of February 6, we began our last day's journey into Hami, we had not the faintest idea of the real situation in the province of Sinkiang, torn by rebellion and civil war. On the Etsin-gol and at Ming-shui we had picked up by wireless random messages saying that peace and quiet prevailed, and only one short communiqué had something to say about a local revolt among the Turki population east of Hami. But this revolt ought to be over by now, and perhaps we should be able to cross the border of Sinkiang without any adventures.

No one had any doubts. The Chinese and Mongols in our expedition were as determined as the Swedes. We did not even hold a council of war when we approached the outskirts of the oasis, and paid little attention to the few countrymen who stood staring outside occasional farms. We just drove ahead. *Jacta est alea, transibimus Rubiconem !* It was a step big with fate. But we continued.

In front of us the road divided like a fork, the right-hand branch leading into the village of Hwang-lu-kang, while the left-hand branch led past a tent. On both sides of us some twenty soldiers appeared, some on horseback, but most on foot. They threw themselves down along the road and held their rifles at the ready. Yew, who was driving with Serat, realized at once what a critical moment it was, and ordered the car to be stopped by the tent. If he and Serat had gone a few yards farther they would have been exposed to a murderous short-range fire. When Yew

[1] This chapter is a summary of my earlier book *Big Horse's Flight*. It has been inserted to preserve the sequence of the story.

opened the door and jumped out, with arms held up to show that he had no weapons, the rifles were lowered. Yew called up the commander, who advanced cautiously to the car with finger on trigger.

"Who are you?" he asked brusquely. "Where do you come from? Where are you going? Have you passports? Are you armed?"

Yew replied calmly. Meanwhile the convoy had come up. I showed our passports. The garrison of the outpost crowded round us. Our passports were examined and stamped.

Then we were disarmed. We were told to stay where we were until orders regarding our treatment arrived from Hami. Soon the reply came that we might proceed. We resumed our places in the cars, which were also manned by soldiers, and the heavy convoy moved off again through the dust into the village of Hwang-lu-kang. Twice the road was barred by bands of soldiers with rifles at the ready before we at last drove into Hami safe and sound and stopped outside the commandant Chang's *yamên*. Here we were well received. Our passports were shown again and the impounded rifles and pistols were returned to us.

So our lot was cast. Our situation was, to say the least, exciting. The talk of things being quiet in Sinkiang, which the wireless had circulated, was far from being true; on the contrary, the war had evidently just reached its decisive and bloodiest stage, and we had got right into the midst of this war!

It would have been best for us to turn back from the military post at Hwang-lu-kang, where the road through Kansu via Suchow and Anhsi joins the route we had travelled from the Etsin-gol, and make straight for Anhsi and China proper. But according to the instructions we had received from Nanking, we were to examine one of the three roads which led to Chuguchak, Kulja and Kashgar. And there was not one member of the expedition who thought for a moment of returning eastward before this part of the programme too had been carried out.

Besides, it was too late to turn back! We had crossed the frontier, and were in the hands of General Ma Chung-yin,

Big Horse. He alone could decide our fate. We begged
Commandant Chang to ask whether the road to Turfan was
open to us. The reply came that we were welcome.

We therefore proceeded to Turfan. Everywhere we
were received with consideration and courtesy. Rooms
were kept in readiness in the places through which we
passed. We were not even allowed to pay for the supplies
we needed ; everything was placed freely at our disposal.
We were shown the arsenal at Turfan, were allowed to
witness the enrolment of troops and enjoy unrestricted
freedom. Only the road to Urumchi was, naturally,
barred, for Ma was occupying the mountain passes at
Dawan-cheng, between that town and Turfan, and there
ran the front between the contending armies. On the
other hand, we might travel unhindered via Kara-shahr,
Korla, Kucha and Aksu to Kashgar, and letters of instructions addressed to the commanding officers in all these
towns were given to us at General Ma's orders.

But what we did not know, and what no one dared to
hint to us, was that General Ma's own fate hung on a
thread just at that time, and that in a few weeks he and the
whole of his army would evacuate their positions and
retreat to Kucha, Aksu and Kashgar in hurried flight along
the same road we intended to follow westward. Thus we
were placed between hammer and anvil in an even higher
degree than we had feared.

The road from Turfan to Kara-shahr via Toksun led
through devastated or burning villages, and we met or
drove past small parties of fleeing country people. The
commandant at Kara-shahr received us civilly, and we
obtained all the help we needed to transport the five cars
over the Khaidu-gol, the ice of which was just breaking up.

We were now in March, and a time began which was
beyond comparison the worst and wildest I had experienced
in Asia since, in 1885, I set out upon my first expedition in
the great continent. It would be unfair to make General
Ma Chung-yin himself responsible for the acts of violence
committed against us by his troops. These were for the
most part Tungans—Chinese who had embraced Islam and,
during previous Tungan rebellions, made themselves

notorious for their bloodthirstiness and bestial cruelty. They have always had a special hatred for the Chinese.

When we reached Korla in pitch darkness on the evening of March 4 we found the town occupied by troops of this kind, professional man-slayers, veterans from the last wars in Kansu, where, a few years before, they had slaughtered at least 10,000 of the civil population in the oases on the southern edge of the desert. When our convoy of motor-cars, by the light of a few lamps, thundered into the main street of the bazaar of Korla, we went straight into a nest of robbers and handed ourselves over to the mercies of the cruel soldiery.

Ma's chief of staff, General Li at Turfan, had, when we left that town, given us an escort of five men and begged us to take them with us as far as Aksu, or, if possible, to Kashgar. This "escort" soon showed themselves to be dangerous companions. On the journey they fired to right and left out of sheer mischief, and in the village of Kumush one of them, through sheer carelessness, was within an ace of shooting Dr. Hummel. Their commander Chang was a graceless whelp, who put on insolent airs in dealing with us and was backed up by two scoundrelly subordinates.

On March 5 the escort asked if they might "borrow" one of our lorries and a driver, on the ground that they had received orders to take an important message to the front at Aksu. I refused emphatically. Our cars belonged to the Government, and we had no right to dispose of them. At 10 p.m. two other men appeared and asked me to come to headquarters at once to answer important telephone messages from Kara-shahr. I took Yew, Georg and Effe. We drove in the small car, unarmed.

Effe remained in the car while we went into headquarters. Chang again put forward his demand for a motor-lorry in a dictatorial tone. I refused absolutely to hand it over. He continued roughly:

"I shall have one of your lorries to-night whether you allow it or not."

I rose and went out to the cars. Yew accompanied me. I took my seat in the car. Yew had grasped the handle

and was about to get in when three soldiers rushed forward
and dragged him away by force. He resisted. I shouted,
" Keep calm and go with them," and myself hurriedly got
out of the car, whereupon I likewise was seized by some
soldiers and pushed back into the courtyard with rifle-
butts. Effe and Georg too had been arrested. What
followed was the work of a few minutes. Rough, horny
hands gripped my wrists as in a vice, preparing to bind my
hands behind my back. The three others were already
bound with ropes that cut into their flesh. One fellow
ripped off my jacket, while another pulled up my shirt to
tear it off. Savage soldiers, forty in number, filled the
courtyard. A candle was burning in the room, and its
faint beams were the only illumination that reached the
yard, where the most hideous scene I have witnessed in my
life was taking place.

Everything was prepared for the execution. The rifles
clattered and rattled as they were made ready to fire. All
that remained was to put us up against the wall. Then
Hummel, Bergman, Kung, Chen and our drivers and servants, who had remained in our quarters, would be shot,
our cars and our property confiscated, and all traces of the
expedition wiped out. New drivers could be found in the
ranks of the Tungan army.

It was a matter of seconds. The forty soldiers who surrounded us were no men, they were beasts, demons, to
whom human lives—one or a thousand—meant nothing.
My whole life flew past me. What sorrow there would be
at home when month after month passed without news !
The Turki population of Korla could only report that we
had arrived on the evening of March 4 but after that had
disappeared. There were no witnesses of the murder,
and the murderers would certainly hold their tongues.
Were the motor-roads from Peking and Nanking to
Sinkiang really worth such a sacrifice ? Ought I and my
comrades to throw away our lives in so foolhardy an
enterprise ?

But now it was too late ! We were already facing the
barrels of our murderers' rifles, and throughout the process
of stripping us and binding our hands each of us had had a

couple of Mauser pistols aimed at his heart. If one of that
rabble of soldiers had stumbled, or accidentally put his
finger to the trigger, the first of us would have fallen, and
the fate of the rest would have been sealed. I saw terribly
clearly that a minute at most remained. No, it *must* not
happen! Perhaps it was too late. But an attempt must
be made. The psychological moment had arrived when
all were waiting for the word " fire ! " Just one spark of
fury or hatred in Chang's heart would suffice for the order
to be given. I shouted to Georg : " We'll be shot ;
promise them the car to-night ! "

Georg spoke calmly. Chang gave an order, and I was
led into the room alone. The minutes I sat there, with
armed soldiers on each side of me, seemed an eternity. I
expected each moment to hear the three volleys from the
yard. But at last Yew was pushed violently into the room,
and then the two Swedes. And then negotiations began,
the result of which was that the car was driven up to the
gate and it was agreed that Georg should be ready to drive
it to Aksu at daybreak.

There was not much sleep in our quarters that night !
Before we parted, Georg begged me to read a few Swedish
hymns. We had a feeling that we were seeing one another
for the last time. Our plan had been to split up the
expedition at Korla. Bergman and Chen were to go with
two motor-lorries to the New River, the Kum-daria, and
Lop-nor, while we others, with three cars, would follow
the high road to Kashgar to find out what was required in
the road-making line to make it entirely suitable for motor
traffic.

Now the situation had suddenly been transformed. We
perceived clearly that our position was most insecure, and
that the Lop-nor party was lost if we left it to its own
devices. Georg begged and prayed to the last that we
should *all* go as far east into the Lop desert as possible and
seek for regions where there were neither roads, inhabitants
nor villages. But I assured him that not one member of
the expedition would be poltroon enough to leave a comrade in the lurch. Everyone agreed, and we decided to
start for Kucha and Aksu next day.

We had left the large village of Bugur, after two days' travelling, and had reached the outlying village of Chompak when Bergman, who was driving my car, called out :

" Here comes Georg ! "

We halted. A cloud of dust had sprung up on the high road, and the outlines of a motor-lorry became distinguishable. It drove up to us ; Georg jumped out ; and another weighty council of war was held. Georg told us about his adventures. When his passengers, the twelve wild beasts, had jumped off at Kucha, Georg, unwatched for a moment, had turned the car and dashed back towards Korla in wild flight. But he had seen and heard enough to realize that it would have been extremely dangerous for us to proceed to Kucha with the whole convoy. At Chompak we were in a mouse-trap. West of Kucha, in the village of Bai, was a detachment from Ili belonging to the northern army, i.e. General Sheng's troops at Urumchi. To eastward, on the road to Korla and Kara-shahr, we had Ma Chung-yin's defeated Tungan hordes.

We remained halted in the middle of the high road for over an hour. I would have preferred to go on to Kucha, try to break through the front at Bai and then proceed to Aksu and Kashgar. But when, in discussing the matter, I found that all my colleagues, and above all Georg, insisted that we should return to Korla and try to make our way to the Lop-nor district, we decided in accordance with their views. We were in the midst of the theatre of war, although the district was quiet at the moment—the calm before the storm. I would have liked to go to Kashgar and so carry out an important part of our programme—a detailed examination of one of the three roads (to Chuguchak, Kulja or Kashgar). Where should we get petrol and oil without a visit to Urumchi ? But what might not have happened if we had proceeded from Chompak to Kucha, which was only a few hours away ? Perhaps our lorries would have been taken, with petrol, oil and drivers, and used for the transport of war material, ammunition and troops between Kucha and the front. Perhaps the fugitive troops, to prevent the cars from falling into the hands of the

victorious Urumchi army, would at the last moment have
burnt them and shot the drivers.

We were between two fires, and our lives would be in
danger whichever way we turned.   The country to eastward still acknowledged General Ma Chung-yin, at whose
orders we had been hospitably received.   If we could only
get away from the mob of soldiery in Korla, it ought not
to be hard to find our way eastward out into the Lop
desert, where we should be far from all theatres of war and
could keep hidden for a time.   And this time should be
spent on the problem how best to use the New River, the
Kum-daria, for irrigation purposes, and to the exploration
and revival of the old Silk Road, famous from the days of
the Han dynasty 2,000 years earlier.

We drove into Korla on the afternoon of March 11.
The whole countryside seemed de-populated.   Peasants
told us that there were scarcely a dozen Tungans in Korla,
as the whole garrison had marched out to the northward
along the road to Kara-shahr, where a battle was just then
being fought.

We had arrived at a fortunate moment !   After half an
hour's visit to the town authorities, we drove out of Korla
by the road which led to the village of Shinnega, to the
southward.   We had gone 3 miles, and were driving along
a willow avenue flanked by narrow irrigation canals between
low earth ramparts.   Suddenly horsemen appeared on both
sides of us, obviously keeping our convoy under observation.   When they reached a place where the ground was
covered with bushes, they dismounted and opened a fierce
fire on us.   We jumped out of the cars and sought cover
behind the canal banks.   Georg and Yew ducked simultaneously when a bullet whistled between their heads.
Another crashed against a willow at my side.   Twigs fell
from the trees ; bullets hummed through the cars and
baggage.

"No firing ! " I ordered at once.   If we had replied to
the fire not one of us would have escaped with his life.
The firing lasted for nine minutes, and fifty-five rounds
were fired at us.   By a miracle no one was wounded.   We
were under the protection of the Almighty.

When we made no reply, a Tungan advanced towards us, stopped a hundred paces away and asked one of us to come over for a parley. Kung went forward.

" You must return to Korla immediately," the Tungans' ultimatum ran.

To refuse would have meant a fight. We returned to our quarters, a house belonging to a Turki named Abdul Kerim. This was our first imprisonment—at the hands of Ma Chung-yin's Tungan garrison in Korla. Curiously enough they did not surround us with guards. But as conditions were very insecure, and fleeing Tungans were beginning to stream in from the northward, we employed three Turkis to act as night-watchmen, while two of our fellows were always on guard, turn and turn about. For that matter, we had little sleep on those nights. All the dogs in Korla barked ; we heard rifle-shots, cries, and the neighing of horses. Savage bands of soldiers thumped on our gate with their rifle-butts, shouting, " Open the gate, or we'll fire." They would have liked to steal our provisions and our silver and take our weapons.

March 13 was rather an eventful day for us. In the morning the town was swarming with Tungan troops, and it was said that the defeated general Ma Chung-yin himself had arrived. He sent some officers to our quarters, regretting that he could not come to call upon us himself and that he was obliged to ask for the loan of our four lorries. Hummel was sent for to see one of his staff,[1] who had been wounded in the leg.

Meanwhile our courtyard was filled with officers and soldiers. The former came to take over the lorries, while the latter loaded two of them with machine-guns and other war material. While this was going on the noise of aeroplanes was heard, and a noisy bombardment of the little town began. The yard was emptied as by the stroke of a magic wand. The bombers would certainly pay some attention to the lorries ; so we and our servants thought it best to withdraw to a large open yard north of our Turki house. The machines were Soviet Russian, and twenty-

[1] Ma Ho-san, general of cavalry.

nine bombs were dropped. Only one or two people and
a few donkeys were killed.

When this was over, the lorries were got ready, the
drivers—Georg, Effe, Serat and Jomcha—took their seats,
we shook hands with them, entrusted them to God's protection, and watched them roll out of the gate. We had
the most serious fears for their safety, for it is the way of
the Tungans to wipe out the traces of their misdeeds by
killing and burning.

Outside the town the convoy drove right on to Ma
Chung-yin, who took a seat in Effe's driver's cabin.
According to Effe's account the two young men—aged
twenty-three and twenty-one—got on admirably during the
drive to Kucha. On their arrival there, General Ma
regretted that he was not in a position to replace the petrol
he had consumed, but had a corresponding amount of
photogen handed over to Georg. He also gave Georg his
portrait, and asked him to convey to me his (Ma's) apologies
for having commandeered the cars. But most important
of all was the pass he gave Georg, forbidding anyone in the
Tungan army to stop or impound the cars on their return
trip to Korla. Whatever else may be said of Ma Chung-
yin, his personal behaviour to us was irreproachable.

On the night of March 13 fresh bands of fugitive Tungan
soldiers poured into Korla, and the town was ruthlessly
looted. Ma's army was in wild flight ; all discipline had
ceased to exist. We kept a sharp look-out at our quarters.
We heard that aeroplanes were now passing by the town
and hovering over the high road to Kucha, which was
packed with fleeing troops, on horses, donkeys and camels,
in carts or on foot. Long trains and caravans with food
and war material choked the roadway, which was at the
same time crawling with peasants, their wives and their
children. A pale yellow cloud of dust hovered over this
chaotic mass of humanity, and the airmen dropped their
bombs right into the thick of it. One or two aeroplanes
made a detour over the southern part of Korla to drop
bombs upon the Tungan troops which remained there.

On the morning of March 17 two of our men, on visiting
the bazaar, found the main street full of Mongols and

Russians and their horses. This was the victorious northern army, which had reached Korla and was immediately continuing the pursuit of Ma's fleeing army. It was said that the latter had lost 7,000 men on the way from Dawan-cheng to Korla.

The same morning a Cossack came and ordered me to go at once to the general in command of the advance guard, who had established his headquarters in the same house which Ma Chung-yin had occupied a few days before.

General Volgin interrogated me for an hour on end— he could not but believe that we belonged to Ma Chung-yin's army in one capacity or another, although the passports from Nanking, which I showed, spoke another language.

In the evening General Volgin sent four soldiers to our quarters. We were ordered not to go outside our gate. We ourselves had been made prisoners for the first time on March 11, when our cars were taken. Our imprisonment by the Tungans lasted only till March 16, when the advanced troops of the northern army entered Korla ; then our second imprisonment began.

On the afternoon of March 17 our quarters were honoured with a visit from two White Russian officers, who asked for a conversation with me. They were invited into our simple room, where we were just having tea. One of them, Colonel Proshkurakoff, was a tall, lean, sinewy, weather-beaten man, with a large nose and a serious aspect. He introduced himself as adjutant to the commander-in-chief of the northern army, General Bektieieff, who had just arrived at Korla and had ordered him to obtain information from me.

The examination began, in Russian. I answered all the questions in accordance with the events to which they related. After an hour and a half's conversation the colonel rose and said :

" Lastly, I have to convey to you General Bektieieff's great surprise and regret that you should have placed your abilities and your experience at the service of a dangerous rebel."

" I don't understand what you mean," I said, quite calmly.

" General Bektieieff means that by lending Ma Chung-yin your lorries you helped him to escape from our victorious army, which is just about to capture him."

He received an appropriate answer.

The colonel smiled, and replied, in a gentler tone than before : " I have only carried out my orders, and have now to report to the general."

Next day Colonel Proshkurakoff appeared again and asked if I would go with him to pay a visit to General Bektieieff, which I did all the more willingly in that I had already expressed a wish to this effect.

The general received me in the same house in which I had met General Volgin a few days before.

He listened to my story with great interest, and did not even hint at the regret which his adjutant had expressed with so much ceremony the day before. We parted the best of friends, and I was escorted back to our quarters by a Cossack. That they were not sure of us was shown by their action in confiscating our wireless apparatus, which was only a receiver. At Turfan we had managed to conceal it. When I told Bektieieff that we had one, he declared that he must take charge of it for a time.

On the following day General Bektieieff came to pay us a return call. He told us that he was leaving for Kucha immediately, and I begged him to do all that was humanly possible to save the lives of our two Swedish and two Mongolian drivers and, if he could, restore our motor-lorries to us. He promised to do this, and to let me know what had happened to the drivers as soon as possible. When I asked him whether he thought their lives were in danger, he replied that, with his knowledge of Tungan methods of warfare, he felt unable to reassure me. He considered their predicament to be more than awkward.

The small car was the only one we still had. I placed it at his disposal if he should need it for short trips, an offer which he gratefully accepted.

The weeks of our second imprisonment passed slowly and monotonously. We were closely guarded by at least six Cossacks, who always carried rifles, stood on guard at the gate, walked up and down the courtyard, came into our living-room and sat and stared and talked. We could not even pay the most innocent little visits to the northern courtyard without being escorted by a soldier, rifle in hand !

During the first days we spent in Korla Dr. Hummel treated daily wounded Tungans and sick Turkis. He had placed a large red cross on the street gate. His clientèle grew, and often he was unable to deal with all those who came. The Tungans disappeared when the troops evacuated the town. But the Korla Turkis continued to come. After the northern army had entered Korla all further treatment of the sick was forbidden. The object was clearly to isolate us completely. Our imprisonment was much stricter under the Russian regime than in the Tungans' time.

March 22 brought an event that made us rejoice. Serat and Jomcha, the two Mongolian drivers, suddenly appeared in our courtyard, escorted by a couple of soldiers. They had just arrived to fetch two lorry-loads of war material for the northern army. They brought, too, letters from Georg and Effe. Thus we heard that General Ma Chung-yin and his staff had succeeded in reaching Kucha in our lorries. Far from committing any acts of violence, they had restored to our men their complete freedom.

Our drivers, on their way back, had naturally met the northern army, and this in turn, at General Bektieieff's orders had commandeered the four cars, which were now being used for transport purposes at the front. Through the help we had thus given, willy nilly, to the northern army we had in fact been neutral.

On the afternoon of the same day Serat and Jomcha returned to Kucha taking money, food and letters to the two Swedes, for whose safety we now need no longer feel any anxiety.

Our wireless was returned to us, damaged. We were asked not to use it during the next ten days.

On March 27 four Russian colonels—Naleika, Salomakhin, Nikolaieff and another—appeared in our mess. Colonel Naleika, speaking with a military bearing and in military tones, declared that an order had just arrived by wireless from General Sheng, the highest authority in the province, asking our expedition in its entirety to go to Lop-nor, because the road from Korla to Urumchi was still rendered unsafe by roaming Tungan fugitives and marauders, and by Kirgisian and Mongolian robbers. The general could not, therefore, make himself responsible for our safety on that road. But in two months it would be cleared, and we could travel to the capital in complete safety. He proposed that we should spend the two months in the Lop-nor region, where we were far removed from all dangers and complications arising out of the war.

" General Sheng asks you to start at once," the Colonel added.

This communication from General Sheng Shih-tsai, which was expressly declared not to be an order, but a kindly-meant proposal, was to all of us—and especially to myself, who had so long wished to pay a fresh visit to the newly formed Lake Lop-nor—an extremely pleasant change in our lately so precarious situation. I had talked with General Bektieieff of the new course of the Tarim and of Lop-nor, and thought he had induced General Sheng to send us to this region in order to do me a service. We regarded this as a proof that the higher authorities at Urumchi were particularly favourably disposed towards us and our undertaking.

But in this belief we were mightily mistaken. We were sent to Lop-nor simply and solely to keep us as far as possible from the theatre of war and make it quite impossible for us to observe the troop movements which were taking place round Korla in connexion with the pursuit of Ma Chung-yin, the conclusion of the war, the rolling-up of the fronts and the departure of the troops. It was not desired that unauthorized persons should see these movements, and, least of all, that emissaries of the Central Government should be able to see *Russian* troops, aeroplanes, motor-cars and other war material being used for the benefit of one side in a *Chinese* civil war.

On the morning of March 29 I was awakened by a lot of noise in our court-yard. The gates were thrown open, and in drove Georg, Effe, Serat and Jomcha with the four lorries. There were shouts of joy, embraces, handshakes.

At the breakfast-table the new-comers were exposed to a raking fire of questions, and told, bit by bit, their marvellous story.

On April 1 we were ready to leave Korla, where we left a lorry and all the luggage we could dispense with in charge of Captain Deviashin, the commander of the garrison. The three other lorries and the small car were to be carried along the foot of the Kuruk-tagh to the new river Kum-daria, and a base camp (no. 70) was to be established near the Yardang-bulak spring.

From Kara-kum I made a two months' voyage with Chen along the Kum-daria to the new Lop-nor, on the northern bank of which we were picked up at the end of May by Kung and the small car.

Yew, Kung and Effe carried out in April a reconnaissance to Altmish-bulak with two cars ; Hummel collected birds, insects and plants by the river above Yardang-bulak, and Bergman made a desert journey to the southward along an arm of the Kum-daria delta. Work went on, therefore, in many directions. The results were so important that I shall in due time devote a separate book to them.

XI

A DASH TO URUMCHI

ON the evening of May 30 I set out from our base camp
no. 70 on the Kum-daria near Yardang-bulak, where I
left Dr. Hummel and his servant, and drove across the desert
to Yew's temporary camp by a lorry which had been
damaged on an expedition. I reached the place just before
nine. The small car's headlights were seen a long way
off and told them I was coming. They were all outside
the tent and received me with cries of joy.

We had hardly sat down in the tent when I asked Yew:

" Are you ready to come with me to Korla, or possibly
Urumchi, to-morrow morning? "

" Yes, delighted, this moment if you like. I shall be
travelling just as I am."

We sat chatting till far into the night. I and one or
two of the others preferred to sleep in the open air, as the
tent was too crowded. I had not fallen asleep when
a raging east-north-easterly storm sprang up and swept
clouds of dust over our camp. But I crept under the
blankets and took no notice. The thermometer fell to
70; we were certainly in no danger of being cold.

We had a lot to do on the morning of the last day of the
month, and not till eleven did Serat, Yew and I take our
seats in the small car. Yew sat by Serat and I was alone
in the back seat, which was also encumbered with petrol
tins, beds, provisions and the insignificant personal equipment we were taking with us.

Our goal was Korla. Since Big Horse and Bektieieff
had plundered our supply of petrol we had only just enough
left to take the convoy to Urumchi. Our lubricating oil was
all but finished, and without oil the convoy was helplessly
tied to base camp no. 70. The Russian commander had

promised that quantities of oil and petrol, fixed by ourselves, could be fetched from Korla in the middle of May. But as on May 30 we had still not heard a word of the promised supplies, I had no choice but to go to Korla myself and investigate the position. And if the oil had not yet reached Korla, I was quite prepared to extend my trip as far as Urumchi.

I am about to describe what happened to Yew and myself, and show how the simplest things can be muddled in Central Asia. Our experiences provide a picture of life and events in a part of the earth from which even a faint echo very seldom reaches the world outside.

Serat drove Yew and me north-westward. To our left extended a completely barren desert, with fragmentary and irregular blocks of *yardang* rising here and there. To our right were mountains. A water-course led us to a cross-road from Shindi to Ying-p'an. The road ran between *mesas*, past a cairn and the skeleton of a camel. About noon the Kum-daria appeared, only 2 or 3 miles away to the left. A few antelopes were going towards the river-bank, but turned and fled when they heard the noise of our car.

A little trouble with the generator caused an unwelcome delay. But Serat knew the car, and put matters right. We came back to the Shindi road and rolled down the dry bed of the Bujentu-bulak, leaving the spring and its beautiful green poplars on our right. We lost ourselves among lesser gullies full of coarse gravel and small blocks and here and there clothed with luxuriant tamarisks, but we gradually found our way out of the tangle and steered westward.

At three o'clock we were out on a good road again and stopped a little while for lunch. Then we drove over alluvium cut by innumerable water-courses. So it did rain sometimes in the Kuruk-tagh ; and the rain-water in the course of countless centuries had washed down soil and levelled the *saj* or heaps of gravel at the mountain-foot.

The evening was coming on. We drove now on hard gravel, now through valleys running down from the mountains. We had come to a wonderland in which the light of the sunset tinted the cloud-masses in the east blood-red, and deep purple reflections fell upon the earth. Late in the evening we wandered among the gullies of the Kurbanchik valley until at last we found the right one and pitched camp no. 93, having covered 65½ miles.

It was nearly ten; the sky was covered with threatening black clouds, and once or twice a few drops of rain fell. Our camping-ground was idyllic, beside a thick tangle of tamarisk, with dry, dead trunks and branches rising out of the living green bushes. We broke off some of them and made a fire close to the brushwood. The flames rose high into the air and lit up the whole of our surroundings— the erosion terraces, the undergrowth and the shining car. In the bright light we removed the worst stones and spread out our beds by the fire. The flames streamed this way and that, spreading unchecked, and soon the whole of the undergrowth was on fire—crackling and snapping, muttering and smouldering. The midges, which had been troublesome, were driven away by the smoke. We had to remove our beds hurriedly to a safer place and lay our dinner of mutton, eggs, bread and tea at some distance from the conflagration. The wonder of the scene was enhanced by the Kurganchik brook, whose lovely clear water chattered sharply among its rocks and stones.

It was delightful, on the morning of June 1, to have a good wash in the cool, pure water of the brook and, after breakfast, drive up higher through a gully and at last reach the top of the right-hand erosion terrace. We had broken hills on our left and continuous mountains to our right. The former soon came to an end, the second became a jagged mountain-ridge in changing hues of grey, brown, gold and violet. Along the road there were many traces of donkeys and camps, but the tracks of our motor-lorries had been obliterated by heavy rain on May 14 and subsequent falls.

We reached a deep, roughly hewn gully and followed the high road, the same which the lorries took in the spring and which is marked in some places by large bundles of dry stems and branches.

About noon we left on our right the water-course which

comes from the Örtang-bulak; this we crossed at a place where many dry poplar trunks indicated that there were copses higher up the valley.

A little later we crossed a fresh gully and left the Konteibulak on our right. From the mouths of one or two valleys there were splendid views up into the mountains. Another half-hour, and the Suget-bulak was on our right; something like a hundred dry poplar trunks lay in the bed of the stream, although the name means " Willow Spring ".

Our course was south-south-west, while the mountains ran towards the north-west and the colours grew more subdued as we moved farther away from them.

In the afternoon we met three Turkis, who were going from Konche to Turfan with 150 sheep, a horse and a donkey and meant to camp at Örtang-bulak-aghsi. We rested for lunch in the shade of a high tamarisk cone. We crossed just there a belt of these characteristic vegetation-clad mounds, which at some points were so close together that we had to worm our way between them.

Our course was now westward, and poplar groves were sighted in the distance. At a quarter-past five we were at Sajcheke, which we passed quite close without stopping. The river itself was for the most part hidden behind dunes, mounds and trees, and when we turned to the north-westward we lost sight of it altogether.

A mile or two farther on we drove past an old watch-tower on the ancient Silk Road, passed tamarisks sometimes in ones and twos, sometimes in masses, and at Gerilghan drove through a dense growth of reeds, poplars and scrub. I had travelled by this road with camels in 1896. We wound between many poplar trunks, one after another— a lovely sight after the parched desert. Soon after six we came within a few yards of the left bank of the river, but left it again immediately. Then the road ran along a now cut-off bend of the river, and soon afterwards we were by the stream again. I could see at a glance that it had fallen since I went down it with our boats two months earlier. At our base camp the fall during our absence had been as much as $9\frac{1}{2}$ inches.

Our road now ran through thick reed-beds, and the

wood became thinner. At a *satina*, or shepherd's hut, we found a young shepherd who showed us the right way. Twice more we touched bends of the river; then we left them for good and drove through an area which was a transition stage between steppe and desert. We drove between isolated poplars, both standing and fallen, and a belt of *yardang*, with or without dead tamarisks. These grew lower and lower and finally were no more than yellow undulations in a darker soil. The Yar-karaul watch-tower had a shattered *mesa* as its foundation.

At a second Suget-bulak we got so badly stuck at 9.30 p.m. in a deep ditch that we thought best to stay the night, having covered 84 miles. There was no fuel, but we were able to boil the water for our tea with the help of a few dry weeds. After that we could not help sleeping after the day's exertions.

It was not long next morning before, driving north-west, we reached the outlying farms and fields of Shinnega. Immediately afterwards we met people; they showed us to a neighbouring farm inhabited by our friend Seidul Hsiang-ye's uncle, who invited us to tea.

We had not heard a word about the war for two months and had no idea what the situation was. Now we received the first news, very obscure and uncertain. Our informant thought that Russian troops from Urumchi had occupied Korla, Aksu, Shah-yar and Maralbashi, and that the Tungans held Kashgar and Yarkend and were fighting against Khotan. We could understand that things were bad, and that Colonel Salomakhin's prophecy that the war would be quite finished within two months from April 1 had been too optimistic. Although our Turki friends could not or dared not say much, we could understand from their words and manner that our position was not as comfortable and advantageous as we had hoped on April 1, and that Korla might be a bad place for us, as it had been in March.

After a couple of hours' rest we drove on through the belt of desert and reached the Korla oasis and the willow avenue where we had been fired at on March 11. It was a little after two when we stopped outside the Russian

garrison's headquarters. There we met the pleasant commandant, Captain Deviashin. After a short talk he
accompanied us to Abdul Kerim's house, where six soldiers,
turn and turn about, had been keeping guard over our
property all the time we had been away. The captain now
proposed that both the motor-lorry and the packing-cases
should be removed to the Russian headquarters, where
they would be safer. Certain vital parts of the engine
were at camp no. 70, and the lorry was therefore dragged
away by thirty soldiers on the morning of June 3, we having
first taken out the clothes and provisions we should need
at Urumchi. For, as we had feared, there was not a drop
of oil or petrol in Korla, and a letter to the authorities in
the capital had not yet been answered. We realized at
once, therefore, that our trip to Urumchi was an absolute
necessity.

We bought rice, tobacco and a quantity of other things
for those who were left behind at camp no. 70. I wrote
to Hummel and Bergman and sent them 4,000 taels. We
drew up an agreement with Abdul Kerim in Turkish by
which he undertook to drive the consignment to Seidul
at Shinnega himself and arrange with him for it to be sent
on to our men. We were told that, without an agreement
of the kind, all the money would be stolen and not much of
the rest would arrive.

The captain gave us the cheering information that the
road we were going to take to Urumchi was anything but
safe, and that on several recent occasions merchants and
other travellers had been attacked, robbed or killed by
Kirgisian and Mongolian robbers. He was, therefore,
responsible for us, and demanded that we should take a
Russian officer with us as escort. I said that we had no
room in the small car and that we meant to travel so
fast that no robbers could catch us. But he was
inexorable, and introduced our escort, a second lieutenant
named Yaroslavieff, as big as a smallish elephant and
armed to the teeth, but otherwise good-natured and helpful.
When all the baggage had been stowed away and the
baby elephant had taken his seat, I was so squashed that
I could hardly move. But again we had no choice. It

was a matter of only 400 miles, about half of it on a good road.

We spent only one night in Korla, that of June 2, and slept in the mess-room of our former prison. We were awakened in the morning by a well-dressed European, who entered and greeted us. I did not recognize him, but he gave his name—Plavski, one of two Polish travellers we had met at Turfan in February. We had met him again in March on our return journey from Bugur. It had then been his intention to travel home via Kashgar; but he had not succeeded in doing so, and he was now making for Urumchi instead.

We had a great deal to do, and the time passed quickly. A little while before we started a prophet of evil appeared and warned us against going to Urumchi.

" If you aren't put in prison, you're sure to be kept there six months or a year—or more," he said.

He painted a depressing picture, but it did not make much impression on us. However much oil we had had, we should not have withdrawn from the game by going to Kansu via Altmish-bulak and Tun-hwang. We were on an official mission to Sinkiang to prepare the way for road-making and improved communications between China proper and the great north-western province, and we were bound to pay a visit to its ruler Sheng Tupan, who had conquered Ma Chung-yin and frustrated his plans of conquest under our very eyes. We did not know what our reception would be like, but we felt that we were on our way to a new adventure.

In my letter to those who remained at the base camp I hinted in veiled language that they ought to cherish no illusions and that they might have to wait a long time. But we should do all that was humanly possible to obtain at Urumchi the oil the motor-lorries needed—six poods — which Yew, Serat and I meant to take by car to Korla and Konche and thence down the river by boat to base camp no. 70. The petrol we required would at the same time be sent to Kara-shahr or Korla.

It was after half-past three when we took our seats and rolled across the bridge, over the pass and into the pictur-

esque gorge of the Konche-daria.   Now and again we met
travellers on horseback, on donkeys and in carts.   We
asked them if the road was quiet, and they replied that they
themselves had not been attacked.

The road through the reedy plains had, since we last
saw it on March 4, been turned to a morass by the deep
wheel-tracks left by the fleeing Tungans, who had swept
through like a deluge to Korla and gone on to Kucha.

It was nearly half-past six when the magnificent poplar
groves of Kara-shahr lifted their green tops ahead of us
on the banks of the Khaidu-gol.   It took only half an
hour to cross the main arm of the river by ferry and its
smaller arm with the help of natives.

Safely over on the left bank, we drove straight to the
young prince of the Torgut Mongols, who, apart from his
high rank as a lama, was also commandant of Kara-shahr
and general commanding a division.   He was not at home,
but a relative showed us the way to his *yamên*, where we
sent in our cards.   The prince, accompanied by his
adjutant, met us in the court-yard and invited us into a
large room, where we sat down at a long table.

The prince asked us about the object of our journey,
and said he had sent my letter about the oil to the supreme
authority at Urumchi, but had so far had no reply.

I reminded him of the great kindness his uncle Sin Chin
Gegen had shown our previous expedition, and especially
his courtesy to the King of Sweden in presenting him
with a complete lama's temple *yurt*, handed over to the
king by Henning Haslund.   The king, as a mark of gratitude, had presented the prince with his portrait and a
valuable gift.

Sin Chin Gegen's young successor declared that he knew
all about this and that the king's gifts were now in his care.
But he broke off the conversation about his uncle with
unexpected haste, and suddenly turned to quite a different
subject, the object of our journey.   It was evident that he
did not like talking about his kinsman.   We had already
heard—and the reports were confirmed later—that there
was a very ugly story behind the Kara-shahr Torguts'
change of ruler.

When the Tungans invaded Sinkiang a few years before, the then governor-general Chin Shu-jen, who in some mysterious way had taken up the post after the murder of the able Marshal Yang, had mobilized the forces of the province as well as he could. He had also called upon the Torgut prince Sin Chin Gegen, who was a " living Buddha " and also held supreme temporal power over the Torguts during the minority of his nephew, the real prince, to take the field against the invaders with his Mongolian cavalry. Sin Chin Gegen had not obeyed; but he had been incautious enough to obey a later request that he should come to Urumchi for a conference with Governor-General Chin.

He went to the capital with only a few attendants and was well and courteously received. While he himself was with the governor-general, his attendants were told to wait in an outer court-yard. Probably no one now living knows what was discussed—except the governor-general himself, who was later imprisoned at Nanking for a variety of offences. When the conversation was over Chin escorted his guests across the inner court-yard. Before they had reached the gate, several rifle-shots were heard from the outer yard. The prince started and asked in alarm what this meant. He received his answer at once—a bullet through the head.

Why did not his people, the Kara-shahr Torguts, rise in protest and rebellion against this cowardly murder of their revered chief?

But they kept quiet and in course of time Chöngshin Mentsuk Kampo, scarcely twenty years old, became their khan or prince. It was with him we were now sitting and talking—little about the uncle, not a word about the murder, of course—but of quite different things. We talked at length of my friend the Tashi Lama. When we visited this exalted arch-priest at Beli-miao, I had asked if I might have a letter written with his own hand to the Torguts' holy man at Kara-shahr, and he had gladly given me such a letter, stamped with his own seal.

Unfortunately I had neglected to bring the letter with me, but no damage of consequence was done. The young prince could have done nothing to help our expedition; he was powerless under the new regime. It might even, perhaps, have excited suspicion against us if we had stood in any at all intimate relationship to the Torgut prince; and perhaps, too, it was best for the Tashi Lama, in the existing precarious situation, not to have any contact with a prince who commanded a Chinese division.

At last an order was sent to the mayor to find us quarters for the night. At these we were well received, and were given an excellent room and a Chinese dinner. We did not pay a farewell visit to the prince next morning because he had not returned our call. We saw him again later at Urumchi, in conditions which showed how light a weight he then was in the scales of Sinkiang's internal politics.

On the other hand, we drove to pay a farewell visit to the pleasant mayor before going on. When we were in Kara-shahr before it had been in the hands of Ma Chung-yin and the Tungans; now it was in the hands of Sheng Tupan and the Chinese. Yet numbers of harmless Tungans—*bourgeois*, farmers, disarmed soldiers—remained in the town, as well as eight Russians and a medical orderly, all in Chinese service.

And then off we went along the road we knew already. It was more thickly bordered with carcases of fallen animals than before. At half-past four we were at Kara-kizil and an hour later at Kumush, where four families were living. Here the road branches off to the right which runs southward over the Kuruk-tagh; the 500 Russians, who had marched to Korla via Shindi, Ying-pa'n and Tikkenlik, had taken this road.

Barely an hour later we crossed the watershed, whence the ground falls all the way to Arghai-bulak. We reached that wonderful spring in the twilight, and encamped just below the gush of cold, crystal-clear water, as thick as a man's arm, which spurts from the sheer rock wall.

We had driven 112 miles and our camp was no. 97. We had met a couple of carts on the way down to the spring. The rain of May 14 had severely damaged the fantastic road over the high stone block in the narrow defile, but Serat got the car down safely, although it got a bit rubbed against projecting boulders. There was a fearful stench of dead horses and soldiers in the valley, and I declared emphatically that we must camp at a respectful distance from the corpses. On the morning of June 5 we found that we had the body of a Tungan eight yards from our camp. We had no fuel at all, but the evening was still and we could keep candles alight in the open air. In the night the temperature dropped to 70·5, which seemed cool after the heat of the day.

That morning Serat was filling the tank, and had poured in half the contents of a tin we thought contained photogen when he found that it was water. The tank had, therefore, to be emptied, and then we had fuel for only 120 miles, whereas the distance to Urumchi was still 141 miles.

We started at half-past eight and followed the spring along the valley for an hour till it stopped—at Su-bashi. In this neighbourhood we passed the " armoured car " which had been made at Urumchi, taken by Ma Chung-yin, and abandoned by him for lack of petrol.

We were soon out of the mountains. At Toksun we could only obtain seventeen eggs and a few loaves of bread. We stopped only a short time. On the plain outside the town we had 106·3 degrees in the shade, a record for the whole expedition.

We rose gently over barren *gobi* and approached the first hills, where the track was under water for some distance, crossed a ridge among red and black hills and the point where the caravan road from Turfan joined our road, and where I came once more to a region I had known since 1928. Our route was picturesque, winding among savage mountains. Then it rose uphill along a brook among bushes and trees. We turned off to the right from a lovely little copse and ascended steeply to the Dawan-cheng pass. It was seven when we reached the top. Some soldiers were guarding a string of carts, but did not stop us. Bogdo-ula, God's mountain, was enveloped in clouds —like our destiny at Urumchi. We encamped for the night at the village of Po-cheng-tse, having covered 80 miles.

We lay down to sleep in the open air as usual. At half-past three it began to rain—at first lightly, then harder and harder. We had to roll up our things and creep into the car.

On the morning of June 6, Swedish Flag Day, there was a fresh breeze from the north-west, but the sky was clear. The temperature had fallen to 59·7 ; we had reached a cooler climate. Not till ten o'clock did we begin our last day's journey on the road to Urumchi. In an hour's time we were driving over open steppe with mountains on all sides. The road was bad. The wind howled and whined round the car, and seemed to be blowing up for a storm. A puncture in one of our back tyres caused half an hour's delay. The road was incredibly vile ; we bumped over rough places, holes and tussocks of grass.

Our course was north-west. Earth and dust had got into the connexion pipe between the tank and the motor, and we had to stop again. It took three hours to repair the wretched thing, and it looked as if the small car simply *would* not convey us to that place of mystery Urumchi.

Meanwhile I talked to Yaroslavieff. He was a Cossack from Orenburg, and had been in the Cossack Guard Regiment before the war. He was in St. Petersburg in 1914, was sent to Holland and England and returned via Norway, Stockholm and Finland. In 1919 he fled to Sinkiang by way of Orenburg, Akmolinsk and the Kara-sarik pass, with Dutoff, hetman of the Orenburg Cossacks, who was later shot by the Reds. In the following year he came to Urumchi, and had lived in that town ever since.

Like other White Russians, he joined up for the war against Ma. He had belonged to the Russian corps which, as mentioned above, marched from Kumush to Korla through the Kuruk-tagh. General Ma had captured eleven guns at Urumchi, which had been buried near Turfan during the retreat. Sheng Tupan had quite lately sent men to look for them. Six had been found and were lying on the carts we had seen at the Dawan-cheng pass.

At last we were able to drive on, the road winding between low mountain crests. A caravan of twenty camels came along, laden with cotton. We were again attacked by heavy rain on a little ridge. It was half dark and unpleasant; we were clearly unwelcome. We had only three and a half gallons of petrol left; would it be enough? Now we went ahead; we crossed the brook at the mountain-foot and drove through the large village of Dawancheng unmolested, passing loopholed walls behind which Ma had had his headquarters for a considerable time.

At half-past six we entered the outskirts of Urumchi and drove in through the gate of the Turco-Russian town. We passed the former Russo-Asiatic Bank, where we stayed in 1928, and where Norin and Ambolt and Professor Yuan remained for a couple of years. Ten minutes later we drove through the gate of the Tungan town and at last reached the first gateway of the Chinese town. All went well, but at the second gateway armed soldiers ran forward shouting, " Stop ! "

We stopped at once, not wishing to be shot. An officer came forward and asked us the usual questions in an authoritative tone. A large crowd of people collected round the car. The narrow gateway was crammed with soldiers and ragamuffins. We had to wait while they telephoned to Sheng Tupan's *yamên*. Meanwhile Yaroslavieff was allowed to get out with his bundle and disappeared from the scene for ever.

The young officer took the Cossack's place in the car and showed Serat the way to Sheng Tupan's *yamên*, at the gate of which we stopped. The officer took our passports and visiting-cards and hurried in. He returned quite soon with a message from the ruler of Sinkiang, who had said that we were bound to be tired after the long journey and must go to bed early. But he would see us next day, and would send us an invitation to come and dine with him.

Then the young officer escorted us to Sheng Tupan's guest-house, where we were to be his guests during our stay in Urumchi. Neither rooms nor food were to cost us anything. A large room with five beds was placed at our disposal. A Chinese traveller was already staying there. The officer had water brought in to us for washing and declared that he had received orders to be entirely at our disposal. We had only to inform him of our wishes.

Here one chapter in our story ended and another began.

From base camp no. 70 we had driven 491½ miles in only seven days. So far all had gone well. What the future had in store for us God only knew. We were cut off from the expedition. That we should not stay a day longer than necessity compelled us was certain. And it is equally certain that neither Yew, Serat, nor I myself will ever forget the months we were forced to wait in the capital of Sinkiang.

Yardang : furrows cut deep by the action of wind and water between sharp ridges of clay.

Mesas : blocks of clay, the remains of deposits left by erosion.

XII

OUR CAPTIVITY AT URUMCHI

OUR first day in the capital of Sinkiang was a long one. It had rained all night, and it went on pouring all day. But that was not why we kept indoors. The governor-general Sheng Shih-tsai, called in everyday talk Sheng Tupan, had informed us through his own adjutant that he wished to see us at dinner. We waited for the invitation, and the hours passed so slowly, and the rain splashed monotonously on the paving-stones of the court-yard on to which our room looked, as did the rooms of several other official guests. At 8 p.m. we sent a message to Sheng Tupan's *yamên* to find out how the land lay. Sheng Tupan sent an answer that we should be received at eight the next morning.

We were there at 8.15. An adjutant told us that his Excellency was to give an address at the cadet school at 8.30, and asked us to return at 5 p.m. We asked tactfully whether in the meantime we might visit the Soviet Russian Consul-General and the Danish head of the post office. Yes, certainly we might.

We therefore drove straight to the Russian Consulate-General. The Consul-General, Garegin Abramovitch Apresoff, received us immediately, accompanied by two of his officials. He made a favourable impression; he was open, genial and cheery. I told him what the object of our mission was, and he thought it was sensible of the Nanking Government to make motor-roads to Sinkiang. There was no obstacle to our proposed visits to Kulja and Chuguchak, but he advised us to go there within a week, or else we should be prevented by the height of the Manas river. On my asking whether we could buy petrol and oil at Urumchi, he replied that only Tupan himself could give permission for this, and advised me to speak to him about it. Our adventures in Korla and its environs interested him very much, and he congratulated us on having escaped from Ma Chung-yin's troops with our lives. But Apresoff, like all the Russians with whom he spoke later, cherished an unconcealed admiration for Big Horse—his courage, daring and vigour.

We on our side clearly made a favourable impression on the Russian Consul-General, for he asked us to dine at his house as early as June 11. It was of great importance to us to be on good terms with him. It was in his power, if he chose, and if he suspected us of secret intentions contrary to Russian interests in the province, to have us arrested and detained for an indefinite time, and to bring the whole expedition to nought.

To be just, we were bound to admit that the Consul-General was fully entitled to suspect us. Both the previous emissaries of Nanking, General Hwang Mu-sung and the Foreign Minister Lo Wen-kan, had failed in their missions, and it had been made clear that their role of mediator and " peace commissioner " was neither desired nor necessary. What could be more natural than to suspect that we, the third set of emissaries, had been charged with a secret political mission under the guise of road-making ? Our position was, therefore, extremely delicate from the beginning, and we had to behave with the utmost tact and shrewdness. Our tactics were very simple. Yew and I were in agreement on all points—our policy was complete honesty ; we had nothing to conceal ; anyone who liked could spy on us as he pleased. The most important of all the instructions we had received at Nanking was under no circumstances to concern ourselves in, or seek information about, the province's internal or external policy. Our line was therefore simple and clear. And yet our stay at Urumchi was this time an absolute purgatory—a time of the most fearful tension, which tested our patience to the utmost. My story will show how the winds changed and listed hither and thither. We had spent only a few days in the town when we realized that it was a perfect nest of intrigue.

After two hours' conversation with M. Apresoff we drove to the post office, and were received by its chief in the court-yard. Harald Kierkegaard was no stranger to me, nor I to him. We had often corresponded during the main expedition, and he had helped us in hard times, not least during the period when Ambolt had disappeared. He came running towards me with arms outstretched, and we embraced—an almost theatrical meeting, which tickled Yew.

Kierkegaard was a man of forty-eight—white-haired, lively, jolly and genial, like most Danes. I had discovered in a few minutes the cause of the irrepressible joy which was evident in all he said and did. He had completed his service, and was to leave that pestilential hole, Urumchi, for ever in a week. Wherever he went, it would be paradise compared to that wretched town.

We went up to his study. There we made the acquaintance of his countryman Mr. Egtorp, an engineer, who had wanted to set up a chemicals factory and had been promised heaven and earth, but, after waiting vainly for six months, had considered the position hopeless and decided to accompany Kierkegaard home to Copenhagen.

We also made the acquaintance of Mr. Chen, Kierkegaard's assistant, who had been appointed to succeed him. The postal service in Sinkiang had been managed by Europeans for many years—by the Englishman McLorn during our main expedition, before him by an Italian. But Sheng Tupan was now going to put an end to this custom. Chen was a good fellow, quiet, honest and reliable. Our acquaintance with him was soon to be very intimate.

Our letters from Korla had reached Kierkegaard safely, and he had got them through without being censored, which as a rule is absolutely impossible. We heard hair-raising accounts of events at Urumchi, Kashgar and other places. The Russian Tartar Gmirkin, whose acquaintance we had made in 1928, who had been head of the garage and later had risen higher and higher in rank, had been shot ! His successor was an old acquaintance of ours, Ivanoff, whose position was considered to be strong. Kierkegaard gave us this golden advice : never talk to anybody ; let the

others talk, listen, but appear indifferent ; believe nobody—
they are all liars, spies, informers and traitors ! Anyone
may disappear at any time, and it is best not to ask where
he has gone.

But the hours rolled on, and it was time to drive to Sheng
Tupan's *yamên*. This, like Kierkegaard's private house and
the official guest-house in which we were staying, were
inside the wall of the Chinese town. The distances, therefore, were not great, but the roads were shocking.

After crossing a few court-yards we were met by the
great man himself. He led us to a reception-room, where
we were asked to sit down at a table. Sheng Tupan was a
man of fairly prepossessing appearance. He had searching
eyes, which, nevertheless, avoided ours. He began by
asking us what sort of a journey we had had. He had seen
our passports and found everything in perfect order. To
all our requests he replied promptly and clearly. He would
himself send petrol and oil via Aksu to the expedition on the
Kum-daria. We could not go to the Tarim for three
months, by which time he would have cleared the country
of robbers. It was his chief object to improve and develop
the province of Sinkiang, neglected and left in darkness as
it had been, and he was glad of the help we were to give
him in this task. He had heard that we should like a
quieter place to stay in, and he had therefore ordered a
three-roomed flat, with European and Chinese cooking, to
be prepared for us. If we needed any spare parts for our
cars, we could get them from scrapped cars at the garage.
And we could have as much money as we liked ; it was
printed as desired by his own press.

One could hardly have desired a more kindly reception
from the highest official in a province which was about to
break off all connexions with the motherland, and in which
two earlier emissaries had been so curtly turned away.

On getting home I wrote two telegrams, one to my
family in Stockholm and one to our chief, the Minister for
Railways. In both I emphasized the kindness of our reception. We had to weigh our words, for no telegram was
sent off unless stamped with Sheng Tupan's own red
stamp, and no one but himself could apply this. We

were, therefore, under the strictest censorship, like every-one else. A telegram containing a hint of a complaint, or any news of the real conditions in Sinkiang, was never sent.

Next morning a Russian colonel, Paul Alexandrovitch Pao, appeared at Sheng Tupan's orders. The Chinese called him Pao Fan-kwei; he was the governor-general's chief interpreter and a master in the Chinese language. He looked as if he was dying, and was evidently in the last stage of consumption. During the siege of Urumchi, at the beginning of 1934, he had sat at the telephone night and day, and all orders had gone through him. Sheng Tupan had now told him to arrange for two comfortable bed-rooms for Yew and myself and a sitting-room with two writing-tables and carpets. Russian cooking was to be provided. This would all be ready in three days.

At the garage we met our friend Ivanoff. There was not a drop of petrol, but he was waiting for fifty tons from Manas, and when they arrived we should get what we wanted. It all sounded very promising—but those rooms were never ready, and not a word was ever heard about the petrol from Manas.

We called on another friend from 1928, Antonoff, then a modest business man, now general and head of the con-tingent of Russian émigrés, which had stormed the *yamên* and driven out the incapable Chin Shu-jen in April, 1933. Antonoff was acting Russian commander-in-chief while Bektieieff was operating in the field against the Tungans.

At lunch at Kierkegaard's we met two more old friends, Father Hillbrenner, of the Societas Verbi Divini, and Dr. Pedashenko.

Rumours buzzed in the air like bees over summer meadows. Now it was said that one of the Big Horses, a relative of Ma Chung-yin, was on the way from Anhsi to Hami with strong forces to invade the province afresh. If this army was defeated at Hami, it would probably return by a southern route, and might be a danger to our cars which we had left on the Kum-daria. But like other rumours, there was nothing in it.

The Consul-General Apresoff was kind enough to send all my telegrams intended for Stockholm to the Swedish

Legation in Moscow. They were written in Russian, but in Latin characters for the telegraphist's sake. Our telegrams to China were written by Yew in Chinese and went through Sheng Tupan.

We spent June 10 at the German Catholic Mission with Fathers Hillbrenner, Laedermann and Haberl. They told us strange and terrible stories of the rebellions and the civil war.

On June 11 we had a number of quite uncommon experiences. First, Georg's brother, Herr Gustaf Söderbom, came to see us. His position in Urumchi was if possible more dubious than our own. He had come there by car from Peking a couple of years before—for the second time—in the hope of being able to open a traffic route between Urumchi and Kwei-hwa. But he had been unsuccessful, had got into difficulties, and was now unable to leave the province. Some time ago he had gone into the service of, or into partnership with, a rich Chinese, who was trying to improve agriculture with the aid of imported machinery.

At one o'clock we had been invited to dinner with the Russian Consul-General and Madame Apresoff. In their drawing-room we found some twenty guests, among them Mr. Chen Teh-li, who was at the same time Foreign Minister and Finance Minister, wore European clothes and spoke Russian fluently; also the whole staff of the Consulate; Kierkegaard and Egtorp, and several Chinese dignitaries, all with ladies. At three o'clock the governor-general Sheng Tupan appeared with his wife—punctuality is not a virtue in China. Yew and I were the guests of honour.

Our hosts were Armenians from Baku. M. Apresoff had served for five years in Persia, as consul at Resht and Meshed and as Chargé d'Affaires in Teheran, where he used to play chess with Shah Riza Pählewi. He had also lived at Tashkent. He had been transferred to Urumchi in November, 1933—only seven months earlier—but he had had more than enough of the place and longed to get back to Moscow.

We sat down round the table, which groaned under

whole batteries of bottles—brandy, vodka, liqueurs, Madeira, port, Caucasian wines—and an equally liberal display of *hors d'œuvres*. We had had enough when the main dishes began to go round—cabbage soup and sour cream, chicken with cucumbers and rice, cutlets with green vegetables, pudding, fruit, jam and marmalade.

The guests were in festive mood—not surprising at such an entertainment in the heart of Asia, in the midst of rebellion, war and brigandage. Our hostess was pretty and charming and spoke excellent French, our host unwearying in his attentions. We joked, chatted, told stories and drank one another's healths. Sheng Tupan sat in silence. His searching eyes never left us. Once only he observed :

" You must be old friends."

" Yes, indeed," we replied, " we've met twice before."

Then we adjourned to the drawing-room, and fresh mountains of tarts, cakes, salted and candied almonds, coffee and liqueurs. Then we went in procession to the avenues of the park and inspected the Consulate's new club-house, and ended up on an open square where a game of football was beginning, in which Sheng Tupan took part.

M. Apresoff told us that when, four months previously, the news of our arrival in Hami, Turfan and Korla had reached Sheng Tupan's ears, he had been annoyed, surprised and most suspicious. But the Consul-General had reassured him and told him of my previous journeys in the province. The day was a great success for us, as Yew put it, thanks to M. Apresoff's hospitality. The powerful Tupan, the military governor-general, had realized clearly that we could not be treated as spies.

It was a tremendous banquet, and lasted for seven and a half hours. The last act—further refreshments in the drawing-room—began at twilight. At last Tupan rose to go. We followed his example, and offered to drive him and his wife to their *yamên* in our car. They accepted the offer. Serat put on full speed, and the fifty horsemen of Tupan's escort had great difficulty in keeping up with us. There was a trampling of horse-hooves in the mud between the Turki shops, a rattling of rifles and sabres, and the tormented townspeople must have wondered what was happening.

Next day we called upon the "president of the provincial council", or civilian governor-general Li Yung, a stout, amiable old fellow of sixty-six with a goatee beard, born at Barkul, formerly a rich business man, owner of silver mines, talkative and frank. He had formerly been *tao-tai* or governor of Hami, and had been sent to Peking by Marshal Yang to obtain from the President Tuan Chi-jui support for the development of Sinkiang, the construction of motor-roads and railways, and so on. For this money was needed. About the same time England had repaid the "Boxer indemnity" to the tune of 20,000,000 Mexican dollars, and Tuan had promised Yang a part of this sum. But Tuan fell, and his successor Chang Tso-ling needed the money for his wars. After his return Li Yung became adviser to Yang and later to Chin Shu-jen.

When Sheng Shih-tsai assumed the supreme power in the spring of 1933 and became military governor-general, he made Liu Ting-shan civilian governor-general. But the latter fell for reasons connected with Hwang Mu-sung's visit; he was now kept under military guard in his own house at Urumchi and was allowed no communication with the outer world. So I, too, was unable to visit this old friend of ours from 1928. Li Yung had taken up his exalted post only three months earlier, at the beginning of March, 1937. He did not conceal from us his hatred of Chin Shu-jen, who, he was convinced, was to blame for all the misfortunes which had befallen Sinkiang since the summer of 1931.

I had consented to a request of M. Apresoff that I should lecture in the hall of the Russian Club on my journey through the Takla-makan desert in 1895. The hall was packed with 250 Bolsheviks and a few Chinese who understood Russian, among them Chen Teh-li. A few polite words of greeting from M. Apresoff opened the performance, after which I rose and delivered my lecture to a most appreciative and friendly audience. Above and behind me, from a fiery red cloth on the wall, there flamed in golden letters a sentence of Stalin's declaring that war was a curse and " we want to live in peace with all the peoples of the earth ! "

Then a balalaika orchestra struck up, and a ballet of boys and girls in Ukrainian dresses executed the dances of their homeland with charm and grace.

We chatted for a time over our tea in the club restaurant. And so the petrol and oil question came up. Our plan of travelling to Bakhti and buying there broke down because everything in the way of transport animals and ox-carts had disappeared during the war. M. Apresoff proposed that he should telegraph to the Russian Consul at Kulja telling him to send what we needed over the Tien-shan to Korla, 375 miles in twenty days. This plan too, came to nothing. But Sheng Tupan had promised us petrol, and we trusted him, and the days passed.

A Chinese wedding was a rather unusual excitement ! Sheng Tupan's younger brother was the happy man, and Yew and I had been invited to the wedding, which was being celebrated in the village of Shui-mo-ko, " Water-mill ", a quarter of an hour's motor drive from the town to the north-east. The hamlet was idyllic. With the thermometer standing at 95·4, it was delicious to enter the solid vault of shady trees. The road was packed with soldiers and horses of Sheng Tupan's escort, little blue Peking carts, telegas and Russian droshkas, a picturesque mingling of ancient, old-fashioned vehicles. Our car was the only one of its kind present. The governor-general preferred riding to driving in a car, and his subordinates, therefore, felt themselves unable to use the most comfortable of all vehicles. I once asked him why, and he replied that as there was a shortage of petrol, and the supplies which were available were needed for military purposes, he was anxious to set a good example by his own frugality.

An outside staircase led up to a pavilion, at the back of which was Sun Yat-sen's portrait surrounded by a decoration of flags. Pillars supported the roof, carpets covered the floor. Several hundred Chinese were invited, including Li Yung and Chen Teh-li, as well as a number of Soviet Russian officers, some of them generals acting as military advisers to Sheng Tupan.

The bridegroom advanced to the table by Sun Yat-sen's portrait. Then came the bride, accompanied by her bridesmaids. She wore a thin pink dress and a veil of the same colour on her head, like a turban or a bridal crown. She held a bouquet of flowers in her hands. She was young and pretty and walked with bent head, shy and embarrassed.

The bridal pair, with their attendants, formed a semi-circle before the picture of the great revolutionary. The marriage contract was read, and the newly married pair bowed to Sheng Tupan and to one another. Speeches were made by Tupan, the bridegroom and one or two others.

After the bride and bridegroom had disappeared dinner was served. At dinner Chen Teh-li spoke of my lecture at the club, upon which Tupan asked me to give a lecture on Lop-nor one day. I promised to do so. But I waited in vain for the invitation, and as much came of that plan as of all others from that quarter.

Yew and I did not hesitate to accept Kierkegaard's kind invitation to move into his house with our goods and chattels, a minimum which we had brought with us from the Kum-daria and Korla. The house had been built by the General Post Office at Shanghai. It was a one-storey house in the bungalow style with a large verandah, a big light room on the right, a dining-room on the left, and a number of bedrooms and reception-rooms.

We had no peace in Sheng Tupan's guest-house. There was always bawling, gambling and drinking there, and a telephone rang all day in the passage outside our room. But the worst part was that one was never safe from spies, and that our belongings might be stolen at any time. When, one day, a messenger handed over to us a sum of 20,000 Urumchi taels, about £8, from Sheng Tupan, we had no place in which to keep this gift, but deposited it with Kierkegaard.

One day I went to Colonel Pao and asked him to tell Sheng Tupan that I would no longer consent to inhabit the nasty room he had given us, but intended to move to Kierkegaard's. Next day Pao told me that the governor-general was annoyed at my criticism and did not like my moving to the house of the postmaster, who was suspect and *mal vu* like all foreigners in the town.

About three o'clock one afternoon Yew and I moved to Kierkegaard's. This was evidently reported at once to Sheng Tupan. His method of rebuking us was rather original. At four o'clock he came in his own exalted person to call on us in the rooms he had placed at our disposal and which we had just abandoned. And there he sat and waited for us for hours, and talked to other official guests staying in the house. Finally he invited them all to dinner, an honour which Yew and I missed.

Our new host, with whom we lived regally, entertained us with vivid accounts of the sanguinary events which had taken place in the town before we came to it, and which showed that we in our turn could not consider our persons secure. The Chinese army which had been defeated in Manchuria in 1933, and driven over the Siberian frontier by the Japanese, had been disarmed by the Russians and transported to Sinkiang. Some twenty of its officers had one day been imprisoned at Urumchi and shot for conspiracy against the existing regime.

A young German business man, Herr Dorn, had arrived at Urumchi in 1933 with the object of opening up trade and selling cars to the province. As the above-named Gmirkin, in whose house we had been entertained in 1928, was, among other functions, head of the garage and of all things connected with cars, Dorn went to him and stayed in his house for some little time. At the beginning of December Big Horse was not far off. On the 10th the governor-general gave a dinner in his *yamên*, and Gmirkin was among the guests. Gmirkin was suspected of intrigues with Big Horse, and in the middle of the dinner was arrested and thrown into prison. His house had been searched and compromising documents found, including a list of those who were to hold the highest posts after Big Horse had conquered the province. It was said that Gmirkin had been shot at the beginning of April.

Dorn had been arrested at the same time without the slightest justification, and had had to endure the most horrible sufferings in a Chinese prison for a whole year.

At long last he was allowed to return to Peking, where I met him at the end of March, 1935. He was emaciated and depressed, and had lost everything he had. Gmirkin and he had been in cells on the same little court-yard. Dorn told me that Gmirkin had been killed as early as January 20. He had heard the half-stifled, gurgling cries the wretched man had uttered when his executioners, after binding him, simply cut off his head with a sharp knife.

On the evening of June 17 an official named Wang, from the foreign department, came to me with a request from Sheng Tupan that I should write a memorandum on how best to develop the production and communications of the province. When, the next afternoon, I was occupied with this work, Kierkegaard burst in radiant, shouting :

" Egtorp and I are going to-night ! "

" What do you say ? What's happened ? "

" Why, the twenty-seven Russian motor-lorries which came here with goods a few days ago are going back to Chuguchak empty, and we've got permission to go with them."

I was delighted at this news for the sake of our two kindly Danes, but how empty life would be for Yew and me when they had left that miserable hole, in which men of honour were the greatest rarity !

The postmaster's house was a scene of activity during the last hours he spent there. He was busy packing. He handed over to us the whole of his library and stacks of the *Berlingske Tidende* and *Veckojournalen*, as well as a number of things of practical utility which were valuable to us.

Several Europeans came to say good-bye to Kierkegaard, who had spent several years in the town. Among them were Herr Schirmer, Dr. Pedashenko, Father Hillbrenner and a German engineer named Schahrt, who had been summoned to Urumchi to make roads, but whose sole dream was now to be able to leave the city, since he was no longer getting his pay.

Finally, the whole staff of the post office came to take leave of their chief. The time for departure was drawing near. Champagne was served and speeches were made. The hour of twilight was approaching, when the town gates were inexorably closed. A final hand-clasp, " love to all at home " ; the two Danes took their seats, and the lorry rolled away.

They left behind them a sensation of emptiness and deprivation. Yew and I sat talking on the verandah for a long time, as the night came stealing over the most hopelessly desolate town in Asia. We were alone now in the big house with the four or five post office employees. And then sleep came and freed us.

When I first visited the capital of Sinkiang, in the spring of 1928, one had got $2\frac{1}{2}$ Urumchi paper taels for a silver dollar. If one wanted to buy silver dollars, one had to pay $3\frac{1}{2}$. On June 16, 1934, 240 Urumchi taels were to be had for a dollar ! But on June 18, only 140 taels were to be had—because the printing-press had got out of order ! The paper tael would now continue to rise in value, the longer the printing-press remained inactive. That day Serat wanted to do some repairs to the small car, but he could not, because all the workmen at the garage were busy on the printing-press !

As a rule this press printed 700,000 taels (or *liang*, in Turki *sär*) daily. For the festivities in April twenty millions had been printed. In 1928 there were only one-tael notes, so that a sum of a thousand taels made a pretty fat bundle. But now 5,000 and 10,000 tael notes were printed, which further accelerated the fall in the exchange. People who had collected their notes and kept them for some time suddenly found themselves ruined.

The Consul-General told us that Kierkegaard and Egtorp had got off at 1 a.m. after the governor-general had tried to induce them to stay a few days longer, in order that he might have the opportunity of giving them a big farewell banquet at his *yamên*. He had also ordered some works of art to be made as gifts for Fru Kierkegaard. But Kierke-gaard had replied by telephone that the great man's dinner and gifts had no attraction whatever for him, and he had got away at last with M. Apresoff's help. After a narrow escape from drowning when crossing a river the two Danes at last reached Chuguchak, where that tireless intriguer Sheng Tupan made a last effort to detain them. This time again it was the Russian Consul-General who gave them a helping hand.

I never succeeded in finding out what Sheng Tupan gained by this peculiar form of paralysing hospitality. All foreigners who for any reason came to Sinkiang were detained month after month against their will. Old inhabitants of Urumchi who wanted to go to Peking waited vainly for their passports. Kierkegaard, when visiting Stockholm, reassured my relations by telling them that in his opinion I should be detained for an indefinite time.

The atmosphere was unpleasant; we had a feeling of insecurity. On the 18th Yew wrote to Sheng Tupan and asked him when he would see us, because we wanted to get our business settled. Above all we wanted to know when we could get petrol and oil, and when we could travel down to the Kum-daria to fetch the expedition.

The governor-general replied: " To-day and to-morrow impossible; I will let you know the day after to-morrow when I can see you."

When, on the 21st, we had still received no answer at all, we sent another message asking when he could receive us. This time he did not answer at all.

No one came to us. We ourselves hardly ever went out. The big villa was silent, abandoned, desolate. We had no peace of mind for work, reading or writing. We were always waiting for a decision one way or the other, and always in vain. Our isolation became more obviously emphasized. We were like prisoners. The postmaster's villa, which was surrounded by a high wall, and whose gate was shut at night, was our prison. To kill the time that passed so slowly we manufactured a game of back-gammon and played far into the night. Late one night, when we were sitting playing by the feeble light of the photogen lamp, a shot was fired just outside our gate. " Now it's starting," we thought; but the night passed quietly.

Kierkegaard's successor, Mr. Chen, was now the rightful owner of the villa, our prison, but preferred to go on living in his simple house a little way off. But he often came to see how we were getting on. He came on the afternoon

of the 21st, and we could see at once that there was something on his mind. He paced up and down the room with
long steps, with bent head and serious expression. At last
he revealed that he had had a visit from an official from the
governor-general's *yamên*, who had asked a number of questions about us with an inquisitorial thirst for detail. How
many of us were there ? what were our nationalities ? how
strongly armed were we ? what had the various members
of the expedition done before ? what were our objects ?
and so on. Our personal passports and car and arms permits already contained exhaustive answers to most of these
questions.

The thumb-screw was being tightened. We were
suspected. What report on us had been sent from the
front ? Ma Chung-yin, Big Horse, had invaded Sinkiang
and besieged Urumchi, and if he had been successful,
neither Sheng Tupan or a single one of his men would have
escaped with his life. It was known too at Urumchi, of
course, that we had helped the defeated Ma to escape by
lending him our lorries. So it was really not at all curious
that we were suspected ; the most curious thing was that
we had not been immediately arrested. Most certainly it
was due to M. Apresoff that we escaped so lightly from the
military-political maelstrom into which we had been
dragged. The Russian Consul-General was an intelligent,
cultivated man, and he realized that the task I had undertaken had no other object than road-making. But it
was another matter to make the leading men of Sinkiang
share this view. The provincial government regarded us
to the last as spies from Nanking. We were treated
as such, and shadowed day and night. The conviction
that this was so kept us in a continual state of tension,
which deprived us of all inclination for any kind of regular
work.

On June 22 we received a huge red card of invitation to
a dinner at Sheng Tupan's at 3 p.m. next day. The names
of all the guests, fifty-two in number, were given on the
card in order of rank—a method which has its advantages
in that one knows whom one is going to meet. The
Russian Consulate did not appear. The others were mem-

bers of the Government, emissaries from Nanking and representatives of out-lying parts of Sinkiang. It turned out later that the names of the Russians had been given in a separate list.

We drove to the *yamên* and were escorted across its court-yards to an inner, square walled garden, beside the house where dinner was laid. Along the paths stood soldiers armed with rifles and pistols. We passed between them, not without a feeling of uneasiness—we knew what might happen at a Chinese banquet in Urumchi!

We were conducted through the dining-room to a neighbouring room, where tea, sweets and fruit were served at a long table. At this the guests first assemble. A few of the Chinese guests had arrived. We sat down and waited. The atmosphere was still uncomfortable. The two rooms had a dozen big windows, and outside these soldiers were posted. Some of them were half sitting in the windows and fumbling with their weapons.

Our host, Sheng Tupan, entered and greeted us. Then came the civilian governor Li Yung and two emissaries from Nanking, Kuo and Kao, who had been waiting to do their business for months and were still detained. Yew and I felt relieved when we saw M. Apresoff come in at the head of the whole Russian Consulate. If he was there, there would hardly be any sensations.

The menu consisted entirely of Russian dishes, and we drank brandy, white wine and champagne. Our host rose and made a speech as long as the dinner-table, in which all the guests of honour were remembered. He turned to-wards me and said a lot of nice things about my travels, and then addressed himself to Yew and Burkhan, to a couple of important representatives of the Altai Kirgises, to the officers of the Manchurian army, and finally to some students from Manchuria who had been in Japan and had now come to Sinkiang to seek occupation.

Sheng Tupan spoke fluently, easily and agreeably, and his words were translated into Russian by an interpreter. Then each of those who had been addressed had to reply; in their case, too, interpreters were available for those who spoke Russian or Kirgisian. The whole thing went off well, and we returned in cheerful mood to the prison within our own walls.

The last few days of June passed quietly. We paid a visit to Chen Teh-li, Minister for Foreign Affairs and Finance, who solemnly vowed that we should get our oil and petrol in a few days.

Then we bought a quantity of provisions and other useful things at the *Sovsintorg*, " Soviet-Sinkiang trade ", which was under the commercial attaché Teskuloff, a Pensa Tartar, and was managed by one Borodeshin ; they were both very civil and helpful. The Russians and Sheng Tupan were interested in our cars and wanted to buy one or two of them. We had no objection ; our economic position would probably compel us to sell them.

An official newspaper was published at Urumchi, called the *Tien-shanjih-pao* or *Celestial Mountains Daily News*, an organ unique of its kind and of a piece with everything else in the town. In it one could read " news " which had been in the Peking and Nanking papers six months before. Information which was thought suitable or reassuring for the inhabitants, seldom containing a word of truth, was printed daily. In the issue of June 30 we read that Ma Chung-yin had captured Khotan and made an alliance with the local Mohammedan government. Then he had come to loggerheads with it, there had been street fighting, Big Horse had been defeated and had fled to Kuku-nor with sixty adherents. Not a word of this story was true ; it was invented to enhance the prestige of the Urumchi government.

We could not check a report in the same paper that the grandson of Shah Maksul, King of Hami, had had his father's titles restored to him. Whether it was true or not, this news would be received with satisfaction by the Mohammedans.

There was a Russian flying school at Urumchi, whose aeroplanes manœuvred over the town daily. These were some of those which had honoured us at Korla and on the way there in March. The petrol which arrived from Russia was consumed by the aeroplanes, and we had to live on empty promises which were never fulfilled.

Food prices rose fantastically. Thus on March 9, at Bugur, 100 catties of wheat flour cost 75 Urumchi taels; on May 22, at Tikkenlik, 550 taels; and on June 26, at Urumchi, 5,000 taels. Later the price rose to 14,000 Urumchi taels, and no one could afford to buy bread. On June 2, at Korla, an egg cost half a tael; three days later, at Toksun, 5 taels; and at the end of June, at Urumchi, 30 taels. Fruit, usually so cheap, rose in price and grew scarcer and scarcer. A melon cost 60 taels, a cucumber 5.

Our fellows were at base camp no. 70, waiting for help. Their food supplies would not last till the end of June. Again and again, orally and in writing, we had asked for lubricating oil for the convoy. We had still, at camp no. 70, enough petrol to enable three motor-lorries and the small car to cover a stretch of 930 miles—i.e. the distance from Korla to Suchow via Hami and Anhsi. But without oil the convoy was absolutely tied to camp no. 70. Our request to be allowed to hire an *arba*, or two-wheeled cart, which should carry oil and necessities of life to the camp via Korla under Serat's leadership, was equally fruitless.

Now we wrote a fresh, vigorously worded letter to the governor-general on the same subject. If the intention was to starve the expedition to death in the uninhabited desert on the river-bank, this was the way to do it. Their situation was not yet critical. They had money, and they could buy flour, maize, chickens, eggs and sheep from Tikkenlik. To promise us petrol and oil from week to week was the method employed to paralyse and detain us. We were fed with illusory promises and sheer lies, and what was the use of protesting? If we " got on our hind legs " and assumed a tone of indignation, they answered quietly : " We are at war with Ma Chung-yin and have everywhere rebellions to suppress. We need every drop of petrol and oil we can get from Russia for our lorries and aeroplanes. We never asked you to come here, so you must put up with having to wait."

Strictly speaking, we never had cause to complain of monotony. We lived, as I have said, in an uninterrupted state of tension. On June 29 I received an infinitely cheering and stimulating telegram from home. We had not heard a syllable from the world outside since we left the Etsin-gol on January 17. The silence of the grave encompassed us. We were prisoners in our own house, and it was said that spies, in disguise, were posted outside our wall. Our servants, or rather those of the post office, were probably spies too, and observed and reported our occupations.

The same evening our host, the postmaster Chen, came into the sitting-room while we were playing backgammon. Again he walked up and down the room with a troubled expression. At last he stopped in front of us and began :

" The authorities have had a message saying that a large army from Nanking started from the Etsin-gol some time ago and may reach Hami at any moment. They expect that the people of Hami will join the Nanking army at once, and it will doubtless come straight on here. An English paper in Shanghai, which I have got, speaks openly of a campaign against Sheng Tupan having already been begun. Will Urumchi be besieged for a third time ? That'll be serious."

We went on with our backgammon quietly, and did not let Chen see the impression his news had made on us. A child could have seen that he too was a spy. He came to see us every day and then reported to the governor-general what he had seen and heard. We therefore held our tongues and did not betray our anxiety. But I could not prevent myself from saying to Chen one day that if the governor-general was afraid of foreigners, he ought not to detain them and so give them an opportunity of making a thorough study of conditions in the province. It would be more sensible not to let them in across the frontier at all, and if they succeeded in getting in all the same, like ourselves, he ought to turn them out again as quickly as possible.

But when the postmaster had gone, Yew and I could open our hearts to one another. It was by no means the first time that rumours of an invasion from Nanking had haunted us ; but this time the rumour seemed to have taken a more positive form. We could not possibly say that it was not true. Ma Chung-yin had been beaten, and the northern army under General Bektieieff was pursuing his fleeing forces beyond Aksu on the road to Maralbashi. Sheng Tupan, leaning on Soviet Russian help, was sole ruler of the whole province, except the strip of oasis from Kashgar by way of Yarkend and Khotan to Charkhlik.

It was not improbable that the Nanking Government, in such circumstances, might fear that Sinkiang would be brought by degrees under Russian domination, as naturally as Outer Mongolia had been. And if it was really true that an army from Nanking might take Hami any day and come on to Urumchi, how would the expedition stand then? The greater part of the expedition and all our motor-lorries were, as far as we knew, at the base camp on the Kum-daria. But I, its responsible leader, and the Chinese engineer Yew were at Urumchi. Surely it might easily be suspected that our expedition had been sent on ahead to mark out a practicable route for the Nanking army and its supply columns and lorries! Was that why we were refused permission to return to the Kum-daria? and did they reckon on our being valuable as hostages? And if an army from Nanking did really appear one fine day before Urumchi, would not Yew and I straightway be arrested or even shot? Our lorries had helped Ma Chung-yin to escape in March. And now we should be suspected of having shown a new army of invasion the way through the desert!

Our situation was not agreeable. I wrote in veiled language to Hummel and Bergman, and enclosed the letters in an envelope addressed to the commandant at Korla.

Thus not a day passed without some new sensation or some new rumour, and we knew nothing of the fate that awaited us. We took rather a gloomy view of the situation. We felt as if a storm was gathering over our heads. The hours passed slowly. We played backgammon, and the profound silence that surrounded us was broken only now and again by the stealthy steps of a servant. We sat talking on the verandah at sundown, and saw fantastic leaden-grey cloud masses rolling away over the crests of the Tien-shan. We envied them their freedom, and would have liked to accompany them on their rapid flight towards the Gobi desert. The midsummer sun sank in the west in a bed of molten gold.   At a fixed time every evening a party of Chinese soldiers marched past our gate, singing to the monotonous accompaniment of pipes and drums.

A more loyal and unselfish comrade than Irving C. Yew during the long months of our third captivity I could never have found.   He was a model of patience and un-ruffled calm.   When we had any wishes to be brought to the notice of the supreme authority, we first discussed the contents in English, and then he wrote out the letter in Chinese in his graceful script—almost always in vain, I am sorry to say : indeed, when vital questions were at stake, such as petrol, oil, or permission to rejoin the expedition, it was absolutely hopeless.   In whatever terms our situation may be described, we had no freedom.

We used to sit on for a little while in the twilight. Darkness came on.   The barking of dogs was heard from far and near ; the cry of an owl ; now and then a shot. Who was being shot—criminals or innocent men ?   We went in to our armchairs by the sitting-room table.   Steal-thy steps were heard in the passage, a pale yellow light fell on the walls, and a boy entered with the lamp.   And once more we bade the casting of the dice bind our wandering thoughts, while the mice scampered noisily under the rafters.

XIII

A RELIEF EXPEDITION

ON the evening of June 30 Yew and I were sitting in our room as usual, killing the time with backgammon, when a servant from the Russian Consulate-General came in and handed me a letter, addressed in Dr. Hummel's writing. The letter had evidently been forwarded by the commander of the Russian garrison at Korla.

My last hurried meeting with our doctor had been on May 31 at base camp no. 70 on the Kum-daria, where three of our lorries were waiting for oil. I had arrived from Lop-nor the same day, and was going on at once to Urumchi via Korla. By a pure chance Hummel came to the camp at the same time. Since the beginning of April he had been on the Konche-daria and Kum-daria with his flotilla of boats and his servants, collecting animals and plants on their banks.

The little menagerie he had started on board included three young wild pigs. A few weeks before one of these had bitten him in the right hand. He had paid no attention to the wound at first, but in a short time the arm swelled, he became feverish and weak, and it became clear that it was a serious case of blood-poisoning. Hummel saw that an urgent operation must be performed if his life was to be saved ; he clenched his teeth and himself made, with his left hand, the necessary incision right down to the bone. After that he felt rather better, but stayed in bed for a week or two. When we met on May 31 he was up and about and carrying on his work as usual. He himself declared that he was quite out of danger. The only proper course would really have been for him to accompany Yew and me that evening, when we left for Korla and Urumchi in the small car.

I read his letter with growing anxiety. The blood-poisoning had grown worse, and the fever would not diminish. He thought he ought not to remain by the river in the summer heat, and had decided to travel on a horse-drawn stretcher via Singer to Toksun, where a car ought to meet him. The letter was dated June 10, and he was to start on the 11th. The fact that he thought it necessary to fly to Peking, or hurry by car and railway to have an operation, was further proof that the case was serious.

Hummel had started on the 11th, and now it was the 30th. He ought to have been at Urumchi long ago. Evidently he had become worse on the journey and needed urgent help. Perhaps he was dead already.

As soon as I had finished reading the letter, and had hurriedly translated it to Yew, we drove to the Russian Consulate-General. A servant told us that the Consul was ill and that the other officials were out, but should be back in an hour. We were standing in the avenue and had just decided to wait, when a short strongly built man in a white summer suit passed us. I had never seen him before. We took off our hats. He introduced himself as Dr. Saposh-nikoff, doctor and surgeon to the Consulate-General. I could have fallen on his neck ; Heaven must have sent him. Dr. Saposhnikoff had just been to see his patient M. Apresoff, who had a headache. He now accompanied us to the house in the Consulate grounds where the vice-consul Koroloff lived—a good-natured man, whose pretty and agreeable wife, French by birth, received us.

When M. Koroloff arrived I translated Hummel's letter sentence by sentence. Saposhnikoff's view of the case was refreshingly optimistic. But there were indications, he said, of a secondary source of infection in which might possibly be a complicating factor. He regretted that he himself had so many patients at the moment, and so much to do in his clinic and two hospitals, that he could not go to Hummel's aid. The latter's route over the Kuruk-tagh was 312 miles, a trifle with a car, but an appalling distance for a sick man without a car.

M. Koroloff, with an energy and rapidity that quite

moved us, went to the telephone and rang up first Chen Teh-li, demanding in an authoritative tone ten poods of petrol and a corresponding quantity of oil without delay. He ordered M. Ivanoff at the garage, in the same tone, to give Serat at once all the help he needed for the temporary repair of the small car. Everything was to be ready next morning, Sunday, July 1.

So far so good. But the very same evening the local authorities started their game of mean, petty intrigue. Mr. Wang from the foreign department came to tell us, with the governor-general's compliments, that we might not leave Urumchi without a special pass.

"Well, why don't you send the pass, then? It's to save a man's life!"

"You'll know at ten to-morrow morning whether you can have the pass or not. If you get the pass, petrol will be sent too."

We were dressed early on Sunday. There was no sign of either pass or petrol. I wrote to Apresoff, and a reply came that he was not at home. The hours passed. Serat came from the garage with the small car; it was repaired, and we had got petrol. Now we needed only the pass to be able to start on our relief expedition. We knew which way Hummel was travelling, and the sooner we could meet him the better.

Late in the afternoon came Mr. Wang, the skilful stage manager of this drama of intrigue. He said, almost mysteriously:

"If you sell Sheng Tupan two of your lorries, you can get anything you like out of him."

"We can talk about that when the cars have come to Urumchi. What we want now is the pass to be able to go and save Dr. Hummel."

"The pass will be here at ten to-morrow morning."

"But you know it's to save a man's life. What's the point of making us lose yet another day?"

He rose with a smile, bowed and went away.

Just then an Italian, Dr. Orlandini, appeared; we had met him at Kwei-hwa at the beginning of November, 1933, when he was on a shooting trip in the mountains.

He had arrived at Urumchi in company with Kemal
Effendi, the Turkish adviser to Big Horse, whom we had
met at Turfan four months earlier. After Big Horse had
been defeated Kemal deserted him, came to Urumchi and
offered his services to Sheng Tupan.

We were on tenterhooks, and had no desire to listen to
Orlandini's adventures. Evening came on, and we had
no choice but to wait for the pass until ten next morning.

The night passed. We got up at seven; ten o'clock
arrived, and there was no sign of any pass. Wang would
doubtless appear in the afternoon and promise us a pass on
Tuesday, and so on day after day till our patience was at
an end and we had no choice but to resign ourselves to our
lot. This is the usual method, the method of exhaustion,
which always secures the desired end—if the victim cannot
secure more powerful help in another quarter. There was,
as we had already heard, only one man in Urumchi who
was more powerful than Sheng Tupan—M. Apresoff.

When it was an hour after the promised time, and the
promise given had proved to be worthless, Yew and I
drove to the Russian Consulate. M. Apresoff had a visitor.
We waited on the little verandah. Suddenly the door
opened, and a tall man whose face we knew well came out
accompanied by one of the secretaries—Kemal Effendi.
But he walked with bent head, looked serious and worried,
and did not notice us. He had obviously had no good
news from the Consul-General.

Our turn came next. We were escorted straight into
the office, where M. Apresoff sat at his writing-table. Full
of humour and high spirits, he gave us a masterly little
piece of acting. He rose with an expression of the greatest
astonishment and exclaimed :

" What ! haven't you gone yet ? Why, your doctor's
ill and in urgent need of help, and you're still sitting here
wasting your time ! I'll denounce you to the Swedish
Government. You've got petrol and oil, and your car's
repaired, and still you don't start ! It's monstrous ! "

" Yes, you're quite right, Garegin Abramovitch. But
the foreign commissariat has told us, through Mr. Wang,
that we mayn't leave the town without a pass from Sheng

Tupan, and although we have continually reminded him about it, and he has promised it repeatedly, it doesn't come."

" Oh, I'll settle that in a moment ! "

He rang up the pleasant, untrustworthy little Foreign Minister Chen Teh-li and spoke to him in a tone of command, as though to a subordinate :

" Dr. Hedin is here, ready to start. I hear he is being detained till a special pass has been issued. No pass is needed in this case. I ask you to give him permission to start now, on the telephone, through me . . . So he's perfectly free to start ? "

Chen Teh-li had agreed to everything. Then M. Apresoff showed us another kindness which I shall never forget. He suddenly exclaimed :

" Why don't you take Vladimir Ivanovitch (Saposhnikoff) with you ? He's a surgeon, and would be useful if any operation had to be done at once ! "

" What do you say ? Isn't he busy with his patients ? "

" I'll give him leave for as long as you need him. His wife's a doctor too, and can do his work while he's away. Go to him and ask him to get ready at once ! "

I could have embraced the Consul-General. No one could have done me a greater service at that moment than that which he had offered me. In a few words I told Yew of the position. Yew then proposed without hesitation to give up his place in the car to the Russian doctor, well knowing that the available space was needed for provisions and sleeping-bags.

After heartily thanking M. Apresoff, we hastened to Dr. Saposhnikoff's hospital close by. His waiting-room was full of patients. I told him of the Consul-General's decision, which delighted him. He had never been in the country south of Urumchi. He would be ready in an hour. Meanwhile we drove home, packed my things, and had dinner ; then I said good-bye to Yew and drove to the hospital, where the doctor was waiting in the court-yard with his camp-bed, a blanket and pillow, a bag containing surgical instruments, a syringe and drugs, as well as a large parcel of cigarettes.

In an hour we reached a little stream. Here half a dozen carts were waiting ; their horses and mules had been taken out of the shafts and were standing eating out of their maize and corn bags. Three Catholic missionaries in black and grey Chinese dress came up to our car and greeted us—Father Moritz, Father Möller and Father van Oirschat. Father Moritz had formerly been stationed at Suchow, and had done great services to several members of our expedition there. It was a pleasure to me to be able to thank him now, if all too hurriedly. A little later we met a Russian droshka, in which the new bishop of the Sinkiang mission, Loy by name, was driving with Father Allroggen. There had just been a change of personnel in the Societas Verbi Divini.

We drove on over the hills on the long desert and steppe road, with Bogdo-ula to the left. Infinitely beautiful, with blinding white fields of eternal snow and shimmering blue glaciers, God's Mountain raised its three peaks in regal pride over the heart of Asia.

We left five gallons of petrol at the village of Dawancheng for our return journey. We spent the night in the yard of a miserable caravanserai, totally destroyed by the war. Our camp was no. 100. We sought shelter under a clay wall. It was blowing hard and the dust whirled round us. After a simple supper we wrapped ourselves in our blankets and lay down on the ground beside the car.

Next morning, July 3, Serat and I were waked just after four by Vladimir Ivanovitch, who thought we had got dust enough in our lungs. We drove to Toksun along the well-known road and made our way through the narrow bazaars to the mayor's house. The mayor, Kasim Beg, was a frank, intelligent young man, who received us hospitably in his garden in the shade of acacia and mulberry trees. We sat down at a table. While the teacups were being laid out I asked with trepidation whether Kasim Beg had heard anything of a Swedish doctor who was ill. No, he had heard nothing ! Splendid ! So there was still hope that Hummel was alive. The news of a death can make its way through the most desolate wildernesses.

It was a quarter to eight. Hot morning winds were

already blowing through the dense foliage. We had not yet begun to sip our tea when a servant laid a European visiting-card on the table before Kasim Beg. I took it up and read " Folke Bergman " ! I thought I was dreaming. I spun round, saw the gate just opening, and in he came, tall, quiet and smiling as usual. I hurried towards him.

" This is like being in heaven ! " he said.

" Yes. Is Hummel alive ? "

" Yes, he's alive all right ; at any rate he was alive when I last saw him the day before yesterday, and he was clearly on the mend."

" Thank God ! Where is he ? "

" At Kirgis-tam, ten li south-east of Kumush."

" Then we may meet him at any moment ? "

" His animals are done for, and there's no pasture and no fodder. He was taken in a lorry from the camp on the Kum-daria to Singer in the Kuruk-bagh—Georg squeezed out the last drops of oil. At Singer, where the air is cooler, he stayed a few weeks to recuperate. Since then we've been going step by step through blazing hot desert mountains."

All the misery, all the annoyances, and all the trials of patience inseparable from journeys in Central Asia are more than amply outweighed by the unforgettable moments which just now and again fall to our lot. Nor would Bergman quickly forget our breakfast together in Kasim Beg's garden. He had heard that all was well in his home in Stockholm.

Kasim Beg received orders to get three good horses and 150 catties of fodder, which a young Cossack named Constantine—who had been with Hummel on his river trip, and had now come to Toksun with Bergman—was to take to Hummel's caravan at Kumush.

But we had to hurry on ; we said good-bye to Bergman and Kasim Beg and drove up into the Su-bashi valley. With mountains on either side of us, we drove uphill over the fine, treacherous sand of the valley bottom and in its little winding channel. At 1 p.m. we stuck fast. Two carts were just coming down from the pass ; and for a handsome *quid pro quo* we were able to borrow two of their horses, which pulled us out. But it was not long before we got stuck again, in the middle of the channel. We made desperate efforts, but nothing was of avail. We sat for hours discussing what was to be done. Should we return to Toksun, hire horses and ride to Kumush? At last Saposhnikoff, who was accustomed to operations, built a little stone dam, which diverted the water of the channel past the car; and then we were able to get it out.

The brook disappeared higher up the valley, where the sand and gravel lay absolutely dry. Twilight was coming on. We passed the jet of clear water that springs from the cliff on the left, arrived at the foot of the pillar of rock which blocked the valley, and took its first steep slope in the gathering darkness. But it was out of the question to risk the car on such ground; the light of the head-lamps was not enough—it was best to wait till daylight.

We halted by the niche in the rock with the memorial tablet.

Large stones were placed behind the wheels to prevent the car from rolling down again. We sat chatting and smoking till 9 p.m., when we lay down among the gravel. About half-past four we were awakened by a light rain, which grew heavier. As day was breaking we went for a walk up the rock. At one point, where the passage was only about 60 feet wide, a ledge of firm scree lay across the road between gigantic blocks, a high step with sand and water at its base. There was no possibility of getting a car over it.

But the rain came on harder, and we returned to the car for shelter. When the rain had stopped, we went back to the ledge, while Serat steered the car up with the greatest care. On the left-hand side of the passage he discovered a shelf, over which the car could possibly be hauled up. While we were trying to repair the road, a cart came down from the pass. The horses were taken out of the shafts just above the difficult ledge, led down the valley by some of the men, and hobbled. The men, seven of them, turned, twisted and lifted the cart over and between the blocks. They actually succeeded.

I spoke to the owner, Abdul Semi, and promised him a

substantial sum if he would let us hire the cart and horses and one or two men, to help us to Kumush. That was impossible; he had no maize to give the horses for the extra distance. But his men would gladly help us build a stone bridge over the awkward place. They began to do this, but we soon saw that it would be a failure. Sharp points stuck up in the middle of the track; to cover them we should have to fill up the whole valley. Moreover, the everlasting manoeuvring over that horrible ground had made such inroads on our stock of petrol that we had only nine gallons left. We decided to do nothing more for the moment, and returned cautiously downhill to the spring.

Here Abdul Semi spread out a blanket on the sand, and produced cold mutton, cut in slices, bread and tea. We contributed sugar, Russian cakes and cigarettes. Abdul Semi had been wounded a few months before in the fighting in Kashgar and had been admitted to the Swedish mission-aries' hospital. He grew eloquent in his descriptions of the tenderness and care which had been his portion there.

And so we talked and considered the situation of which that wonderful road was the cause. We asked how people could be content with a road like that, year after year. It would have been a simple matter to make an excellent road through the valley by blasting and using concrete. It was a question of only a few hundred yards. It would have been possible even then, if one had had the man-power, to fill up the track itself with sand and fine gravel. We had found the valley about Arghai-bulak filled up in this way when we had passed through it at the beginning of Febru-ary and the beginning of June. But since then violent rain had swept away all the finer substance, and only the large and middle-sized blocks remained. In time of peace one road like this handicaps all trade and communications; and in time of war it can paralyse the supply services and have fatal consequences. If the governor-general Chin Shu-jen had used the money he squeezed out of the people for making roads, he would have done something useful. But he thought only of himself.

About three o'clock a little blue-draped Peking cart came

up, drawn by three horses. In it was driving a Turki woman with her twelve-year-old daughter. They were related to Abdul Semi. He had some bad news for the woman; she began to weep loudly, and her lamentations echoed through the valley. Then they exchanged carts; she drove up the valley in his *arba* and he down in her Peking cart. He promised to send us fuel and a sheep from Toksun. We paid in advance, but never saw anything of what we had ordered.

In the course of the day other wayfarers gathered at Arghai-bulak to drink its beautiful water. Among them were three merchants from Turfan, on their way to Aksu. One of them promised to take a letter from me to Dr. Hummel. In the afternoon the crowd began to thin; some went up to the pass, others down the valley. About ten still remained, drinking tea, sitting and talking, or watering their horses; but the scene had lost its variety and gaiety. Calm and stillness descended over the narrow valley, and the echoes between its precipitous walls had died away. It was the calm before the storm.

The sky clouded over quickly; leaden-grey clouds gathered heavily over the mountains; it grew dark as though dusk were falling. Now the thunder was heard muttering and coming nearer and nearer, and the echoes raised their mighty voice. There was a thundering like the worst bombardment on a battle-front; there was a banging and crashing as if the whole mountain crest were collapsing into the depths, and the darkness was divided every other second by flashes of lightning. The storm grew more violent; one had a feeling that some fearful natural catastrophe was impending.

Then the first rain-drops fell, big and heavy. From up the valley we heard the noise of a regular cloud-burst. We all three got into the car. The travellers who had lately been sitting about so peacefully rolled up their belongings and crept close to the cliff, which is almost perpendicular just above the spring. At five minutes past four the storm broke in earnest. The cloud-burst had reached us. It rained, streamed, poured down upon our heads, and hailstones as big as hazel-nuts hopped about on the gravel of the valley bottom. The bombardment hurled its projectiles at the roof of our car, and we were only waiting for this to be crushed in over our heads at any moment. The Turki travellers pressed themselves against the cliff at a place where it hung over a little and there was protection against the hail ; but the rain-water streamed down the rock-face, and the unfortunate wayfarers were certainly soaked to the skin. The little inn which had formerly been there had become a ruin during the war.

The horses stood with hanging heads, the water dripping from their rugs. They were restless, and started nervously under the whip-lash of the hail.

Our car was only a few yards from the perpendicular cliff. I thought of the dangers which threatened us ; blocks might break loose and fall and crush us at any moment. And along the very foot of the cliff a swiftly growing stream came creeping down, as yellow as pea-soup. It had already reached our left wheel. Serat realized the menace and backed the car out towards the middle of the valley, which lay rather higher than the two sides of the river-bed.

Here we felt pretty safe. But now a stream came welling down on the right-hand side of the valley too. We were on a broad island between them. The right arm too grew swiftly and—there came a raging torrent, cleaving the island diagonally. It was going right under the car. It grew with alarming speed and in half a minute joined the two others, forming one single roaring, raging flood. It filled the whole valley bottom. Waterfalls with chalk-white foam plunged down on all sides from the clefts in the rocks. The roaring was indescribable. All conversation was drowned, and all the time the rain and hail beat upon the roof of the car and upon the foaming, surging torrent.

Vladimir Ivanovitch saw the danger which threatened us. The fury of the river increased every minute. The water was above the step and was trickling into the car. A few minutes more, and we were lost ! We should be drowned like rats, or, if we succeeded in crawling up on to some boulder in the river-bed, the car was lost. The valley was scarcely thirty yards wide. If the cloud-burst continued, the flood would rise a few feet, and our fate was sealed!

There was still a chance of safety. The gravel lay tightly packed in the river-bed. The engine was still just above water. Serat jumped out, took a look at the ground, and found at the upper end of the gravel-bed a spot where the depth was not great. Soaking wet, he took the wheel again and reversed at top speed. The engine buzzed, but the car did not move. If he could not get it to move we must either clamber up on to the roof of the car or wade to a bank or boulder.

But wait! the car was moving. It worked its way gallantly up the valley, through rushing waves crowned with yellow foam, and was soon in shallower water. On the left-hand side, where a projecting rock stuck out into the valley, was the ruin of an old shelter. We saw there the carcases of several horses, and ragged remains of clothes and uniforms. One more effort, and Serat worked the car up on to the left bank, which rose about three feet above the surface of the water. The rain had lessened somewhat, but white cascades were still leaping from every cleft. A fine waterfall was still bounding down the steep slope of the cone of rock, by the memorial tablet where we had spent the previous night. If the storm had come that night, our situation would have been almost hopeless. Side-valleys run from every direction into the main valley at Arghai-bulak, and every one of them simultaneously was offering its tribute to the flood which rose swiftly in the narrow channel.

But, thanks to the Russian doctor's alertness and Serat's skill, we were now safe and could watch the impressive scene at our ease. We had all but been caught in the watery trap, and if the deluge had continued for another hour our place of refuge would have been flooded, like the rest of the valley.

About six the rain stopped, the last cascades dwindled, the yellow stream sank rapidly, and in another hour there was no longer any running water in the valley. Then we drove down into the middle of the river-bed, sat talking in the open air and took a simple meal. There was no fuel, and we could not have any tea. When it grew dark we got into the car, because the rain had begun again. And once more a terrifying drama was enacted around us. Blue-white lightning flashes flamed over the mountains without a moment's interval. Violent gusts of wind roared through the hills and howled round the car, and thick clouds lay like mattresses over the peaks. We held ourselves in readiness to return to the dead horse. But this time the rain was not serious. At midnight our conversation stopped, and we leaned back against the cushions and went to sleep. We had witnessed a spectacle which, perhaps, no European before us had seen in this part of Asia, where violent rainstorms are rare. And it is equally seldom that one arranges a journey so as to spend a night in a place where there is neither pasture nor fuel, but only water.

When we woke in the morning the sun was peeping over the mountains and drying up the moisture. I obtained shade for my head with the help of my stick and coat.

While we were washing and shaving at the spring Constantine and a Turki named Haidin came along with three horses loaded with fodder for Hummel's caravan. They had some fuel, and at last we got our tea. Some travelling merchants had met Hummel the evening before at Kumush, the distance to which place was 30 miles. As he was travelling very slowly on account of his illness, he could not be at Arghai-bulak before July 6; so we had another twenty-four hours to wait!

After Constantine and Haidin had rested for a little while they had to go on towards Kumush, taking a quantity of provisions and a letter to Hummel.

It was indeed a delightful trip on which I had invited Vladimir Ivanovitch to accompany me! He got no proper food, rarely hot tea, never a camp-fire, and the shelter for the night which was offered to him was anything but attractive. It rained interruptedly all through the night of July 5, not a violent downpour as before, but hard and steady. We had to sit in the car all night. One gets no proper rest sleeping in a sitting position. I was still sitting there dozing at 10 a.m., from sheer weariness, when one of our old friends, the rich merchant Mossul Bai from Turfan, came up to the car and woke me. He told me that Hummel was quite near. I sprang up, half asleep and unwashed, and hurried towards the defile. I had not gone many yards when I saw two horsemen riding straight towards me. The foremost rider, a Turki, was leading the other's horse, and this second rider, as brown as a Hindu, called in the best Swedish :

"Good morning ! Why are you up so early ? Go to bed again ! "

It was my dear doctor ! He had a royal welcome. Thank heaven, he was not merely alive but looked pretty well, if thin and tired after his illness and his exhausting journey. Vladimir Ivanovitch and Serat came up ; we spread out blankets and pillows at the foot of the cliff and made a comfortable bed for the invalid. Soon after Hummel's little caravan of three horses and five donkeys arrived, carrying his kit, including the remains of the stretcher, which enabled us to light a fire and have tea. Finally the young Cossack Constantine also appeared ; he had ridden to Kumush to no purpose, for he had taken a short cut and so had not met Hummel. But now we were all assembled and could have several hours' good rest.

The sound of engines and echoing shouts were heard from the cone of rock. It was two of the Urumchi Government's motor-lorries, returning from Aksu. One of them had broken its back axle on the ledge of rock which had made us stop and wait, and had been left behind as a casualty. Then the road had been repaired sufficiently for the second to get over, knocked about but usable. It had to take over the whole of the wrecked car's load and twenty passengers in all, including Mossul Bai. It was said that the Urumchi Government had acquired eighty Amo cars from Russia, fifteen of which were already out of use.

One wondered what use it was to order expensive cars from abroad before making the motor-roads fit for traffic. That was precisely our task—to examine the roads and submit proposals for their improvement to the Nanking

Government. But we got no help from the Sinkiang authorities in this task, so important to the province. They put every imaginable hindrance in the way of our work and refused us permission to test the roads within the boundaries of Sinkiang.

We drove to Toksun in the afternoon and encamped in the desert at 9 p.m. On the following day, July 7, we had a hazardous journey over the pass by Dawan-cheng and got stuck in the river on the farther side of it. A little Turki caravan which was just passing hauled us up on to dry land for payment. It was past five when we started on the long stretch with Bogdo-ula to the right and the salt lake to the west. It was getting dark; we lit our headlights.

We drove in among the hills, and were only 2½ miles from the south gate of Urumchi when we stuck in the thick mud of a shallow gully. It began to rain. Serat made desperate efforts—no good. We hoped that a horse caravan would pass sooner or later and help us up out of the swamp. But it was too late; the town gates were shut at dark. Serat scratched about with the spade and dug away the mud in front of the wheels. But the car would not stir; it had sunk too deep.

We shut the windows on account of the rain and lit the last candle-stumps. Then we unpacked the remains of the provisions—biscuits, cheese, chocolate, a melon. That was all very well, but we had nothing to drink, and it was impossible to find drinking water in pitch darkness in that place, polluted by carcases and all kinds of uncleanness and putrefaction. We sat in our respective corners and chatted. We had given the convalescent a bad reception. But despite everything we grew sleepy; one after another we ceased to talk and fell asleep.

A horrible night! It is all very well to spend one whole night sitting in a car, but three nights running is too much. I dropped asleep, woke, looked at my watch and found that only half an hour had gone. I longed vainly for day-break. The hours passed so slowly. But at last I began to distinguish the outlines of the nearest hills, little copses and gardens. A little while more and the light grew stronger. A party of fifteen Chinese passed. After some negotiations they agreed to set about the job for 350 taels. And then at last we managed to get loose.

We drove into the town without being stopped, dropped Dr. Saposhnikoff at his hospital and just after 8 a.m. were at Kierkegaard's house, into which his successor Chen, with his wife and three pretty children, had moved during our absence.

It was characteristic of conditions in Urumchi that we had hardly passed through the south gate of the town on our expedition for Dr. Hummel's relief when Mr. Wang of the foreign department went to Yew in a state of rage and excitement and heaped reproaches on his head at the command of the highest authority. Yew explained what had happened, but of course was not believed. Accordingly Wang hastened to M. Apresoff, and, the Consul told me, said:

" Sheng Tupan is most surprised and annoyed at Dr. Hedin having left the town without special permission and without a pass. It is as clear as day that Hummel's illness is an invention, and is only a pretext to enable Dr. Hedin to leave Urumchi, go to his expedition and make a bolt over the frontier to Kansu."

M. Apresoff replied jestingly:

" In the first place, it was I who asked permission of Chen Teh-li for Dr. Hedin to leave Urumchi. In the second place, you ought to know that he came here to get oil, which his expedition has not got. So they can't possibly make a bolt to Kansu. In the third place, my own doctor, Dr. Saposhnikoff, is with him—and *he* won't make a bolt!"

Mr. Wang was silent—it is not easy to talk when one has lost countenance—and was escorted to the door by the laughing Consul.

XIV

HUMMEL AND BERGMAN LEAVE FOR SWEDEN

IT rained heavily on the days that followed, and the streets were turned into rivers of mud. One day Kung appeared, and at about the same time Folke Bergman. They had left our headquarters, camp no. 70, on the Kum-daria with their small caravans and crossed the Kuruk-tagh by different routes. Space forbids me to describe their adventures. Kung's trip had been perilous ; all his animals had died of thirst south of Turfan, and he and his servants had been within an ace of losing their lives.

It is impossible to narrate all that happened during this trying time. We lived in a continuous state of tension during the months of our third captivity. I will quote only a few incidents from my diary to give an idea of the conditions in which we lived our daily life in that barbarously retrograde town.

A Russian visa for Hummel's and Bergman's journey home to Sweden was easily and quickly secured. Even the mighty Sheng Tupan received us amiably and promised them passes and permission to leave the province by way of Chuguchak. Nevertheless, it was nearly a month before they started. Dr. Saposhnikoff wrote out a medical certificate declaring on his professional honour that Hummel, on account of his blood-poisoning, must be thoroughly treated at a special institute for tropical diseases. Painful as it might be, he *must* leave the expedition for the sake of his health. He was certainly convalescent, but his state might grow worse *en route*, and I could not be responsible for letting him make the long, difficult journey alone. There was no one but Folke Bergman who could escort

179

him home, which meant a double loss for me. I will not
attempt to describe what it meant to me to lose my two
Swedish friends and veterans at one blow at so critical and
perilous a time!

How could we repay the Russian doctor for the great
services he had rendered us? He absolutely refused to
accept any fee—he had his Consulate pay, he said. Fortunately, Hummel had left behind part of his medical outfit
in 1928, including a first-class case of Swedish surgical
instruments. This excited Dr. Saposhnikoff's pleasure
and admiration. The drugs were bought by the head of
the Foreign Affairs department Chen Teh-li; he paid in
Russian roubles, which improved our finances at a time
when we were in need of money for Hummel's and Bergman's journey.

Our funds were calculated to last eight months, and we
had been away nine months already. Living was dear in
Sinkiang in war-time. A hundred catties of flour cost
10,000 taels already. And the long journey to Nanking
lay before us. Accordingly we composed a telegram to
our chief, the Minister for Railways, Dr. Ku Meng-yo,
announcing that we had come to the end of our resources
on account of the loss of time occasioned by our captivity,
that we could not leave Urumchi or return to Nanking
without money, and we therefore asked for a supplementary grant of 20,000 Mexican dollars. This telegram
was left unanswered for nearly three months.

A minor relief expedition had to be sent to those who
were still waiting on the Kum-daria, Georg, Effe and Chen.
The Cossack Constantine was instructed to convey the
petrol and oil we had succeeded in obtaining to camp no. 70
in a cart which the excellent mayor had placed at our disposal free of charge, as well as provisions and money.
Two East Turkis were in charge of the convoy, with an
escort of three Chinese soldiers.

Again and again Yew and I called upon Sheng Tupan
at his *yamên*. His reception of us was always polite and
friendly and he promised us everything we wanted.
But he *never* kept his word. Then we wrote letters,
which were answered in a few days. In one letter he

promised us thirty poods of petrol, which never came, and a special house for the expedition, which we never got.

It may be good for the human soul to be purified and hardened in patience, and to learn by personal experience how awful it must feel to be a prisoner for life. All day long we sat on the verandah looking at the sunflowers, tomato flowers and oleanders in the beds below. The hours passed so slowly. And yet we never had any real peace. We felt insecure, and were always waiting for something to happen. We longed for freedom, and saw no limit to the time of our captivity. Day by day we followed with envious looks the ceaseless flight of the clouds over the Tien-shan on the way to God's Mountain. If only we could have travelled back to the desert and the great silence on their blue-grey dragons and galleys! It grew dark. A hurricane was sweeping over Urumchi. Dense clouds of dust whirled round the yard in a witches' dance; the sunflower stems bent submissively before the demons' furious flight. Rain began to fall in torrents, and we retired to our rooms.

Travellers from the north reported that the Manas watercourse and other rivers in Dzungaria were running very high. How would Hummel and Bergman get through? A Russian lorry had overturned at San-chi; two dead, several injured.

Sheng Tupan tried to persuade Kung to stay and help him make roads. Why, that was just what we had come for, but we were kept like prisoners, and treated as spies, and if we only poked our noses outside the town wall we were thought to be meditating a bolt.

Sheng Tupan bought one of our motor-lorries. We tried to get a good price, but he forced it down to 2,500 Mexican dollars. The sum was to be paid into the Russian bank—" to-morrow ". But the money did not come, and the weeks passed, and it was always " to-morrow ".

M. Apresoff had received a telegram from the Moscow Government inquiring about our expedition. They had heard that we had been attacked and were in danger, and asked for all the information that could be obtained.

Apresoff replied that he was meeting me daily, and that all the members of the expedition were well.

After some time had passed we sent Nanking a fresh reminder about the 20,000 Mexican dollars. We could not, unfortunately, say in plain language that we were detained against our will, for the telegrams were censored by Tupan himself. But we said that if we received no support we should have to prepare ourselves for a lean time. If we got no help from Nanking we meant to sell all the cars ; both Sheng Tupan and the Russians wanted them. Then we could try to return by cart along the Silk Road or by train through Siberia. If only we could get permission to leave the town ! Travellers to Moscow via Novo Sibirsk were considered harmless ; but people who went east were dangerous. For there lay Nanking, and the authorities did not want the Central Government to obtain up-to-date reports of the policy that was being pursued in Sinkiang.

On August 1 there was a political mass meeting in the town. It lasted seven and a half hours. Sheng Tupan made a speech in which he said :

" The war is quite finished. Ma Chung-yin is defeated and has fled. Now peace and happiness reign everywhere ; the peasant can go home to his farm and till his ground ; every man can look after his own affairs ; complete freedom prevails ; people can travel freely everywhere. Now the golden time is beginning, the time of construction," and so on, in a style which is not unknown in Europe. But nothing was said about trade being choked by a mass of notes without a trace of cover, nor of its being forbidden to go to Turfan and Hami.

Among the speakers was a girl of thirteen, who boldly emptied the vials of her wrath on Big Horse's head. " We women," she declared, " have suffered more than the men from the violence with which these bandits have treated our sex ! "

Mr. Kou, who had been sent from Nanking to negotiate with Sheng Tupan about the Shanghai-Urumchi-Berlin air route, made a speech which might have cost him his head.

" Sinkiang's Tupan is an excellent governor-general," he said, " but if all his subordinates are bad, and do not care about the welfare of the province, the governor-general will become a new Ma Chung-yin . . . Good communications are necessary both on earth and in the air. It is a scandal that it should take a month to get to Kashgar, when one can drive there by car in a few days and fly there in a few hours."

In the middle of the speech Sheng Tupan got up and went out. But Kou kept his head and, what was more curious, was allowed to leave soon afterwards, having previously waited for permission for over three months.

August 2 also was devoted to a celebration of the victory. A long procession assembled in the fore-court of the governor-general's *yamên*. In front marched 1,500 soldiers in field-grey uniforms and carrying new Russian rifles. Some had shoes, others boots, and their marching was not irreproachable. Little flags and pennons fluttered in their ranks, and broad white or red cloths, stretched on two sticks, were carried across the column. The usual inscriptions, in Chinese, East Turki or Russian, were : " Down with Imperialism, down with Japan ! "

Then followed the cadet corps with its band and banner, various services such as the post and telegraph, with their officials, and school-children, both boys and girls, each carrying his or her little flag. Last came six motor-lorries full of students. The whole scene made quite a festive impression. The six bands played shrilly. Red and green placards had been pasted up at every corner, and house-roofs and shops were beflagged. There was seen the Kuomintang flag—a radiant white sun on a blue ground—and the national flag, which is red, with the Kuomintang flag in the upper part of the hoist.

Five aeroplanes hovered over the town and dropped thousands of red, green and white leaflets with propaganda in Chinese and Turkish. We picked up some of them, and thoroughly enjoyed Yew's translation of their contents. one ran :

" The advance guard of Imperialism has been defeated, but Imperialism itself still lives and is trying to overrun our Sin-kiang in order to conquer the province and the whole of China. In such circumstances the standard-bearers of Imperialism will fight against one another, and then the new world war will be in full swing. We are too weak, fellow-citizens, to be able to have any influence on the second world war, and it will be our fate to suffer as if we were in hell. Therefore we must maintain our demand—down with Imperialism! and remain steadfast enemies of the second world war."

On another leaflet we read :

"Fellow-citizens, comrades! Ma Chung-yin has been destroyed and can never again return to Sinkiang to kill us again. So we have every reason to celebrate. For the victory we have to thank the perspicacity of our new Government. It clearly saw, as we did, the necessity of uniting all races, which saved us from Ma Chung-yin's devastations. Now we are celebrating our victory, and from this moment we must give our new Government all possible support and help it to develop Sinkiang. Then we shall have peace and live in happiness and prosperity for ever."

A third leaflet ran :

"Fellow-citizens, comrades! In the course of the last few years our parents, brethren and other relations have been plundered, our fields and gardens laid waste, our goods and money lost, our trade paralysed, and we are now in a most serious state of financial chaos. All this grievous devastation has been brought upon us by the bandit Ma Chung-yin. He was defeated by us many times and fled, but quite soon after his defeat he came back with a new army, fully equipped, thanks to the support he had obtained from Imperialism, especially that of Japan, which provided him with masses of gold and large quantities of ammunition in order that he might kill our people and conquer our country.

"Therefore Ma Chung-yin is our executioner, but our real enemy is Imperialism, especially the Japanese. But now Ma has been annihilated. This is a proof of the clear understanding and concentrated strength of our fellow-citizens, and of our new Government's wise policy. But although Ma is defeated, his master Imperialism has planned a fresh attack on us. We must stand strongly united on unshakable ground to defend ourselves. We must understand why Imperialism attacks us ; it is because capitalism has turned into Imperialism. To solve the insoluble problem, the Imperialists will fight among themselves and the new world war will begin. We must look back to the former war to remind ourselves how many men were killed, how much money was lost, and how many people had to work hard without compensation. To make a new world war impossible, and exterminate all Imperialists, we must fight against them. When we have crushed them we shall have a peaceful existence in our country, as in all the world."

Other leaflets contained whole strings of political maxims : " Down with the disturber of the peace ! " " Support world peace ! " " Support the new Government ! " " Celebrate victory ! " " Try to keep Sinkiang at peace for ever ! " " All the peoples and races of Sinkiang must stand together ! " " Down with all bloodsuckers ! " " Drive out all intriguers ! " " Destroy not Ma alone, but all Imperialism ! " " Develop the various races' literature ! " " To-day southern and northern Sinkiang are united." " Now that the cruel monster Ma has been destroyed, the people of Sinkiang can enjoy peace." " Strengthen the north-western 'and reconquer the north-eastern provinces (Manchuria) ! " " Do not forget September 18 (Mukden, 1931) ! " " Do not forget our countrymen in the north-east who are so cruelly treated under Japanese Imperialism ! "

The demagogic appeal and its origin were plainly recognizable. The peaceful races of Sinkiang asked nothing better than to live quietly as they had done for centuries under China. An incompetent governor-general, Chin Shu-jen, had opened the door wide to rebellion and civil war, and the people in its distress had turned to the Mohammedan Ma Chung-yin for help. The new governor-general, Sheng Tupan, who saw his rule threatened by Ma, had turned to Russia and got all the help he asked and needed. So Sinkiang was slowly and surely coming under Russian influence, just like Outer Mongolia a few decades before. But the leaflets which rained down over Urumchi contained no warning against this form of obvious Imperialism. Their warnings were not against Russia, but against Japan.

Otherwise, one noticed no Russian propaganda during

the summer of 1934. It was enough for Russia that Sinkiang had passed into her hands militarily, financially and
commercially. The eastern frontier of Sinkiang was
hermetically sealed against all trade with China proper.

Meanwhile the triumphal procession was marching
through the narrow, dirty main street of the town, penned
in between the Turki booths and shops. There sat the
tradesmen and their few customers and stared with dull,
uninterested eyes at the noisy, heterogeneous carnival.
The term "Imperialism" meant little to them, and they
could not believe the promises of a glorious time to come
now that Ma was beaten, when a hundred catties of flour
cost 10,000 taels and the country people who possessed
wheat would not sell their stocks for fear of famine—not to
speak of the obligation to take wheat to the Government
depot.

On the evening of August 4 we were sitting in our room
talking when a letter arrived from the secretarial bureau
of the provincial government, addressed to "the north-
western motor-road expedition". Yew translated it as
follows :

"We have received a telegram from the Ministry of Foreign
Affairs at Nanking stating that the Ministry has been informed
that Dr. Sven Hedin and ten members of the north-western
motor-road expedition, with the postmaster Kierkegaard from
Peking and the geologist Parker Chen, have been attacked and
captured by bandits in the province of Sinkiang and taken to
Aksu. It has been ascertained that these robber bands were
under the command of a certain Mohammedan leader. Please
send men at once to investigate the matter and render help, and
let us have a reply.

"*Signed by the Ministry of Foreign Affairs
on June 13.*

"We should like to know if the contents of the telegram
are true and where the postmaster and geologist in question
are now. Please inquire into the matter and let us have a
reply, for which we thank you in advance."

We laughed till we cried at this quaint letter. The
Nanking people ought to have known that Kierkegaard

was not a member of my expedition, and that Parker C. Chen was an astronomer, not a geologist. This was probably only an echo of the first rumours of the attacks at Korla and the requisitioning of our cars on the way to Kucha and Aksu. It was understandable that Nanking had been puzzled by these reports. But the provincial government at Urumchi, with which we conferred daily, ought surely to have known that I had not been carried off by Big Horse as a prisoner to Aksu any more than Kierkegaard, who had paid farewell visits to the authorities before he went home to Copenhagen on June 18.

If such simple events, which the authorities had to some extent actually witnessed, and the truth about which they could anyhow have ascertained with ease, could produce such a farrago as this, one wondered how any clarity could ever be reached in complicated questions of political import and decisions affecting the welfare of the whole people.

Yew's reply to the secretarial bureau was also worthy of a place in *Punch*. It was very long and detailed, and described our experiences, and the postmaster's departure for home, in as simple, "fool-proof" a style as if it had been intended for the most backward boys in the bottom form of a school.

At 5.45 p.m. on August 7 we three Swedes were in the sitting-room, and Bergman was reading aloud, when a rather violent circular earthquake took place. The tea in our glasses was partly spilled, the plaster loosened here and there, and the window-panes rattled. Hummel and Bergman hurried out on to the verandah and down into the yard. A peculiar curiosity caused me to remain for a moment to see if the ceiling would fall in. It held, but the room went round, I had an unpleasant feeling of giddiness and followed the others. The earthquake did not recur. Three houses had been destroyed not far from us, and it was said that four people had been killed by the fall of a tiled roof.

Two days later we heard that thirty persons had been arrested at two in the morning for conspiring against the Government. One of them was Mr. Soo, head of the provincial bank, and five were White Russians.

The governor-general and the Foreign Minister, Chen

Teh-li, had been present at the examination. The former had asked Soo:

" Have I not always been your friend and shown you the greatest consideration ? "

" Yes, I've nothing to complain of as far as I'm concerned. But how have you treated the poor wretched people in the province ? "

It was said that fifteen of the men arrested had been shot. The prison for political offenders was in the governor-general's *yamên*. If only the walls of the prison yard could speak ! Then one would hear many terrible stories of sanguinary cruelty and inhuman torture. After those sentenced to death had been killed their bodies were flung over the town wall. If they died of sickness, usually typhus, their relatives had the right to take the bodies away and bury them.

We had waited for over a month for a chance for Hummel and Bergman to leave Urumchi. Our doctor's state had not improved ; he was always feverish. The preparations for their departure had taken an unnecessary time, like everything else. But now at last all was ready. A convoy of ten Russian motor-lorries was to leave on the night of August 11 for Chuguchak, Bakhti and the railway. And that this was really true this time was proved by the fact that the Consul-General Apresoff came on the afternoon of the 11th to return the two travellers' farewell visit.

The south gate of the Chinese town was to be shut at 8 p.m., and as the lorries were to start from the Russian quarter, the passengers had to keep an eye on the clock. We ate our last dinner together. The hours crept on. The last hour was approaching, when we were to say good-bye and go different ways to unknown destinies. An inexplicably benevolent Providence allowed us to meet eight months later ; and we could then rejoice together that the evening of August 11, 1934, was past history.

Bergman was ready long before eight. But Hummel took matters quietly, and at 8.30 he was sitting dictating to Yew instructions for my treatment—I had a sharp attack of the gastric trouble so common in Urumchi. Bergman was in despair. If they missed the lorries this

time they would have to wait another month.   It was ten
minutes to nine when the doctor came out on the verandah,
quite unruffled.   The post office carriage was waiting, and
the little luggage they were taking home to Sweden had
been placed upon it.   An embrace : thanks for all your
patience and loyalty—remember me to the people at home !
The gates were flung open by the light of lanterns.   A last
hand-clasp ; the crack of a whip, and the carriage was gone.

Yew and Kung had accompanied them in a Peking cart
to lend a hand if there was any trouble at the gate.   So I was
quite alone, and the silence of the grave brooded over our
court-yard.   I went into the sitting-room and sank into an
armchair.   It is a good thing that one can forget certain
incidents, and that the recollection of them does not darken
one's life for years and years.   In an hour's time Yew came
back and saved me.   He told me that the town gate had
been shut and the sentries had refused to open it.   " One
mayn't leave the town so late—have you passes ? . . . oh
well, we can ring up the *yamên*."

They did so ; the gate was opened, and the carriage
continued its journey to the lorry-park.   The lorries had
not started, and the long and perilous journey begun, till
five in the morning.   The travellers arrived safely at Ayagus,
Semipalatinsk and Novo Sibirsk, where they stayed with
our friend the German Consul Grosskopf, who helped them
on their way with his usual kindness.

Not till August 29—the day on which Hummel and
Bergman arrived in Berlin—did we receive a telegram from
Grosskopf saying that they had passed through his town in
safety.   That was good news ; we need no longer have
any anxiety on their account.

XV

AN EMBARRASSING INCIDENT

ON August 14 came a telegram from the Minister of Railways at Nanking asking how long we wished to extend the time to be spent on the motor expedition,

> "for the time arranged for has already been exceeded . . . You ask to be allowed to return to Nanking, but according to the original programme your expedition was to go to Chugu-chak, Kulja or Kashgar. If the expedition returns now it means that it will not have carried out its mission. Telegraph at once the cause of your request to be allowed to return."

We had hinted to the Minister of Railways that, as we had not got permission to travel along any of the three roads, a prolongation of our stay at Urumchi had no object.

Again—as so often before—we wrote a letter to Sheng Tupan quoting the Minister's telegram, pointing out that our lorries were on the Kum-daria and that we had not yet received the petrol we had asked for more than two months before, and asking if we might borrow a lorry and a ton and a half of petrol for a twenty days' trip to Kashgar. We explained in detail how easy it would be to arrange this trip. Seventeen days later our answer came—a polite but absolute refusal. The province was short of cars, and those which it had were required for military purposes.

On the 21st the Minister for Railways sent an express telegram insisting yet again that we must travel along one of the three roads in the province. To reply by telling the truth—that the governor-general barred the three roads to us for political reasons—would have done us little good, for Sheng Tupan's censorship would never have let such a message through. I may mention that Bergman, on his journey to Chuguchak with Hummel, made notes on the condition of the road which later were appended to the engineers' report; so that even on this point we had, in a way, carried out the task entrusted to us.

Our position was to say the least queer. We asked nothing better than to go to Kashgar, but were refused permission. The Minister for Railways reproached us time after time for not going there, and we could not tell him the reason. We wrote letter after letter to Sheng Tupan demanding a reply to our questions. Two tons of petrol and eight poods of lubricating oil had been promised us from Russia, but could not be handed over till we had paid. Sheng Tupan had bought one of our lorries for 2,500 Mexican dollars, but would not pay the sum till he had got the car. And the car was on the Kum-daria, and could not be fetched without oil and petrol.

Worse was to come! In obedience to our instructions, we had carried out no excavations on the way to Sinkiang. But when Bergman, Parker C. Chen and I found half a dozen graves some thousands of years old on the banks of the New River, the Kum-daria, we excavated them and took away the objects we had found in them, including human skulls, with the intention of handing these over to the proper authority at Nanking after having taken note of anything which, in one way or another, could throw light on the old Silk Road.

The marking out of new routes for motor traffic through Central Asia was, as I have already pointed out, an undertaking which of its own nature was closely connected with archæology. For one could be sure that a motor-road from Sian-fu to Kashgar would follow the old Silk Road for nine-tenths of the distance.

On August 26 I received a telegram from the Minister for Railways, despatched on July 7, which led to the culminating point of the drama. It ran:

"I have received from the Minister for Education a letter which says:

" 'Dr. Sven Hedin is digging for archæological treasures without permission at Lop-nor and on the river Tarim. This is contrary to the laws of the country and the Minister's instructions. Please point out to the Minister for Railways

that his department must be held responsible for this mis-
conduct.'

" I have been asked by the Minister for Education to investigate the affair and inform him of the result.   Dr. Sven Hedin
and the members of his expedition have not permission to dig
for archæological treasures, which was definitely stated in the
instructions previously given.   As I have been asked to investigate the matter, I must say—if the report is correct—that your
action is certainly not justified and that you must stop the
excavations at once.   If you have found anything, every item
must be handed over to the Minister for Education.   I
await your immediate reply."

When I had read the telegram through again carefully, I
was in no doubt as to the attitude I should take up towards
the Minister for Railways.   I told my friend Yew that I
could not remain in the Ministry's service one day longer,
but intended to send in my resignation at once.   Yew was
in despair and would not hear of it.   Kung was equally
alarmed ; he declared that the expedition could be saved
only by my name and my foreign nationality, and that if I
left it all its members would be arrested for an indefinite
time.

We decided, however, as a beginning to send the Minister
for Railways an objective reply, which was to be despatched
by telegraph the same day.   It was a very long story.
First we recalled the expedition's aims and objects.   We
told him how we had got right into the middle of the civil
war and had nearly been shot, and how at the end of March,
on Sheng Tupan's instructions, we had withdrawn to
Lop-nor for two months.   We had divided into two
parties, one of which was to look for a road eastward
through the Kuruk-tagh, the other to go to the Kum-daria
and investigate the New River's suitability for irrigation.
Then we told him how we had found the graves, and
pointed out that these graves could at any moment be
destroyed, wiped out by wind and weather, and above all
by the shifting waters of Lake Lop-nor.

" As these graves," we said, " were calculated to throw some
light on China's past, we did not feel that we could pass them

by, but opened them and took away what we found in them, to be handed over to you . . . Your telegram has greatly astonished us. The representative of the Minister for Education did not take part in our trips to Lop-nor. How can he, with no witnesses, and with no knowledge of where we have been and what we have done, accuse us of digging for archæological treasures ? The objects we have found we shall hand over to you personally at Nanking, as we may need them to prove what kind of ' treasures ' we have dug up."

The telegram was signed by myself and the Chinese members of the expedition and sent to Sheng Tupan to be censored. It came back in two days' time with a notification that it was too long. We therefore sent it as a letter, and Yew made a résumé of the main points, which was telegraphed.

On August 29 I sent the following express telegram to the Minister for Railways :

" I have received and considered your telegram of July 7. It astonished me, as it is based on false statements. The fact that your Excellency gives credence to lies and makes accusations against me in the telegram in question has seriously undermined my prestige and injured my honour. As I do not intend to expose myself to any further insults of this kind, I herewith submit my resignation and inform you that I am preparing to start for Sweden as soon as I have obtained permission to leave the province."

Not till this telegram had been sent off did I hear of another which had been sent to the Minister for Railways at the same time as my own and signed only by the Chinese members. Later I received a copy of it. It was very flattering to me and stated, among other things, that the expedition would be completely broken up if I left it.

Sheng Tupan's censorship did not return the two telegrams to us until September 2. They had clearly entertained him, for on my telegram of resignation he had written " will be sent off at once " with his own hand under his red seal, and on the message of the Chinese " will be sent off without the least delay ".

My telegram to the Minister for Railways, Ku Meng-yü,

had been sent off on September 2. The reply came on September 5, quicker than ever before.

It was in English, and ran as follows :

" Extra urgent. Dated September 3, 7.30 p.m. Nanking. Adviser Sven Hedin Suisan (Suiyuan-Sinkiang) Highway Expedition, Urumchi.

" Your wire dated August 29 duly received. The inspection work for the Suiyuan-Sinkiang highway, extending if possible to Kashgar, is very important. Your knowledge and experience are well known and cover a wide field. Your name is well known over the world. You took up your work with great responsibility and energy, which fact is very admirable and gratifying. I am urging you to stay and continue your work to fulfil the mission.—Ku Meng-yü."

After this it was not long before we received a telegram saying that the additional sum we had asked for had been granted and deposited in the German-Asiatic Bank at Peking. Our position was thus secured.

About six on the evening of September 4, Yew and I were on our verandah when a well-known hooter was heard outside the court-yard gate. We hurried down ; the gate was thrown open, and one of our lorries, the trusty " Edsel ", rolled into the yard. Georg, Chia Kwei, Chokdung and the Cossack Nikolai jumped out. Georg hurried towards us, tall, cheery and sunburnt.

" Where are the others ? Are they alive ? "

" All well, all in splendid form ! "

What joy ! All our cares were dissipated.

Three weeks earlier we had sent Serat, with a sufficient quantity of petrol, in a cart to Korla, where he had met the whole convoy. If everything had been ready, they would have been able to start for Urumchi at once and would have been with us a fortnight earlier. But Colonel Proshkurakoff, General Bektieieff's adjutant, had passed through Korla with a lorry about a month before and had found there the lorry we had left in charge of the Russian garrison. Proshkurakoff had taken from it certain vital parts of the engine which he needed for his own car, with the result that Georg had had to travel the whole distance from Korla to Toksun twice over. This had meant that a good deal more petrol was used, and the convoy as a whole had not been able to get farther than Toksun, whence Georg had driven " Edsel " alone to Urumchi.   He therefore had to return to Toksun on September 6 with a fresh supply of petrol and fetch the others.   But on September 8 we were all gathered together, Parker C. Chen, Effe and Jomcha having now arrived, and we had a dinner to celebrate it—one of the really happy memories of the expedition.

Some of the baggage we had left behind at Korla had been stolen by Russian soldiers.   The parts of the engine taken by Proshkurakoff were never restored, the consequence of which was that we later on had to leave the damaged lorry at Urumchi.   We ought almost to have known that anything one handed over in that country would be stolen.

How much longer were we to be kept in that miserable hole ?   Instead of helping us on our way, now that we had all the members of the expedition and all five cars at Urumchi, they hit upon a new dodge to prevent us from leaving.   On the 13th one of Sheng Tupan's adjutants appeared at our house with orders that all archæological finds should remain within the province, as the law forbade them to be taken out.   He also informed us that one or two other adjutants had been ordered to go to Lop-nor to find out what we had done and where we had been— a brilliant idea, seeing that we had visited only uninhabited regions.

Next day orders came that all our luggage should be taken to the guest-house for examination.   Only the two big cases with archæological contents, i.e. the objects we had found in the graves, were left sealed on our verandah.

An adjutant repeated that an expedition was to start for Lop-nor to search for the treasures we had hidden there. " If we find them," he said, " you'll all go to prison."   We must wait at Urumchi as long as this expedition was in the field.   What was the use of our swearing on our honour and conscience that we had not hidden so much as a collarstud, either at Lop-nor or anywhere else ?

We were all six invited to lunch that day at M. Apresoff's hospitable house, and I told him how we were placed.   He then told me that he had heard that Sheng Tupan had been told that we had found valuable treasures during our excavations at Lop-nor and had hidden them in or near Korla. The reason for our repeatedly expressed desire to go to Kashgar was simply this—that we wanted to stop at Korla on the way, dig up the hidden treasures, take them with us to Kashgar, entrust them to the British Consul-General there, and with his help have them sent on to India.

Sheng Tupan had believed this story, and that was why the objects we had found in the graves had been sealed up and were to be kept back.

On September 17 we were all six received by Sheng Tupan. He was sitting at a long table conferring with his Government. In an adjoining room, through which we were conducted to the audience-chamber, sat ten Turkis and Chinese, waiting to be received.

We had not long to wait before the governor-general came in and sat down among us and the usual teacups.

To begin with, he asked us not to smuggle any gold out of the country, because the ban on the export of gold was still in force, and he had found that considerable quantities were being smuggled out through Turfan.

" We need all the gold we can get hold of in Sinkiang ourselves, to pay for the other war material we have bought from Russia."

We asked permission to leave as soon as two damaged motor-lorries had been repaired.

" You can have passes whenever you like," he replied. " How long will it take to repair the lorries ? "

" About ten days."

" Then let's say that you leave Urumchi on October 1."

He added : " I have had orders from the Central Government in Nanking to forbid and prevent all kinds of archæological excavations, and in particular the opening of graves. If anyone disobeys this order, he will be imprisoned at once."

We told the whole story of the discoveries. Bergman had found a fair-sized burial-ground, which had been almost entirely plundered by Turkis ten years ago or more. Only a number of parts of skeletons and rags remained. " Someone has told your Excellency," we said, " that we have found valuable treasures and hidden them near Korla. That is not true."

Finally, we asked permission to use the road via Kuchengtse for our return journey.

Sheng Tupan was pleased to jest with us.

" As you're so fond of Sinkiang, Doctor," he said, " and the people like you, stay here and help us develop and improve the province. We should find Mr. Yew and Mr. Kung valuable too. It's not easy to get engineers up here from the coast, and we have been compelled to apply to Soviet Russia."

After pleasant audiences like this we used to telegraph to the Minister for Railways, because we knew that Sheng Tupan read all the wires himself. He thus gained prestige in Nanking and learned how highly we valued his courtesy.

September 18, the third anniversary of the fall of Mukden, was celebrated with a mourning procession through the town and a fiery speech from Sheng Tupan.

Even then the dirty Eastern town, with its heterogeneous mingling of Chinese and Turkis, presented an animated scene. The gateways were packed with arbas, telegas, Peking carts, horsemen, donkey caravans with cotton from Turfan, travellers, pedlars, ragged boys, dervishes and vagabonds.

A fiery red leaflet bore the following instructive text :

" On September 18 three years ago the Japanese Imperialists conquered our territory of Manchuria, to protect themselves from danger and complete their unworthy occupation of our country. The Government abandoned Manchuria without resistance and allowed thirty millions of our countrymen to be crushed by the Imperialists, which was the result of September 18. But the invasion has caused the Imperialists certain economic difficulties. A war will break out between the Imperialists one fine day as a result of the unequal distribution of colonies. Before the second world war breaks out, the various Imperialist Powers are preparing to get firmer ground to stand on. The Japanese Imperialists conquered Manchuria in a very short time by a simple military adventure. They will doubtless continue their invasion into China without

delay. Thus, for example, at the end of the fighting along
the Great Wall the Japanese seized all economic and military
privileges in Northern China.

" And now Japan is sending her officials to stir up unrest
in Sinkiang with the object of conquering this province also.
With this object the Japanese Imperialists have planned the
prolongation of the Peking-Suiyuan and Lunghai railways to
Hsing-hsing-hsia, whereby they will be able to invade Sinkiang.
We, fellow-citizens of Sinkiang, must have our eyes open to
this danger, and kill all these dirty dogs or drive them out of
this province.

" To honour the memory of September 18 we must do our
best to defend the whole province of Sinkiang, its privileges
and territories, and firmly to unite all the different races, attack
the Imperialists and recapture all the territory they have taken
from us. If all the different races are to be welded together
into a firm whole, they must be placed on the same level and
treated in the same way. When this has been done, it does
not matter what secret conspiracies Imperialism directs
against Sinkiang, for we shall be able to crush them. We
must be resolutely on our guard every moment against the
Imperialists and give them *one* answer only : that is, *blood.*
Down with Imperialism ! "

It was alleged that the outburst about dirty dogs was
addressed to our expedition ! The fact that our task was
imposed on us by the Central Government at Nanking,
and that it was to make roads fit for traffic to and in Sinkiang for the benefit of the Chinese and the races over
whom they ruled, was never mentioned. Our long deten-
tion, and the refusal to allow us to travel along the three
roads I have mentioned, proved clearly enough that we
were regarded as enemies and spies, not as friends working
solely in the interests of the province.

The political orgies which took place on suitable occasions under the blue and white Kuomintang banner and
the red national flag were the only entertainment that was
offered a visitor to that utterly tedious and sinister town.
There were no cinemas and theatres, though there were
cafès and restaurants of the simplest kind, and prostitutes
—Russian, Chinese and Mohammedan. A life of unre-
strained debauchery—immorality, drunkenness, gambling,

opium-smoking—was lived in the squalid night resorts of the place by the light of reeking oil lamps. Urumchi was a dirty place in every sense of the word.

People got married in Urumchi, and from time to time dead bodies were carried out of the town. The old civilian governor Li Yung lost his wife at the beginning of September, but on the 19th of the month the stout, genial old grey-beard was ready to marry again. His choice was a widow of thirty of phenomenal ugliness.

The bridal party drove up in twelve carriages. Hardly had they passed our gate when a judge's funeral procession came by. Huge paper lanterns were carried at the head of the procession, then a stretcher, then swaying palanquins in many bright colours, and a few banners on long poles. A party of small boys followed in red dresses with pointed caps, gigantic parasols, red-robed priests of Buddha, Taoist monks. The dead judge's spirit drove in a four-wheeled covered carriage decorated with white cloths, escorted by a company of soldiers carrying rifles with fixed bayonets. The near kinsmen drove in white mourning robes, a band at their head, while other relations walked in the mud. Then came the coffin, on a bier under a white canopy, carried by sixteen bearers. The judge's daughter and other white-robed ladies filled the street with loud weeping. The judge's body was being carried to a temple, there to await patiently a favourable day for the burial.

A dinner at the Foreign Minister's developed into a rather barbaric entertainment. The dishes were Russian, the cooks and waiters likewise. Most of the Chinese grew more or less drunk. One of them, a fairly high official, staggered about pouring rice brandy over the hair of those whom he liked (I was not one of his favourites). Mossul Bai and two other East Turkis sat as silent and dignified as images, without touching the strong drinks and without moving a muscle of their faces. But one can guess what they thought. They had to attend the dinner for the sake of peace and quiet. But they did not give tongue with the pack ; they hated their host and his people, and were ashamed to be under rulers who got drunk.

On September 22 I paid a fairly long visit to the Russian
military adviser, General Malikoff, who was Sheng Tupan's
right-hand man in military matters and a very powerful
personage.

I took the opportunity of talking to the general about
young Hanneken's tragic fate. Hanneken had travelled
from Peking to Lanchow in the autumn of 1933 and had
there met a Russian Tartar, who took the young German's
ꜰᵃⁿ⸱ through his knowledge of languages. Hanneken had
⸱ ꜱ ꜱᵃ that the man had served a term of eight years'
⸱ ⸱ ⸱ ꜱᵒⁿment for murder. Hanneken had arrived at Hami
⸱ⁱ September of the same year and proceeded to Chi-ko-
ching-tsᵉ ᵗʰere the road forks, the right branch going to
Kucheng⸱ ⸱, the left to Turfan. Hanneken had chosen the
latter, but had not gone far when the Russian Tartar advised
him to take the road to Kuchengtse. Hanneken had taken
this road, but he never reached Kuchengtse, and nothing
more was ever heard of him.

The Catholic fathers had done all they could to find out
what had happened to him. They told me that Hanneken
had had a greyhound bitch, which was always his faithful
companion. One of Ma Chung-yin's soldiers from Suchow
had seen Hanneken and had specially noticed the dog and
its black and white spotted skin. When the soldier returned to Suchow late in 1934, he told how in the previous
winter he had seen by chance, at a skinner's in Hami, a
dog's skin which he was convinced was that of Hanneken's
greyhound, for he was sure there could not be two dogs'
skins with that peculiar marking. As the soldier had
noticed the animal's fidelity to its master, he had himself
formed the opinion that the two had been killed at the
same time. Loy and Father Haberl were convinced that
the young German had been murdered, either by Kirgises
on the road between Chi-ko-ching-tse and Kuchengtse, or
by the Russian Tartar. They had given up all hope of his
reappearance.

I now told this sad story to General Malikoff. He
listened to my narrative most attentively and asked a
number of questions. When I apologized for taking up
his time, he replied:

" Not at all, on the contrary, I'm grateful. Detective stories have always interested me."

He noted fully all the details of my story.

" I'll do my best to clear the thing up," he said. " To start with, I'll find out which of our officers were stationed on the road between Chi-ko-ching-tse and Kuchengtse in September and October, 1933, during the war against Ma Chung-yin."

" Even if Hanneken is dead, which I'm afraid is the most probable thing," I replied, " it would be of the greatest importance to get confirmation of it and find out exactly what happened to him. Perhaps his diary may be found, or other belongings of his."

I also told the general that the lost man's mother, General Hanneken's widow, had sent Bökenkamp to look for him with a letter from President von Hindenburg, who was an old friend of the late General Hanneken. Hindenburg died soon afterwards.

As I mentioned above, on my last visit to Sheng Tupan I asked to be allowed to take the main road via Kuchengtse and Chi-ko-ching-tse. I chose this road for the special reason that I hoped to meet some of the Kirgises living in those parts and question them about Hanneken. Unfortunately I miscalculated. We were detained so long that the springs in the valley between the two places froze and covered the whole of the bottom of the valley with a sheet of ice, absolutely impossible for our heavy lorries. But I feel sure that the Kirgises, if they were guilty of murdering a European, would have withdrawn hastily into the mountains for fear of punishment when they saw armed Europeans, with an escort, approaching their tents.

XVI

OUR LAST DAYS IN URUMCHI

TOWARDS the end of September we were informed that no collections might be taken out of the province. An exception was made for geological and botanical specimens. As we now sold a lorry to Sheng Tupan, and another had been damaged as a result of the Russian colonel's petty larceny, the convoy would be reduced to three cars for the return journey along the Silk Road. We therefore cut out everything we could dispense with, and five packing-cases were to be sent to the Swedish Legation in Moscow, two to a Chinese firm in Peking. Herr Schirmer undertook to send them off. Among the Moscow packing-cases were two filled with Dr. Hummel's birds from the Kum-daria.

On September 27 an adjutant and two Chinese Tcheka police came to the guest-house, where Georg, Effe, Chen, Kung, Serat and our boys were staying, to examine the packing-cases. This was done with painful thoroughness. Hummel had packed each bird's skin with care, filled it with cotton and cotton-wool, wrapped it up in paper and tied string round the parcel. The police unpacked every single bird. The parcels were literally as light as feathers, but this did not prevent our sleuths from saying they must make sure that we had not stuffed the birds' skins with gold!

The day brought us one minor victory. We had received orders to take all our luggage, every scrap of it, to Sheng Tupan's *yamên*. All the boxes containing personal effects, instruments, and so on were stacked in one room. In two others, on long tables, we had an exhibition of all the things we had found in the graves at Lop-nor. There lay in long rows all the apparently insignificant scraps of silk and cloth, caps, shoes, sandals, wooden or clay bowls, stools, bows and arrows, ritual and symbolical objects. To the un-initiated eye the whole lot looked like rubbish flung on a dust-heap.

And now the display began, a little comedy whose pro-gramme had been drawn up by our shrewd sympathizer M. Apresoff. The members of the expedition were to be there at 8.30 a.m. A little later M. Apresoff arrived with his colleagues Yassinovsky, Starkoff and Michelmann from the Russian Consulate-General. Then Chen Teh-li appeared, and last the governor-general Sheng Tupan.

Sheng Tupan went round the exhibition most thoroughly, with a serious expression, clearly determined to let nothing escape him. He stopped a little while at each object, took it up, turned it over, examined it from all sides, and asked the most searching questions. Yew and I went round with him and answered everything. At times Parker C. Chen, who had taken part in the digging at Lop-nor, took over the duties of cicerone.

I myself was most nervous about the private luggage, which contained all my diaries, sketches and maps, and all the excellent maps of the lakes on the southern bank of the Kum-daria, right down to Lop-nor, which Chen had drawn during the summer. In Yew's and Kung's boxes were their and Bergman's maps of the northern motor-road through the Gobi, and Bergman's maps of the river-arm which flows southward from the Kum-daria, and which was one of our important geographical discoveries. The adjutants had already threatened to allow none of these materials to be taken out of the province, which would have meant that the whole journey had been made in vain and was a total failure. I had already expressed my anxiety to M. Apresoff, and he had, with his customary goodwill, promised to speak to Sheng Tupan. He now came up to me during a pause and whispered:

"None of your private luggage is to be opened. All the boxes will have official labels and Sheng Tupan's stamp, certifying that there is nothing in them to which exception can be taken, and no contraband. Then your boys can load the boxes up on the lorries again and drive them away."

Splendid ! So far the expedition was saved.

And now the time had come for the great effect of the drama. Sheng Tupan assumed a veritably theatrical attitude, made a gesture over the table with his right arm and said :

" Gentlemen, these things have no value to us and are of no interest whatever to my province. You can pack them all up in your boxes, and you will receive a special pass from me entitling you to take your discoveries and the rest of the luggage out over the frontier."

Then he withdrew to his office, as haughty as a Cæsar. M. Apresoff and his subordinates went to their own place, when we had heartily thanked the Consul-General for having, as he certainly had, saved the expedition. We had been long enough in Sinkiang to know that it was not for our own sake, but for M. Apresoff's, that the governor-general had treated us so accommodatingly and with such great generosity. For we were nothing but an unwelcome gang of spies, who had caused him anxiety and inconvenience ; but the Consul-General had helped him to win the war, and without that help Sheng Tupan would have had to surrender the throne of Sinkiang to Big Horse.

Two or three miles from the town lay the temporary aerodrome which had been constructed after Big Horse burned down the old one at the beginning of the year. A sports ground had now been established there, with a race track 400 yards long. The great " Olympic Games " of the year were held there on September 30. We were formally invited and were received at the entrance by Sheng Tupan himself, who conducted us to a large spectators' marquee with chairs and tables, where the prizes, silver cups and other trifles, were displayed on a table.

The newly married civilian governor-general, the Russian Consul-General, and all the dignitaries of the town were there ; and round the track was a crowd of White Russians, Red Russians, Chinese, East Turkis, Torguts, Kirgises and others.

I now made the acquaintance of Hodja Nias Hadji, the East Turkis' leader, the standard-bearer of the native Mohammedan population, the Mecca pilgrim, who was

also the bearer of the honourable, semi-religious title of
hodja. He did not make a very agreeable impression; he
was coarsely built, boorish, black-bearded. Although I
talked to him in his own language, he only answered "yes"
and "no", and he did not speak to anyone else either.
Presumably he felt that if he uttered a single word that
could arouse suspicion he might be a head shorter.

His position was difficult. In the war he had first sided
with Big Horse, who at least was Mohammedan, then
against him, and had been beaten in several fights. He
had had a royal reception from Sheng Tupan, and had his
own court and his own bodyguard. But his own East
Turki people could not approve of his going over to the
Chinese, whom they hate in the mass as heathens, *kaper* or
unclean. Sheng Tupan had shrewdly and skilfully paralysed him by selecting him to be vice civilian governor-
general, an empty title conferring no power, which tied
him to the capital and placed him under direct supervision.
To see him going about in an ordinary yellowish-grey
European overcoat and an equally European cap was an
offence to all faithful Mohammedans, who consider the
Prophet's headgear, the turban, the only one worthy of a
hodja and *hadji*. He was bound, therefore, to excite con-
tempt in all quarters, on both national and religious grounds
and it was not at all surprising that he preferred to keep
silent, wait and see. As for ourselves, we had been so
slandered that practically everyone avoided friendly inter-
course with us.

There is not much else to say about these Olympic games
in the heart of Asia. There was an obstacle race, a relay
race, wrestling, a marathon race and all the usual events,
not badly arranged for such a barbarous country. Dinner
was served in the tent, and at last we were able to go.

The games were continued next day, and Sheng Tupan
took part in a short-distance race. When the prizes had
been distributed he made an eloquent speech about the
importance of physical training for the defence of the
province, and did not lose the opportunity of saying a lot
of nice things about Imperialism and Japan.

On October 2 I was taken ill. Dr. Saposhnikoff was

sent for, and looked serious. Next day he gave Yew instructions about my treatment and advised the greatest care.

" Is it typhus ? " I asked.

After a moment's reflection the doctor replied :

" Well, since you ask me, I'm bound to say it's as likely to be typhus as anything else. If your temperature keeps up you must move to our hospital."

I was moved to the hospital on October 5, well wrapped up. Everything was conspiring against us. We were to have started on October 1, and now ? I wrote a long telegram to prepare my sisters in case the last great departure was at hand. M. Apresoff, who came to see me several times, took charge of the telegram. When I was out of danger, he confessed to me that he had not sent it off, as he did not think those at home ought to be frightened before it was necessary. I blessed him for his high-handedness. My temperature rose to 103·6. Luckily we had all been inoculated by Hummel at Korla.

Typhus—that was the only thing not yet included in our chapter of accidents ! Typhus—the word has an awe-inspiring, terrifying sinister ring, like Titus, Timur and typhoon. It connotes strength without mercy, swift devastation, ruthless cruelty. It was as hopeless to resist Timur, or to bring a fleet of junks through a typhoon, as to fight the typhus bacilli.

I was not long in hospital. Saposhnikoff looked after me splendidly, and I cannot thank him warmly enough for what he did. There were thirty beds and ten Russian and Tartar nurses, who lavished on me the tenderest care and shortened the long hours by telling me their life-histories.

Even now rumours were buzzing through the air like dragonflies. It was said that my illness was feigned and that I was using it as a pretext to await the arrival of some strong man from the coast. It was affirmed that Ma Pu-fang in Ching-hai, in alliance with Yollbars at Hami, was to conquer the whole Turfan basin. It was reported that hostilities had broken out between Chinese and Tungans in the country east of Anhsi, just where we were going to travel along the Silk Road.

The days passed slowly ; winter was coming on. On the night of October 10 the temperature was 27·4 and on the night of the 12th 19·4. But that day was my last in hospital. My temperature was normal, and I was allowed to drive home to the postmaster's house, where the whole expedition was waiting for me and welcomed me.

The last few days were spent in farewell visits. Sheng Tupan owed us 3,500 Mexican dollars, and after months of waiting we got the sum in gold billots from the Altai and a special certificate that we had permission to take it out of the country. It was a dangerous cargo to have with us in the regions we were to pass through.

After Dr. Saposhnikoff had declared that I was restored to health and that we could start whenever we liked, we thought that all possible obstacles had been cleared away. But that belief was too optimistic. Chen Teh-li informed us that two buses were to start on the 21st, and that Sheng Tupan wished us to leave at the same time so that the same escort could take charge of both parties. After long discussion it was agreed that the day of departure should be the 19th. About the same time an adjutant came and declared that the supreme authorities wanted a detailed report on the roads in Sinkiang—those same roads which they themselves had obstinately barred to us.

On the afternoon of the 16th Yew and several other Chinese were summoned to a conference with Sheng Tupan. It was a long time before Yew came back, and this boded no good. The subject of the conference had been our return journey and that of the buses, and the guard we were to receive. Sheng Tupan had said :

" I shall bear the responsibility if anything happens to Dr. Hedin. If he is attacked and killed, the whole world will say that I arranged the attack, and my reputation will be ruined everywhere. I must give him adequate protection within my province. I shall telegraph to Pichan to-night ordering detachments to be sent to Chi-ko-ching-tse and Cheh-kou-lou. The order cannot take effect before the 20th, and you can start on the 21st.

" Let no one know that you are starting on the 21st. For Kirgisian robber bands have their spies in the bazaars ;

these send word to the chiefs and the raids are planned accordingly. I warn you also about the road from Hami to Anhsi. Yollbars reports that a robber band sixty strong has its headquarters at Hsing-hsing-hsia. Think the matter over carefully. I advise you to return by the way you came, through the Gobi. A convoy of twenty-one carts, on its way from Kuchengtse to Chi-ko-ching-tse was attacked and plundered by Kirgisian robbers quite lately. The whole party was murdered.

"Up in the north, on the frontier between Sinkiang and Outer Mongolia, and in the Altai, Kirgisian bands are raiding far into these territories. The Soviet authorities there have complained and asked what attitude I think they ought to take up. My answer was, 'Kill them.' So the raiders are being pursued far into Sinkiang. Once a Soviet aeroplane killed eighty robbers by dropping bombs. We have agreed with Outer Mongolia to have pickets on both sides of the frontier. The bus company's cars can run from Kwei-hwa to Hami, but no farther. Sinkiang's own buses can bring on the mails and passengers after they have been examined."

We were afraid that the next dodge to delay us would be to postpone the farewell banquet, without which no one could possibly start. But on the 17th an adjutant came with a red card bearing the names of all the guests —one confirmed one's acceptance of the invitation by signing one's name.

The dinner was copious and Russian, with plenty of wine. It was a good quality in Sheng Tupan that he neither drank nor smoked and left his guests alone. Some queer speeches were made. The host spoke first.

"This simple dinner," he said, "has been arranged by the Government to say farewell and welcome again to our guests of honour—first and foremost to Dr. Sven Hedin, who has been in Sinkiang many times to study its geography, natural history and archæology. He has now returned here and found a lot of very old things. When these collections have been taken to China and carefully examined, they will throw light on historic events in China which are of interest to other parts of the world also. In

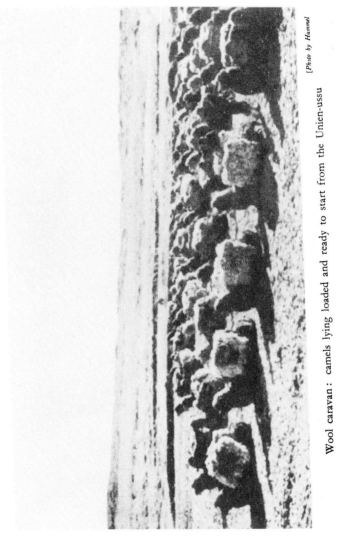

Wool caravan : camels lying loaded and ready to start from the Unien-ussu

[Photo by Hummel

[Photo by Hummel

Parker C. Chen

Khalkha Mongols' temple *yurt* on the Etsin-gol

[*Photo by Hummel*]

Camp in the Pei-shan

[*Photo by Bergman*]

Small car in the river at Dawan-cheng

[Photo by Dr. Saposhnikoff

[*Photo by Ambolt*]

Urumchi, Western Park

A military parade at Urumchi

[Photo by Ambolt

Town wall of Anhsi, with sand dunes up to the top

[Photo by Chen

The Great Wall about 3 miles east of Shan-tan

[*Photo by Chen*]

Bridge over the Su-lo-ho close to Yü-men

[*Photo by Bergman*]

Chia-yü-kwan, the western end of the Great Wall

Stuck in the ice near Hou-shui, January 24, 1935

[Photo by Yeo]

The Ku-lang-ho and Imperial Highway, with avenue planted by Tso Tsung-tang

[Photo by Chen

Lou-tai-chiao bridge, west of Lanchow

"The End of the Road" at Sian railway station

[Photo by Kung

addition to his geographical researches, Dr. Hedin has this time also studied communications, which can be of great importance to Sinkiang and China . . ."

It was to Sheng Tupan's credit that he concluded his speech with the words :

" I am very sorry that the seriousness of the times prevented us from giving him more vigorous help and better treatment than he has actually received."

The speech was translated into Russian by an interpreter, and my reply was translated into Chinese.

Then came several rather amusing speeches, a regular bombardment of diplomatic and undiplomatic civilities across the table. Tupan thanked the Consul at Chuguchak for his splendid help in the civil war, but in his reply the Consul disclaimed all honour and assured us that the victories gained over Ma Chung-yin had been won solely by the gallant Chinese generals. The young Torgut prince spoke in Mongolian and thanked the Russians for the help of their troops, who had saved the province from being conquered by Big Horse. Of course, such a thing ought not to have been said, as it might cause protests from Nanking and other quarters. But the little prince had no idea of the sacredness of political secrets, and continued to skate on thin ice quite unruffled.

At last, when everyone had said what he wanted to get off his chest, we separated the best of friends.

At eight next morning I was waked by Yew, who called to me :

" Sheng Tupan's come to pay a farewell visit with his wife and daughter ! "

I jumped out of bed, made an imperfect toilet without washing, and found the great man with his family waiting patiently in our sitting-room.

Tupan now handed me a pass written with his own hand, which authorized us to take all our luggage out of the province without customs or military inspection. It ended with threats of severe punishment for anyone not complying with the instructions in the pass.

He gave me also two portraits of himself and his family, a large piece of jade and a black lambskin.

Finally, he asked us to go with him to the military parade which was to be held that morning outside the town. But we excused ourselves, saying that we had not had breakfast and would appear later.

We drove to the parade-ground, where all the usual guests of honour had assembled on a raised platform. The troops marched past in brilliant sunshine, about 1,300 infantry, a dozen batteries of artillery with mounted supply columns, cavalry on splendid horses, a number of armoured cars, and so on. The band played and a festive atmosphere prevailed. Tupan's civility was striking. When we left, he accompanied us to our car and saluted as we rolled away.

And so the last day came, removing the uneasiness which in recent times had lain heavy upon us like a nightmare. It had been said that Tupan's own brother and a few other Chinese notables were to come with us in our cars, which would have meant that we lost our freedom of movement. But fortunately it was decided at the last moment that these gentlemen should travel in the buses.

One more good-bye—to the Rev. Mr. Hunter and the Catholic missionaries. At 7 p.m. we were at Sheng Tupan's for the last time.

The two lorries stood ready in our court-yard, with the new supply of petrol we had obtained from Russia thanks to M. Apresoff, provisions and baggage. And so the last night descended on our prison yard.

XVII

THE HOUR OF LIBERATION

THE hour of our liberation came on October 21, 1934, a year to the day since we had started from Peking. At 8 a.m. the passenger car and the two lorries rolled out of the gate, through the southern gate of the Chinese town, the Turkish quarter Nan-kwan and the Russian Jang-hang, all separated from one another by more or less ostentatious gates.

We stopped at the Russian Consulate-General to say good-bye to M. Apresoff. He came running, cheerful and lively, in a real Sunday morning humour, and declared that he meant to intercept us 10 miles or so outside the town. While we were halted at the bus company's office to take leave of Chen Teh-li, Apresoff drove past; he was going to arrange a farewell snack with vodka and wine by the roadside. The guard at the last and southernmost gate let us pass unmolested, and we left Urumchi behind us with a feeling of indescribable satisfaction. We sat in the comfortable car, leaning back in care-free attitudes, and gazed once again at the magnificent scenery, the mighty peaks of the Tien-shan and Bogdo-ula far to the eastward. It was delightful to feel the wheels going round—each revolution took us farther away from Urumchi and nearer to Nanking, Peking, home.

We did not see M. Apresoff again. His driver had evidently turned off along a side-road too soon, and presumably he sat waiting for us in vain. I was sorry not to be able to thank him once again for all his kindness.

We drove along the familiar road to Dawan-cheng. It was getting late, and the shades of evening were falling over the village. The silver of the moonlight grew brighter and brighter. It was dark in the valley when we came to the river. The road had given way for a short distance on the left of the valley, and we therefore had to cross the river three times. At the first crossing we followed the lorries and got stuck in mid-stream, but were hauled out by six men. The second crossing took us across foaming rapids, where the water forced its way into the car and we got stuck again. We had to save in haste what could be saved. Cables and ropes were produced, and a lorry towed us out of the rapids.

At last we had accomplished the third crossing, and looked for a place on the bank where there was a space free from boulders and large enough for a tent. Here our first camp was pitched. Chia Kwei served up mutton, bread and butter, cheese and tea, and it was delightful to sleep in the open air again with the noise of the river in our ears and the wind rustling through the branches.

In the cool of the morning we drove up to the narrow defile of the Dawan-cheng pass and ran steeply down its farther side. We met a few caravans of horses and donkeys carrying flour and cloth—local trade was beginning to revive. A month earlier two Russian Amo cars with Chinese drivers had gone down the pass. The drivers had lost control of their cars, which had dashed downhill at a furious pace and overturned; four men had been killed.

Through picturesque red defiles, with brick-red clouds of dust hovering round the convoy, we drove to the point where the road divides, one branch going to the right to Toksun, and the other to the left to Turfan. The sun set, but the full moon raised its yellow face over that ragged landscape with its complex of ridges and ravines. We were going downhill all the time, and soon the altimeter showed that we were at sea-level.

Next day we drove out through the east gate of Turfan and were soon in the picturesque Sängim valley. At the commandant's office at Pichan an officer told us that guards had already been posted along the road and that we could continue our journey without fear. We drove across irrigation canals and queer bridges under slender, formal poplars, and were soon out in barren desert again. When we had gone 86 miles we encamped. It was a cold evening, and the minimum temperature fell as low as 14·9.

On we went eastwards. A party of Turki horsemen told us that they had met several patrols, which were out to keep the road clear for us. We rose higher again through winding valleys.

It was 5 p.m. when we reached the critical point, Chi-ko-ching-tse, to which fifty soldiers had been sent on our account. The officer in command said:

" If you want to go on along the road to Hami, you must have twenty soldiers with you on the lorries. The road is unsafe, and we are responsible for you."

Our guard clambered up on top of the two loads, and we proceeded. The moon rose, and we were soon in the desert again.

We continued our journey on October 25, a brilliantly clear and still morning. According to the speedometer the small car had now covered 7,000 miles.

Another night was approaching. Twilight came, and then the dark, before we were among the outermost cottages of the Hami oasis. A curious reception awaited us there. Serat was driving ahead, and Yew, Chen and I immediately behind in the small car, with Effe as chauffeur. At a little bridge over a canal a dozen soldiers ran forward with rifles pointed at us. They ordered Serat to stop, which he did at once. We got out and asked what the trouble was. They in their turn asked in an arrogant tone who we were and where we were going. They sent a mounted messenger to Yollbars for instructions. Meanwhile we had to wait. They all kept their fingers on the trigger, ready to fire if necessary.

After a time the answer came that we might drive into the town. A crowd of soldiers climbed up on to the lorries, others stood on the running-board of the small car; and we drove slowly into the dark street, lit only here and there by an oil-lamp flickering in a shop. The cars stopped in front of Yollbars' house. There stood the general himself, the all-powerful ruler of Hami, Yollbars Khan or the Tiger Prince, surrounded by his bodyguard of thirty soldiers. I greeted him, talked with him for a little while and invited him to enter my car; but he replied that he must first fetch the Chinese civilian governor Liu and, in his company, pay an official visit to the house he had prepared for us.

We drove to the same house in which we had stayed in February. The two buses, which had left Urumchi at the same time as ourselves, were already standing in the little court-yard.

Soon the powerful Tiger Prince and the governor Liu appeared and talked to us for half an hour. The two buses were to stop at Hami for a few days to obtain provisions, and we ought to wait one day because Yollbars wanted to give a dinner in our honour. I told him we had had more than enough of that kind of thing at Urumchi, and that we absolutely must start for Anhsi next day, October 26. It was accordingly decided that we should breakfast with Yollbars at ten the next morning, and continue our journey at noon. The road to Anhsi was safe; the robber bands which had been marauding around Hsing-hsing-hsia had been driven away. The commandant at Anhsi had asked to be informed by telephone of the time of our arrival. The Government at Nanking had ordered him to give us the best possible reception.

Herr Bökenkamp, who, as I have already mentioned, had been sent to Sinkiang by Frau Hanneken to look for her son, had stayed three months at Hami and had left the town the day before our arrival, evidently on the road to Anhsi. His departure had resembled a flight, and he had left at his lodgings two boxes full of rubbish to delay a possible pursuit. But Yollbars did not seem to have any interest in pursuing him. To my question whether he thought there was any hope of tracing Hanneken, he replied diplomatically:

" I have not seen his body, and so cannot swear that he is dead. But I don't *think* he is alive, and I feel that there is no hope for him."

When we left Urumchi fourteen persons had asked to be allowed to travel in our cars, and several of them had offered to pay handsomely for the lift. But they had all met with a hard-hearted refusal, for it was laid down in our official instructions that we had not the right to take passengers. One of them was Gustaf Söderbom, who had left Urumchi on the pretext of going to Manas with his two camels, turned and cut back to Hami, and reached that town at the same time as ourselves. But at the west gate of Hami he had joined a caravan which had made a detour outside the town and encamped in the desert to the eastward. If he had kept himself hidden, and gone on eastward with his travelling companions, he would probably have got right to Kwei-hwa. But he was rash enough to visit the bazaar at Hami to make some purchases. As, after our departure, he was the only European in Hami, he did not escape the notice of the Tcheka police, and was arrested and imprisoned. Then he was taken back to Urumchi, where he had to stay till he was freed by diplomatic intervention.

One more trial had to be faced on the following day before the hour of our liberation struck—the breakfast with Yollbars. Quantities of *ash*, *shislik*, *mante* and tea ; a speech by Yollbars in East Turki, to which I replied— and a slight uneasiness lest we should be detained at the last moment. The passengers by the bus company's two vehicles were at the breakfast, and begged us insistently to travel in company with them across the Etsin-gol to Kwei-hwa, so that we might defend them with our weapons in the event of our being attacked by robbers. But once more we were hard-hearted ; we hurried to our quarters, finished our packing and drove away from Hami, escorted by Yollbars and Liu. They stopped ten li out and took a last farewell of us ; and we put on all the speed of which our engines were capable to get away from their dangerous proximity.

The motor-lorry in which Yollbars and Liu escorted us had been sent to Hami by Sheng Tupan, with another like it, to fetch Hodja Nias Hadji's family, who lived there. Yollbars had sent off several members of the family and one of the cars, but had kept back the other, and the Hodja's brother, daughter and concubine, as hostages.

The cultivated belt soon came to an end. To the north

the spurs of the Tien-shan rose like a huge cape running out into the sea of the desert.

We were on the ancient caravan route between Hami and Anhsi. It was sometimes not bad, sometimes difficult, and here and there it ran through belts of hard, dry, yellow grass. We encamped for the night in the little village of Chang-liu-shui, " Long Flowing Water " ; our camp was no. 109.

We had left Urumchi with 500 gallons of petrol, and had now only 200 left. This was enough to take us as far as Anhsi, but what would happen afterwards if we could not replenish our supply in that town ? It was not without a certain nervousness that we faced the indescribably desolate, lifeless desert road between the two towns. If the worst came to the worst, we could scrap the cars at Anhsi and proceed by cart or camel.

Not a blade of grass was to be seen. The desert spread itself before our eyes, as flat as the surface of the sea in every direction. Only to northward were the mountains still visible in a faint purple hue. We drove past a mounted mail-carrier. The man told us that he got sixteen dollars a month, but had to find his own horse or donkey and food. Poor fellow ! One must have either a soul as hard as steel, or no soul at all, to be able to spend one's life on that ghostlike, dead-alive road.

Although the minimum temperature had fallen to 21·6, it was blazing hot in the noontide sun. One searched in vain for a blade of grass. The surface of the desert was sometimes hard and comfortable to drive on, sometimes bumpy. The mountains faded out and disappeared in the north-west distance. Now and again we drove past the ruins of very old clay houses, but there was no sign of human beings. The ruins of a watch-tower stood on a hillock. At Ku-shui, " Bitter Water ", the road forks ; the right-hand branch goes to Tun-hwang, the left to Anhsi. The village of Ku-shui, where we encamped, was razed to the earth ; but a couple of mail-carriers were living in a hovel. They narrated to us the following episode :

A short time before Big Horse marched along this road to Hami for the second time, eleven East Turki merchants

from the last-named town had been on the way home with
goods bought at Anhsi and had got permission at Hsing-
hsing-hsia to cross the frontier between Kansu and Sinkiang. Our friend Li, Big Horse's chief of staff, was acting
as governor of Hami at the time. He gave orders that the
eleven merchants' caravan should be attacked and plundered. This was done ; all the eleven were killed and their
goods seized. When this crime became known in Hami,
the dead men's families demanded compensation. Li
declared that the caravan had been attacked by robber
bands, for whose doings he could take no responsibility.
The incident brought fresh fuel to the flame of revolt in
Sinkiang. If Li had been in a bad temper when we were
his guests at Turfan about February 20, he might easily
have treated us as he did the eleven merchants. But he did
not, either because our weapons inspired him with respect
or because he felt his own position more than insecure
after Big Horse's defeat at Urumchi.

We made an early start on October 28 in brilliant
sunshine and a stifling south wind. The desert soil
was firm and covered with hard gravel ; the slight undulations of the ground lay spread before us like a swell
dying down at sea, and to right and left of us low hills
were visible. We met a caravan of forty camels carrying
tea and cloths. The owner, a merchant from Kerija,
had left his native town eight years before with goods
for Suchow. Rebellion and war had prevented him from
returning. Not till now had he dared to start. The
caravan bells rang as solemnly as for a funeral.

We rose 800 feet to the top of an undulation, whence
there was an endless prospect over a fearfully desolate and
barren desert. Not a blade of grass, not a trace of wild
animals ; it was the home of deathly silence. From time
to time we passed the remains of a watch-tower or a ruined
wall, on the lee side of which travellers could find temporary
shelter from violent storms. Sha-chüan-tse, "Sand
Spring", was one of the places on the road—only too easy
to count—where really good water was to be had.

When we had gone 30 miles from Ku-shui we had risen
1,625 feet and at Hsiao-hung-liu-yüan, "Little Tamarisk

Garden ", we were 5,200 feet above sea-level. Then the
road went in among low hills, crests and ledges, and followed
a narrow sunk track between rocks of fine-grained grey
granite, pegmatite and crystalline slate. The mountains
grew higher. We climbed to a low pass 6,040 feet high.
On the right-hand side of it we saw the little temple of
Hsing-hsing-hsia, ruined and abandoned. Innumerable
cairns marked the road to this Buddhist holy place. There
was no priest in charge of the temple, whose ruined walls
shone out red among grey rocks. The little village close
by consisted of only a few cottages, and the postmaster was
its only inhabitant. His runners were out on their travels.
He told us that the evening before some soldiers from Anhsi
had come up to the village to meet us, but as nothing had
been heard of us, they had turned back.

Ruins and walls of old fortifications crowned the hills
round the temple. The frontier between the two provinces
was here, but now no frontier guards watched over it.

After 17·4 degrees in the night, we started early. Num-
berless cairns and pyramids lined the road, which ran now
over sand or gravel, now between blocks. After a time
the valley came to an end, and the country became open,
with an extensive view southward. A narrow defile led
to level country dotted with infrequent tussocks. We
passed an abandoned gold-digging, and a trench bore
witness to the disturbed times.

Our general direction was south-east. We had for a
long time seen on our right a mountain chain running from
west to east and forming part of the Pei-shan. At last we
touched its eastern end, and the chain disappeared behind
us. Scanty tussocks grew in shallow ravines. We met a
caravan of forty-four camels carrying flour from Anhsi to
Hami ; local trade was beginning to look up again. At
Ta-chüan, " Big Spring ", lived a postmaster with his
family and three donkeys. On each side of the road rose
a hill with a little watch-tower, visible a long way off.
The next village, Hsiao-chüan, " Little Spring ", was uninhabited. We were in among low hills again ; they
delayed our map-making. We saw a herd of antelopes a
few hundred yards away.

Camp no. 112 was pitched on a flattish plain, 6,080 feet up. We had brought water from Hsiao-chüan so as to be independent.

We woke on October 30 to find the sky overclouded, which was unusual, but at sunrise it cleared up again, and the south wind was singing round the cars. Our road led through mountains. The once large, now totally destroyed village of Hung-liu-yüan was inhabited by only a postmaster and a few dogs. All the devastation which met us along this road was the work of Big Horse. He had not left the smallest farm standing. Everything was destroyed and in ruin. When he marched this way from Anhsi to Hami in 1933 he destroyed all the villages and farms, partly to hinder possible pursuit by an army from Nanking, partly to prevent his own soldiers from deserting and returning to their homes.

Soon after 11 a.m. a most unusual sight met our eyes— a motor-car in a cloud of dust. It had come to bid us welcome to Anhsi. The owner, a Balt named Herr Tamberg, was himself at the wheel. He was in the employ of the Oppenheimer Casing Company, and had come to Anhsi with five cars to fetch sheeps' intestines from Sinkiang. Young Almblad from Kalgan, the missionary's son, was in his service. A third passenger was a German, Herr Pauck, in charge of the Eurasia Air Company's petrol stores in Anhsi. Among a number of Chinese should be noted a Mr. Lo, who welcomed us on behalf of the mayor and commandant. After a little conversation we proceeded in company beneath small rocky ridges and ledges and across level desert, through a few villages, past small caravans and ox-carts to Lung-wang-miao, which is consecrated to the divinity of the river Su-lo-ho. It was four o'clock when we reached the right bank of the Su-lo-ho.

The river ran between bare flat banks and was divided into two arms, partly frozen and now hardly carrying 27 cubic feet of water a second. We left the lorries, but crossed in the small car ourselves and drove along a wretched road, with irrigation canals and raised banks, to the crenellated wall which surrounds Anhsi. We were stopped at

the west gate by soldiers, who had to report our arrival
before we could be let in.

Then we made for the mayor's *yamên*. He received us
courteously, and had five rooms reserved for us. While
he was talking to Yew and me, Herr Pauck arrived and also
our friend Bökenkamp, who had ridden from Hami to
Anhsi in the record time of five days.

Anhsi is a miserable, very poor little oasis. The whole
population was estimated at 900 families, 300 of which were
in the town itself. Anhsi had also a garrison of 450
soldiers, Tungans, under the orders of Ma Pu-fang at
Sining. Tun-hwang, which has a garrison of fifty men,
is considered larger and more prosperous than Anhsi.
The garrison lives on the peasants, who receive no compensation and so grow poorer and more miserable in pro-
portion to the number of soldiers they have to feed.

Another source gives the oasis 6,000 inhabitants and the
town 4,000. It is, of ocurse, impossible to obtain any
idea of the size of the population in a country where there
is no census. A tax-collector whom we met farther east
assured us that the whole Anhsi district was inhabited by
940 families, while 960 families lived at Yü-men and 2,500
at Tun-hwang. There were 100 families at Chia-yü-kwan.
These little oasis towns generally have one or two schools.

At Anhsi a heavy shower of news and rumours descended
on us. The Europeans in the town had heard that we had
been made prisoners by Big Horse and taken to Kashgar.
Several hundred motor-lorries full of soldiers were on
their way from Sian and Suchow to reconquer Sinkiang.
For this purpose an aerodrome had been built at Suchow
and 100,000 gallons of petrol conveyed there. Our adventures were evidently not over. On our way eastward
we should meet this army, whose leaders might have need
of our experience and compel us to turn back and serve as
guides.

If we had passed Hsing-hsing-hsia a little earlier we
might have fared badly. Eight robbers had been lying in
ambush there. They had a spy at Hami, who had reported
that a caravan of seventy camels, laden with carpets and
other goods and gold-dust from Khotan, would leave

Hami for Anhsi on a certain day. When the caravan reached the narrow valley at " Stars' Pass ", Hsing-hsing-hsia, the robber band had attacked it, killed some of the merchants and captured the camels and their valuable load. The survivors of the caravan had fled to Hami. Soldiers had been sent out in pursuit from that oasis and from Anhsi. They had found four robbers and taken them to Anhsi, where they were to be beheaded one of these days. The rest of the band, with the captured goods, had fled to the Ma-tsung-shan, where they were now being pursued by military patrols.

Herr Pauck was occupied at the moment in laying out the new aerodrome, which was intended for the Shanghai-Urumchi-Berlin air route. It was 1,100 yards long from east to west and 850 yards from north to south. A hundred and fifty workmen were employed. The aeroplanes, which had hitherto covered the distance from Suchow to Hami in two hours and a half, would in future be able to land at Anhsi if rough weather was predicted. For the time being there was no flying.

When Count Bela Szechenyi, with Loczy and Kreitner, reached Anhsi in 1883 after crossing the whole of China and Kansu, it was rightly held in the geographical world that he had done something remarkable. Often, in years long past, I talked to Szechenyi and Loczy at Budapest of their brilliant journey, so rich in results. When now, more than fifty years later, I myself approached Anhsi, I had a feeling of being, if not nearly home, at least a good way on the road.

From Anhsi we made a most interesting and adventurous expedition by car, by Tun-hwang, westward through the Pei-shan, and south of the Ghashun-gobi to the Lop-nor basin. That a long journey like this was at all possible was due to the great kindness of the head of the Eurasia Company in allowing us to buy as much petrol and lubricating oil as we liked from the store under Herr Pauck's supervision at Anhsi.

Thus we, who had succeeded in getting out of Sinkiang, after so many troubles and so severe a trial of our patience, now returned to that province of our own free will, and could easily have been taken prisoners. If this had happened, we should doubtless be rotting in some dank prison to this very day, for they would have been justified in suspecting us of espionage.

But this trip through the unknown heart of Asia is so closely connected geographically with the Lop-nor problem that I will keep my description of it for the book *The Wandering Lake*.

XVIII

THE SILK ROAD

IN the year 138 B.C. the great Emperor Wu-ti, of the older
Han dynasty, sent an embassy of a hundred persons,
headed by Chang Ch'ien, to the Yüeh-chih, a people who,
since they had been driven westward by the Huns, had
settled in Ta-yüan, the modern Ferghana.

The Huns were China's most dangerous enemies, and
Wu-ti's object in sending the embassy was to secure the
co-operation of the Yüeh-chih in a war against them.
Chang Ch'ien failed completely in his diplomatic mission,
but was able, after many adventures and ten years' captivity
among the Huns, to return and make a report to the
Emperor which greatly interested Wu-ti.

Chang Ch'ien told him not only of the oases and people
in what is now Eastern Turkistan, but also of the routes
to the western countries, to India, Persia and vast territories
stretching as far as the Caspian Sea, of peoples of high
civilization and great wealth. The Emperor understood
at once what this wealth might mean to the development
of China's trade and the extension of its power westward.

Another piece of news Chang Ch'ien was able to give
the Emperor was the existence of a strange kind of " blood-
sweating " horses, the progeny of supernatural stallions
and mares.

The Emperor's cavalry had previously been mounted
on little Mongolian steppe horses of the same kind as
the Huns', and he now calculated that with the help
of blood-sweating horses from Ta-yüan he would be
able to improve the native breed and set up a cavalry
through whose superiority the Huns would quickly be
defeated.

Wu-ti sent several well-equipped emba⸱ ⸱es to Ta-yüan

with the object of acquiring a sufficient number of its noble horses; but they all returned empty-handed.

Finally the Emperor sent an embassy taking to the king of Ta-yüan a thousand gold pieces and a horse of solid gold. The ambassadors were made prisoners; they succeeded in escaping, but were murdered on their way home.

When the news of this outrage reached Wu-ti's ears, he resolved to take a bloody vengeance and sent an army against Ta-yüan, including 6,000 cavalry. A large part of the army was lost on the march through the fearful waterless desert west of Tun-hwang, and the portion which reached Ta-yüan in a miserable state was defeated. Only a tenth of the original force returned to Tun-hwang alive.

Then Wu-ti was still angrier, and he equipped a new army of 60,000 men, 30,000 horses, and oxen, donkeys, carts and camels to carry supplies. Half this force reached its destination, besieged the capital of Ta-yüan, and forced the king and his people to hand over thirty blood-sweating horses and mares of less good, but still excellent breed. China's prestige had been saved, and the Emperor was able to found studs for the improvement of the native breed.

Through these two campaigns, which are recorded in the annals of the Han dynasty, the Chinese came in contact with Western civilization. New roads were opened for the exchange of goods, art and thought, and, not least, for the introduction of Buddhism into the Central Empire.

The man who by his intelligence, courage and capacity had brought about these great historical events was Chang Ch'ien, one of the greatest of all geographical explorers in Central Asia.

In the meantime the Huns were driven out of southern Kansu and a main artery for traffic with the western countries was opened. The Great Wall, begun by the Emperor Shih Hwang-ti, was extended westward by the Emperor Wu-ti and provided with watch-towers to protect the road and its trade. This road, the Imperial Highway, and its fortifications and defence works were thoroughly investigated and described twenty years ago by the archæologist Sir Aurel Stein.

No goods which were exported from China proper along

the Imperial Highway could be compared, either in importance or in extent, with the beautiful Chinese silk, which two thousand years ago was the most highly esteemed and the most sought after of all the articles of world trade.

About A.D. 100 the Macedonian silk merchant Maës Titianus had his agents in Eastern Turkistan; they went to the land of the Seres, the silk-producing people, and returned to their master with an account of their journey. From Maës Titianus these descriptions came into the hands of the geographer Marinus of Tyre, who in his turn became a valuable source for the famous Alexandrian geographer Ptolemy's account of "Scythia extra Imaum", or the country we now call Eastern Turkistan.

After the close of the Han dynasty, A.D. 220, there followed, in the time of the "three empires", a period of division and depression in China, but the silk trade continued more or less unaffected on its long road from the shores of the Pacific to the Mediterranean. About 260–280 there was still a flourishing life and commerce in the Chinese town of Lou-lan, whose ruins I had the good fortune to discover on March 28, 1900, near the shore of the old, then dry lake Lop-nor in its northern location. Lou-lan was a fortress, a garrison town, and an important junction on the main traffic artery. To get to Lou-lan the caravans had to cross a long stretch of fearfully barren desert from Tun-hwang, the most westerly outpost of Chinese culture, before they reached Lop-nor; Lou-lan was the first oasis in the Tarim basin.

Professor Conrady, who translated the manuscripts found by me and preserved in the Royal Library at Stockholm, speaks of the ancient world route which went westward over desert and steppe to Khotan and thence to India, Persia and Europe and eastward via Tun-hwang and Suchow to China proper.

In one house I found fragments of silk, yellow, sea-green and dark blue. One of the translated letters mentions a consignment of 4,326 (?) bales of silk bought for the inhabitants of Lou-lan, which, as Conrady says, "indicates a respectable population". The silk, which came via

Tun-hwang, was of importance to the population, because it was used to pay for wheat.

Not only did the silk trade through Lou-lan come to an end, but the town itself was abandoned by its inhabitants. This was because the river, the lower Tarim, which hitherto had supplied the whole region with water, changed its course about A.D. 330 and began to flow south-east and south to form the lake Karakoshun or south Lop-nor, discovered in 1876 by N. M. Prshevalsky.

Before the abandonment of the town a large part of the silk trade had already begun to take the sea route to India, Arabia, Egypt and the coast towns of the Mediterranean.

Lou-lan itself was forgotten as completely as if it had been swept from the surface of the earth. When Marco Polo, in 1273, made his famous journey from west to east, and passed not far south of Lop-nor, the old town, of whose existence the Venetian could of course have no idea, had already been asleep for a thousand years. And Lou-lan was to go on sleeping for nearly six hundred years longer, till it was suddenly awakened from its long sleep, and, through the discoveries made among its ruins, threw fresh light on the ancient world route and the connexion between China and the west two thousand years ago.

I have already said that the Chinese call their great trade route through Shensi and Kansu all the way from Sian, and probably as far as Chia-yü-kwan, the farthest gateway to westward in the Great Wall, the Imperial Highway. Thence as far as Kashgar its western continuation still bears the name Tien-shan-nan-lu, or "road south of the Celestial Mountains", which name is also applied to the part of the province itself which lies south of the Tien-shan.

The name "Silk Road" is not Chinese and has never been used in China. Professor Baron von Richthofen was probably the inventor of this descriptive name. In his famous work on China, he speaks of *die Seidenstrasse*, and, on a map, of *die Seidenstrasse des Marinus*. In 1910 Professor Albert Herrmann published an extremely valuable work entitled *Die alten Seidenstrassen zwischen China und Syrien.*[1]

[1] "The old silk roads between China and Syria."

North-west and west from Sian, as far as the Tun-hwang region, the Silk Road is one single road. From Tun-hwang, or Yü-men-kwan, "the Jade Gate", not far west of it, it divides, as Herrmann shows, into three branches, one running by Khotan, one via Lou-lan, and a northerly route by Hami and Turfan. There are other branches as well, beginning in the western part of Eastern Turkistan. One road goes by Issik-kul, where the Wu-sun people acted as intermediaries in the silk trade by exchange of goods. Another went through Ferghana to Samarkand or Tashkent, through the country of the Alani by the Aral Sea, and from the Usboi, the old course of the Oxus or Amu-daria, to the Caspian Sea; whence it continued up the Kura to Phasis, the Black Sea and Byzantium.

A third road crossed the country of the Yüeh-chih or Tokhars, Bactria and Margiana, thence through Hekatompylos, the Parthians' capital, Ecbatana in Media, and Palmyra to Antioch or Tyre, where the manufacture of silk was highly developed.

Herrmann also mentions an old silk road from Yarkend over the Pamir to the country of the Yüeh-chih, and another by way of the "hanging passages" in the Hindukush to Gandhara in north-western India, Kabul, Southern Iran, Hormuz, Bushire or Seleucia to the Persian Gulf and Southern Arabia, whence barter trade was conducted with Egypt.

Silk was undoubtedly exported from China even before Wu-ti's time. Silk has been found in ancient Greek colonies near Kertch in the Crimea, and Alexander the Great's strategist and admiral Nearchos speaks of "Serian cloths" which had come to India from the north.

But the precious, easily transported and sought-after commodity has not left many traces on the Silk Road within the frontiers of China, and even fewer farther west, where the silk cargoes split up on to different caravan routes in farther Asia.

I mentioned above the few fragments of silk I found in 1901 at Lou-lan, which were probably the first of their kind from the Chinese Silk Road.[1] Stein found consider-

[1] A photograph of these appears in Conrady's book on Lou-lan.

able quantities of the silk at the same place in 1906 and 1914. The French archæological expedition to Palmyra collected in graves fragments of Chinese silk, described by R. Pfister.[1]

P. K. Kosloff, on his last journey, discovered considerable quantities of silk in Northern Mongolia. Folke Bergman's collection of Han dynasty objects found on the Etsin-gol in 1930–31 also contains a fair number of fragments of silk, as well as other textiles. On our trip down the Kum-daria to the new Lop-nor, in the spring of 1934, Parker C. Chen and I found, in the graves dating from Lou-lan's last years of prosperity, a silk shroud round a young woman, while Bergman, at the same time, found similar remains in fairly large quantities in graves in the desert south of the Kum-daria.[2]

The section of the Silk Road which is briefly described in the subsequent chapters is between Anhsi and Sian and is 900 miles in length. From Anhsi, through the Pei-shan and along the north bank of the new Lop-nor and Kum-daria to Korla we find a section of the same road; it is 522 miles long and runs mainly through unknown country. I shall have an opportunity of returning to this section, which was covered by boat along the waterways and in the Pei-shan with two cars, in my book *The Wandering Lake*.

The whole Silk Road, from Sian via Anhsi, Kashgar, Samarkand and Seleucia to Tyre, is 4,200 miles as the crow flies and, including bends, something like 6,000 miles, or one-quarter of the length of the equator.

It can be said without exaggeration that this traffic artery through the whole of the old world is the longest, and from a cultural-historical standpoint the most significant connecting link between peoples and continents that has ever existed on earth. The Chinese merchants at Sian, Loyang, or other places, large and important trading centres a few thousand years ago, had no idea where the innumerable bales of silk, which were borne or driven westward

[1] *Textiles de Palmyre.   Découverts par le service des antiquités*, etc. Paris, 1934.

[2] Folke Bergman : *Newly discovered graves in the Lop-nor desert.* 1935.

by their caravans, ended their journey. The main thing for them was to get their payment from the first middleman. Tokhars, Bactrians, Parthians, Medes and Syrians carried the precious wares farther, but only the Phœnician seamen in Tyre and other Mediterranean ports knew that Rome was the chief market.

The Roman patricians, who decked their wives and daughters in silks, had the vaguest ideas of the popular textile's origin. It was enough for them to know that *sericum* (silk) and *serica* (silk fabric) were produced and exported by a people called the Seres, who lived somewhere in the far east of Asia. The Latin word for silk evidently came from the Chinese *ssu, sse, sser,* in Korean *sir.*

Thus silk became a connecting link between different peoples, and gave rise to the establishment of endless caravan routes.

The Chinese annals tell us as little as other sources of the variegated and certainly most picturesque life of the Silk Road in the centuries immediately before and after Christ. But much can be deduced from the antiquarian discoveries which have been made during the first third of this century. I shall return to these in *The Wandering Lake.* In that book I shall speak of the organization of trade, of inns and shelters, of military posts and protection for transports ; of marching troops, ambassadors and pilgrims ; of water conveyed to the driest parts of the desert, of interpreters, of customs and other controls at the frontiers of languages and empires ; of the ordinary means of transport, ox-carts, donkeys, horses and camels, and of mounted couriers carrying the mails. I shall speak of the Great Wall, too, and of the watch-towers which also indicated the distance in li.

In my memorandum to the Nanking Government, mentioned in the introduction, I stressed the magnificence of a revival of the ancient Imperial Highway, the road along which the silk was carried for centuries in an unbroken stream towards the western lands. It was, indeed, to study this link between China proper and the heart of Asia, and find out what it needed in improvement and upkeep to make it usable for motor traffic on a large scale, that we were now

in the field.   We came to the real Silk Road for the first
time on our journey home from Urumchi, and it is to this
section that the following chapters are devoted.

On that journey we saw the Great Wall, which, mile after
mile and day after day, lay stretched across the desert like
an endless yellow-grey snake, having discharged its duty
of protecting the Central Empire against the barbarians in
the north.   And we saw the innumerable watch-towers
which rose by the wayside, dumb and yet eloquent witnesses
to a vanished time of greatness.   They loomed up through
the dust of the road and the winter fog as regularly as
heart-beats, as though determined to defy the law of
dissolution ; nor had the passing of the centuries prevailed
over them.

We now saw the Silk Road at its lowest ebb, with dor-
mant life and dying trade, the connecting towns and
villages in ruins, and the population languishing in a state
of permanent insecurity and miserable poverty.   Only in
our imagination did we see the brilliant, many-coloured
scenes from the past, the unbroken carnival of caravans
and travellers.   And when we met, as we did daily, the
mail-carriers with their letters in leather bags behind the
saddle, and listened to the tinkling from the collar of bells
which the horse wore round his neck, there echoed in our
eyes a melody which had sounded along that road for more
than two thousand years.

And again we thought we heard the beating of Time's
wings.

The following figures will give an idea of the old road
as a motor route.   It took us from December 18, 1934,
to February 8, 1935, or fifty-three days, to cover the 930
miles from Anhsi to Sian.   We travelled on thirty-five of
these days, so that our average speed was only 26½ miles a
day.   We could have gone very much faster if the map-
making in the oases, with their houses, walls and gardens,
and the narrow, deep-cut ravines, had not taken up so much
time.   On the last day's journey before Sian, where no
map-making was necessary, but the road was consistently
wretched, we covered 100 miles.   If we had been inde-

pendent of the map, we could have covered the distance between the two towns in a considerably shorter time.

I myself had no objection to the slowness with which we crawled along the Silk Road. I had plenty of time to observe both the road and the surrounding landscape, town and village life, people and traffic—in a word, reality as it passed before our eyes.

But, I will readily confess, I lived most in the world of imagination, in the past with its impressive pictures and seething life, and in the future with its splendid prospects

of technical progress and the development of human energy on a scale that makes the brain reel.

I have already said how important it is for China to extend and maintain the great lines of communication with her possessions in Central Asia. Sinkiang's position is most precarious, both politically and commercially, if roads fit for traffic are not made. I have been glad to hear from different sources in China that the Government has already begun this gigantic undertaking. Work has started on the Sian-Lanchow railway. China's finances do not at present permit of the railway line being continued via Anhsi to Urumchi and Kashgar, although there is strong support for such a plan. She would undoubtedly have to be content with motor-roads to begin with, as their construction is incomparably cheaper and requires only a fraction of the time.

During our journey I saw in my mind's eye the new motor-road running across steppes and deserts, with innumerable bridges over rivers, brooks, irrigation canals and ravines, to Anhsi, Tun-hwang, the northern Lop-nor, along the Kum-daria to Korla and on to Kucha, Aksu and Kashgar. And when it reached Kashgar, after faithfully following the caravan and wheel tracks of the old Silk Road, it would by no means have reached its end.

It is said that the Russians are building, or perhaps have already completed, a motor-road from Osh via Terek-dawan to Kashgar. At any rate it is a trifle for modern road-makers to make a road for vehicles, in hundreds of zigzag bends, over the 12,000 feet pass.

At Osh one is on the already existing motor-roads in Russian Turkistan. On them one can travel without hardship or danger to Tashkent, Samarkand, Bokhara, Merv, over the Iranian frontier to Meshed and Teheran, and on via Kermanshah to Baghdad. The Iranian motor-roads are excellent, and the road through the Syrian desert to Damascus or Aleppo is just as good. Thence the road runs through Asia Minor to Ankara and Istanbul, and in Europe the traveller can go wherever he likes.

This immensely long motor-road cannot be an unbroken entity without willing co-operation from the Russian side. But if China makes the necessary financial sacrifices, and Soviet Russia is sympathetic, the undertaking is simple in comparison with many other technical achievements on earth. Indeed, compared with another piece of building carried out by Chinese—the Great Wall—this road-making is a mere trifle.

It is not a fantastic dream to affirm that the time need not be far off when an enthusiastic motorist can start from Shanghai in his own car, follow the Silk Road to Kashgar, drive all through Western Asia to Istanbul, and then travel via Budapest, Vienna and Berlin to Hamburg, Bremerhaven, Calais or Boulogne. If he reaches the Atlantic coast, after 6,600 miles as the crow flies or 8,000 allowing for the bends of the road, with a whole skin and his car in tolerable condition, he will probably have had his fill of motoring for some time.

But he will also have collected a mass of unforgettable experiences, cut a gigantic cross-section right across the old world, and had the most interesting and the most instructive motor journey imaginable on this earth.

He will return with memories of picturesque, swarming China, of the oases on the edge of the Gobi, the mysterious deserts between Tun-hwang and Lou-lan, the wild camels' desolate homeland. He will have seen a glimpse of the wandering lake and the belt of vegetation which is just being born again on the banks of the river Kum-daria. He will have seen the sand dunes on the northern edge of the Takla-makan and the East Turki oases at the foot of the Celestial Mountains. The summer sun of Central Asia will have burnt him, and he will never forget the howling of the sandstorms or the hissing of the snow blizzards in winter. He will have made the acquaintance, if a fleeting one, of travellers on foot and on horseback, and the silent procession of the camel caravans at the side of the road.

From the countries west of Terek-dawan he will preserve the memory of another world—the splendid mosques and mausoleums from Tamerlane's time in Samarkand; the theological colleges of Bokhara, with cupolas and minarets gleaming in gaily coloured faience; Merv with its traditions of learning and knowledge; the mosque containing Imam Riza's tomb, to which pilgrims still throng from all over Iran; the romantic land of Persia, home of Hadji Baba, and Bagdad, the city of the caliphs and one of the principal scenes of the Arabian Nights.

From Ankara and Istanbul he will enter the noise and hurry of Western life, and will think with regret of the great silence and peace in the deserts of Asia. All the same, he will rejoice when, on the Atlantic coast, he feels fresh winds from the sea filling his sand-coated lungs.

But a traffic artery such as this, the world's longest motor-road, should certainly not be made only for pleasure trips. Its function should be a much greater one. It should facilitate trade communications within the Chinese Empire and open a new traffic route between the East and the West. It should unite two oceans, the Pacific and Atlantic; two continents, Asia and Europe; two races, the yellow and the white; two cultures, the Chinese and the Western. Everything that is calculated to bring different peoples together, to connect and unite them, should be greeted with sympathy at a time when suspicion and envy keep the nations asunder.

Those who say that such a plan is impossible and impracticable should not forget that it was actually carried out two thousand years ago, and that the traffic along the Silk Road between Sian and Tyre continued for five hundred years. Many a bloody war was fought out in those days between the countries and empires through which the Silk Road ran, but the peaceful traffic continued uninterrupted, because all saw the enormous importance and advantage of one of the greatest and richest arteries of world trade.

New fields would be opened to exploration, more easily reached than those of to-day, and darkest Asia would be made accessible to culture and development. The Chinese Government which calls the Silk Road to life again and opens it to modern means of communication will certainly have done humanity a service and erected a monument to itself.

Much of the old-time romance is bound to be lost when caravan and horses' bells have been exchanged for the noise of steam-whistles and hooters; but the interior of Asia is large, there is room enough for the old means of transport, and as for the Takla-makan desert, there are no machines but aeroplanes which can disturb its peace. The railway from Krasnovodsk via Samarkand to Andishan has not to any degree affected the ancient, picturesque aspect of life in Western Turkistan.

With such thoughts we set out upon our long journey eastward along the Silk Road, and while the splendid pictures of the past, one by one, sank beneath the western horizon, new and glorious prospects rose up daily in the east under the morning sun.

XIX

TO THE GREAT WALL

ON December 14, 1934, in a suffocating dust-storm, we returned to Anhsi from our adventurous journey through the most God-forsaken desert region in the world. We remained at Anhsi for a few days to repair the cars, pack and load up. Four days later we drove out through Suiyuan-men, the southern gate of the town, and in an hour's time were at the parting of the ways where travellers to Tun-hwang turn off to the left, while people going to China bear away to the right via Yü-men.

To the south low mountains rose, three-quarters of a mile away ; to northward we had steppe in various shades of yellow. We were now on the real Silk Road, which here runs through sheer desert with a fine gravel soil. The Nan-shan came nearer and nearer ; the Pei-shan was faintly visible in the distance. To our left we sighted a direct road, then blocked by drifting sand, to the eastern gate of Anhsi. Our route seemed dead and abandoned. Now and again we passed a cart loaded with fuel, or a few riders on donkeys. Once we met two old men and a boy on foot, singing and joking. How could they joke in that land of poverty and misery ! According to what we had been told, the garrison of Anhsi was to start eastward that very day to be replaced by new troops. The old garrison was to take with it all the wheat which could be collected and 130 sheep, without compensation. There was a likelihood of our meeting the new troops on the road and being skinned alive by those half-savage Tungan roughs.

We passed the first post office to the eastward in the uninhabited village of Hsiao-wan and soon after, 40 miles on, a watch-tower to the left of the road. We could feel that the Su-lo-ho was not far away to the northward ; the ground sloped gently down to it. On the other side of it the ground rose almost imperceptibly to the foot of the Pei-shan. Low *yardang* terraces were to be seen near the banks of the river.

A mail-carrier came along, with a collar of bells round the horse's neck. A caravan of twenty camels was carrying flour westward, the bronze bells clanging melodiously. The same melody was heard in the days of the Han dynasty, but bales of silk are no longer carried along this road.

For long distances the road was sunk as much as six feet in the earth. It had needed many ox-carts and caravans so to wear the soil away, but the road was thousands of years old.

As early as the morning of December 19 our patience was tested by an annoying misadventure. Yew, Chen and I were in the small car, driven by Effe. Effe had also the task of putting in the little red flags that marked the compass bearings for our map of the Silk Road and were collected by Kung, who was travelling in Serat's driver's cabin. Georg came last in " Edsel " and had been out of sight a long time. We had not gone more than about 12 miles when we stopped at the village of Wang-chia-chuang-tse to get into touch again with Georg. His engine was damaged and he required help. Serat had to turn back and tow " Edsel " into the village. A few families lived there, and our tents were pitched close to them. A little clay house was turned into a mechanical workshop. " Edsel's " engine was unscrewed and taken completely to pieces. Two of the bearings had grown hot and had to be replaced. Georg, Effe, Serat and Jomcha worked, filed and scrubbed for days on end.

Meanwhile the weather grew more wintry. On the night of December 19 we had a temperature of -5.8, and next day the whole countryside was white with snow. But the delay had one advantage—that we avoided meeting the marching troops. When we continued our journey on December 23, the soldiers had already passed.

The road was everywhere worn deep into the earth and only 10 feet wide. Luckily the traffic was quite insignificant, and here and there were little side-tracks made to enable vehicles to pass one another. At the narrowest points of this corridor-like road a man runs ahead of a cart shouting and yelling to warn any vehicles that may be coming the other way.

The walls of the little town of Pu-lung-chi (Bulungir) were in ruins, and there was a gaping hole where the town gate should have been. The town was square, and mostly wilderness. We saw old graves scattered about. Only in the north-eastern corner were some thirty poor Chinese families living. Almost the whole population came out to look at us as we drove through the eastern gate, which also was demolished.

We steered south-east over hard grass steppe and left the Su-lo-ho behind us. We met five ox-drawn carts carrying fuel from the steppe to the town. Several times we scared grazing antelopes into flight. Mountains were visible both north and south of us, now faint grey-blue outlines in the far distance. Three-quarters of a mile north of our road ran another caravan road, along which a camel caravan was moving towards A'nhsi. The telegraph line also went that way. Pheasants were running about in the grass. We pitched our camp no. 143 by an old watch-tower in a region which bears the name Chi-tao-kou.

The thermometer fell to — 7.6, and on the morning of Christmas Eve the whole country was chalk-white with hoar-frost.

We crossed a dry river-bed 60 yards wide, on whose steep banks a large flock of sheep was grazing. Then we drove through the actual village of Chi-tao-kou, consisting of a few grey clay houses and walls and farms scattered round about. We bumped up and down over canal banks, where low-built cars were in continual danger of getting caught and hung up. Every time we had to get the spades out, and the whole convoy was delayed.

We drove through a simple town gate into the wind-ing streets of the large village of San-tao-kou, where some of our servants stopped to make Christmas purchases in the shops of the bazaar. There was no great difference between these open booths with stands, poles supporting projecting roofs, the houses and walls of sun-dried brick, the dirty streets, and their counterparts in the Turki towns and villages of Sinkiang. There was practically the same simple architecture, the same dirt and dust and poverty, and the same starving wretches with hands stretched out for alms. Everywhere we saw ruined houses and walls, and we were told that the district had formerly been much more intensively cultivated, but that the population had decreased year after year through emigration, famine and misgovernment. The worst of all the evils which afflicted Kansu was the squeezing of the people by conscienceless generals for the upkeep of their armies. And those armies were used solely to fight other generals in ever-recurring civil wars. When everything is subjected to new contributions, it is not strange that the peasants' savings are not sufficient to keep them alive. Horrible wars have swept over Kansu in recent times, and the fragments of the population which remain are tormented by their rulers. And yet San-tao-kou, " Third Valley," is considered the largest and most flourishing village which is governed from Anhsi. Anhsi is a *hsien* or town, with a town council and mayor, and San-tao-kou is the most easterly place in the district. The next place east of that is Yü-men.

We stopped a moment at a shop in the bazaar, where our excellent cook gave us a Christmas present—a basket full of pears, spices and fireworks.

Then we drove out of the eastern gate of the village and crossed the bed of a river with several branches, 130 yards wide. But on the other side the road was so sandy that it was quite unsuitable for our cars. We therefore turned back and followed the bed of the river ; its bottom, higher up, was covered with ice which bore.

When we had left the bed of the river we came into a curious bit of country, resembling the clay sediment moulded by the action of wind and water into the shape of tables, ridges and balls, which are so characteristic of the Lop region and are called by the Turkis *yardang*.

We saw several herds of antelopes on both sides of the road. The animals did not pay much attention to us, but kept at a respectful distance. Effe stopped the car, took his gun and crept towards the antelopes. He disappeared

among the bushes and rough ground. A shot rang out ;
the antelopes fled like arrows ; but one remained. It was
a pity to kill the pretty creatures, and that on Christmas
Eve. The victim was killed, the intestines removed, and
now we had fresh meat for the evening.

Ahead of us appeared a dark strip of vegetation, clearly
indicating the proximity of the river Su-lo-ho, which flows
past the little town of Yü-men. And in a short time we
had reached the left bank of the river. One of the motor-
lorries, which had the tents on board, had gone on ahead,
and so the camp was all but ready when we reached the
spot. We preferred to spend Christmas evening in the
open air outside the town wall.

The bed of the river Su-lo-ho was about 30 yards wide,
and cut 13 feet deep, and the water in it was about two
feet deep. The Christmas camp was pleasant, with its
view over the bed of the river and the gardens on the
opposite bank. A small bridge crossed the Su-lo-ho at
that point. We were in the eastern outskirts of the
town of Yü-men, and only a few hundred yards from the
town gate, from which we were separated by the river
and bridge.

We had celebrated the Christmas of 1933 in great style.
Then we had just reached the desert river Etsin-gol, and
had our tents pitched in the wood ; and then Hummel
and Bergman had still been with us and had made preparations for a worthy celebration of the year's greatest festival.
But now they had gone ; and on this second Christmas of
my motor expedition the only Swedes I had were Georg
and Effe.

We were fairly tired, and had no time to waste in preparing any special festivities. But the Chinese were Chris-
tians, and had almost the same reverence for Christmas as
ourselves. When, at six o'clock, after a short rest in the
small car I received a message that everything was ready
in my tent, I proceeded thither and found it radiant with
the light of many candles and the table, one of our packing-
cases, covered with a blue enamel tea service and plates
filled with cakes from the Yü-men bazaar. The part of
the tent-cloth which was just over my bed had been adorned

by Chen with a *god jul*[1] in perfect Swedish, in gigantic letters cut out of red paper and fixed to the cloth. A band of paper elves hovered about the Christmas greeting, but we had no Christmas-tree this time.

Dinner was ready at 8 p.m. Then we dipped in the pot and had soup boiled with antelope's flesh ; *shislik*— small pieces of mutton roasted on spits over the embers, with thin slices of fat between them—*pilmé* and beans, chocolate pudding, and finally coffee. In the late hours of the evening the gramophone played the moving old hymn " Var hälsad, sköna morgonstund " and after that " Sverige ", " Du gamla ", " Hör oss Svea " and other patriotic and secular hymns and songs.

But best of all was that we were all safe and well after all the dangers we had been through, and our spirits rose still higher at the thought that we had only another six weeks' journey to the coast.

And so the lights were put out, and the Christmas night stars shone out over the wide spaces of Asia.

On Christmas morning we drove across the bridge over the Su-lo-ho, 42 feet long, 19½ feet wide, and resting on three massive piles, and up to the west gate, Sui-teh-men, with its decorative *pai-lou* or triumphal arch. We were stopped by five soldiers in light grey-blue uniforms and black fur caps. Each carried on his back an overcoat rolled up in straps, and an extra pair of boots. The commander asked for our passports, but had to be content with our visiting-cards, which he sent to the mayor's *yamên*. We were given permission to drive to the *yamên*, where a secretary received us and took us into a waiting-room resembling a prison. The town's highest civilian official, Li Chih-tung, came in and invited us to stay to dinner. We declined, and drove on to the commandant, Ma Yo-ling, who showed us equal courtesy and told us that the garrison consisted of 250 men, Chinese and Tungans from Ching-hai. The civilian population of the town he put at 400 families, of which only thirty were Tungan, the rest Chinese. No Mongols or East Turkis lived at

[1] " Happy Christmas."

Yü-men. The people were poor; they could not afford
to buy clothes or food, and the harvest was uncertain.
The commandant regarded improved communications as
of the greatest importance, and hoped that the Government would make a railway right across Kansu in three
years! Little children were running about the narrow,
dusty, dirty streets between the ruined houses, wearing fur
jackets, but otherwise stark naked.

We were soon driving out again through the eastern
gate, outside which a few monuments and a watch-tower
stood by a canal. The road was still as deeply sunk as it
had been before. We often passed remains of old walls.
In one village a few trees grew. We saw there a few
peasants and carts; a frozen river and springs were crossed
by primitive, rickety bridges.

On December 26 we had the southern mountains close
to us on our right, and to our left low black hills. A
village lay by a little frozen lake, and near it was a well
with good water. The people of the district looked poor;
the year's harvest had been mediocre. In stark contrast
to the actual conditions were the first two syllables in six
village names, Chih-chin, " red gold ". The road, deeply
sunk, ran across bumpy grass steppe. There was excellent
grazing for cattle, camels, horses and sheep, but now the
country was desolate. In front of an old sign-post stood
five small towers, all in the form of mutilated pyramids
and severely weathered.

At midday we were in the Hui-hui-pu valley, about
6,000 feet up. There was a little town there, with a square
wall round it and a bazaar street, in which we bought fuel.
To the left of the road stood a little temple. The country
was something of a tangle with its valleys, ravines and
defiles, through which the road with difficulty found its
way.

In a few hours this landscape of broken rocks came to
an end, and we were out on open steppe again, sloping
gently to the east. The road was marked by small lumps
of clay, about 5 to every 2 miles. We crossed a secondary watershed 6,200 feet high. Then the ground dropped
slowly to level plain, almost entirely barren. At last we

drove through a narrow defile with several cairns along
the sides, and arrived at Chia-yü-kwan, the famous entrance-
gate to the Central Empire. We had reached the Great
Wall, one of the most gigantic structures ever erected by
human hands. The gates with their vaulted arches, gate-
houses and crenellated walls around small court-yards are,
in their present shape, the result of restoration or complete
rebuilding by the Emperor Chia Ching a good hundred
years ago. The whole is a complicated piece of work, in
which old and new are intermingled. We passed a temple
on our left. The town wall is double at this point, and we
drove through both walls under arches. We pitched our
camp no. 146 in an open field close to a small temple and
a cemetery.

Next morning we walked along the top of the walls
round this strange complex of old and new gates, gate-
houses, towers, vaulted passages and picturesque little
court-yards for the sentries between the different gates.
From the top we had a splendid view over the old town,
which spread right under our feet its mosaic of modern
clay houses, streets and alleys inside its peculiar square
town wall, each side perhaps a hundred yards long.

Everything is carefully and solidly built. The vaulting
of the gates, the floors of smooth stone, the gateways with
their wonderful vistas, all are equally tasteful and charming.
The upper part of the towers are built of wood, with
carved roofs ; and round the lower floor is a colonnade.
The whole effect is superb—in truth a worthy outpost of
China proper. The original entrance-gate no longer exists ;
the Emperor Chia Ching replaced it with a new one, itself
noble and stately, a solid, genuine piece of architecture.
The town gates, on the other hand, still remain, and one
of them is a masterpiece.

To reach the top of the walls one clambers up a steep
incline, just as on the Peking city walls. Wooden staircases with high steps lead to the upper storeys of the
towers. Each storey has its wooden floor, and one had
to be on the look-out for gaping holes. In one of the
towers hangs a fair-sized bronze clock, and at several places
little kiosk-shaped temples still remain. From the windows

of the top floor of the towers, where the desert wind sings its ancient melody, there is an amazing view in every direction. Right at one's feet one sees the town of Chia-yü-kwan crowded inside its square, and north-east of it newer groups of houses outside the walls. Our camp by the cemetery was not far from these. The strong crenellated lines of the wall top made a worthy frame for the groups of houses and court-yards below.

We could see the Great Wall stretching southward for about 6 miles, to the banks of the river Pei-ta-ho. In the opposite direction it runs north-east for about the same distance, then south-east, east and east-south-east. We could make out clearly the Imperial Highway or Silk Road, which goes on to Suchow, faithfully followed by its line of milestones. To the north lay the endless spaces of the Gobi desert. To the south, the nearest chains of the Nan-shan stood out, streaked with snow. In this direction, from 20 to 25 miles off, lies a wooded region whose pines and firs supply the timber for new buildings in Suchow and Chia-yü-kwan.

An artist could stay in this wonderful place for months and years and daily make new discoveries for his brush and pencil. It would be worth while to preserve for posterity these masterly creations, now in decay like everything else in China. There is a Society for the Preservation of Antiquities in Peking and Nanking, which would find here an inexhaustible field for its energy and devotion. Here the panelling and lintel of a hundred-year-old gate have been torn down by Ma Chung-yin's hordes; here beams and rafters are wrenched from towers before our eyes and burnt for fuel; there bricks are knocked down from battlements and used to build new houses—all this beauty is exposed to destruction and vandalism without the authorities lifting a finger to preserve it. But if a European goes out into the desert and finds a few wretched graves, not even of Chinese origin, he is accused of theft and robbery and subjected to disgraceful persecution.

Outside the Great Wall, with which we now came into contact at Chia-yü-kwan, are the ruins of an older wall which was explored by Stein. It too has watch-towers and stretches beyond Tun-hwang; that is the westward limit of the Han Emperors' Great Wall.

In olden times, the Chinese soldiers who went into the field against the western countries used to say: "I wish that it may be granted me to come in again through Yü-men-kwan." And those who started from Chia-yü-kwan on their campaigns in the West used to say: "Before us is the Gobi desert, behind us is Chia-yü-kwan," meaning that all they loved in life—their homes, with their wives and children within strong safe walls—lay east of Chia-yü-kwan and inside the Great Wall.

Countless armies and political ambassadors have passed through this gate. Merchants have set out from it with their caravans, and beneath its arches countless ox-carts laden with silk have creaked and groaned on their long road through Central Asia to the West. If the walls of this arched gate could speak, they would have endless stories of romantic adventure to relate.

"Tien-hsia-hsiung-kwan"—"the strongest gate in the world"—these words are cut on a black tablet just south of and outside the great gate. The inscription was put up about 120 years ago by a General Li, who was commander of the garrison at Chia-yü-kwan. The text is most artistically executed.

But the noonday sun reminded us of the passage of time, and we left our lofty viewpoint with regret and went back to our cars, which awaited us among the graves.

XX

SUCHOW AND KANCHOW

HARDLY have you left Chia-yü-kwan behind you when you are out in barren desert again. But the country is not absolutely lifeless. Here is a herd of antelopes, running as swift as the wind, and along a side-road a camel caravan makes its way. The distances are marked by little mutilated clay cones called *pu-t'ai* (*pu* = distance, *t'ai* = tower), of the same kind as on some of the chief roads in Eastern Turkistan. About every five li rises one of the old watch-towers, picturesque in all their simplicity, silent witnesses from a past in which this famous Imperial Highway, the main route of Chinese silk through Asia, had an importance of which modern people have hardly a notion. The watch-towers are usually surrounded by a yard, rectangular like themselves, which a low clay wall encloses. Outside this, in a row and quite close to one another, stand five miniature balls on the side of the watch-tower which looks towards the road.

We crossed a frozen spring by a quite new bridge, an unusual sight in that country. The ground descended in the direction the road was going. The surface was better than it had been. We noticed here an evident attempt to improve the road, in that all the stones had been moved to the side, where they formed two parallel ridges, and inside these was a suggestion of narrow, shallow ditches. Between these the road was about 30 feet wide.

The towers reappeared like protecting guards, grey, ruined, monotonous. One of them seemed to have been entirely rebuilt or restored. Each tower has on its front a small tablet with picture writing. Here was one with the words : " Pei-yü-tun ", or " reserved defence tower ".

A train of nine ox-carts met us, carrying goods to Anhsi

—cloth, cigarettes and wheat. The next tower bore the inscription " Hsia-pa-tun "—" the tower on the low river bank ". The traffic grew thicker the farther east we went. A caravan of twenty donkeys was laden with coal. We crossed an arm of the Pei-ta-ho, frozen hard. To southward, in the Nan-shan, are the coal-mines of Tai-hwang-kou, whence Suchow gets its coal supply. To the left of the road appeared houses and trees, belonging to the Suchow oasis.

At 1.30 p.m. we were at the real river Pei-ta-ho, divided into one large arm and several small ones. It is one of the two sources of the Etsin-gol. Serat did not dare to cross the bridge over the larger arm ; he drove his lorry into the stream just below the bridge and got stuck in the sand. Georg drove " Edsel " across the gravel bottom still lower down, and then towed out Serat. At another bridge some twenty carts were waiting ; and here our cars got over successfully.

We now had the town wall of Suchow on our right and followed it to the north gate of the town. Here we were stopped by soldiers. One of them took our cards and hurried as usual to announce us at the mayor's *yamên*. Meanwhile we had to wait. The life in the narrow town gate was attractive in its Oriental variety, its hurry, its noise and its dust. There came slow oxen drawing creaking carts, urged on by ragged countrymen and noisy drivers with long whips and sticks. Peasants from neighbouring villages balanced baskets containing cabbages and other vegetables on pliable bamboo canes, while a company of soldiers took their horses to water on the river-bank, riding them bareback or leading them. Camels raised their heads and humps, with or without burdens, above the throng, and pushed grunting through the ceaseless whirlpool.

The soldier soon returned with the information that we might drive in through the gate. We went straight to the mayor, and as he was not at home we went on to the commandant, General Ma Pu-kang, one of the " Big Horses " of Kansu. He received us with the greatest civility and invited us to dinner next day. We had better luck with the mayor, Wei Yung-chi, on the way home, and found him a particularly well-bred, pleasant and reliable man.

The very first evening we were entertained to dinner by the mayor, who told us a great many stories about the conditions in his town.

General Ma Pu-kang received us politely when we went to his lunch-party the next day, but he took no part in the festivity because he had to spend almost the whole of Friday in the mosque—he is an orthodox Mohammedan. We heard at Suchow that the military leaders in Kansu— the five " Big Horses "—were decidedly against the build- ing of a railway from Sian via Lanchow and Suchow to Tun-hwang and Kashgar, because then the power of Nan- king would increase in Kansu and their own would be- come illusory. Nanking had indeed become stronger in recent times, since Canton had been pacified and the Com- munists driven back. It had been due to the Kansu generals' protests that the completion of the railway from Tung-kwan to Sian had been so long delayed.

They had also a dangerous rival in Chiang Kai-shek. The marshal had a habit of suddenly descending like a bomb, accompanied only by an adjutant, anywhere where disorders had broken out, in the coastal provinces, the Yang-tse valley, Suiyuan, Lanchow or Sining. He had already made descents of this kind in twelve of the twenty- four provinces ; he had always gone right into the lion's den and talked straight to the lion. The future would show whether he would also, despite the Kansu generals' resistance, succeed in completing the building of the rail- way to Lanchow and later the motor-road westward, the road we had been commissioned to mark out.

At Suchow we had an important plan to prepare. We had already investigated and mapped the northern motor- road ; the second, the Imperial Highway, we were study- ing at the moment. Between the two a road ran along the Etsin-gol to Suchow, and we wished to investigate the suitability for motor traffic of this line of communication also.

We therefore decided that Yew, with Serat as driver, a couple of boys, and one of the motor-lorries, should ex-

amine this route, 240 miles long, while we proceeded eastward. We heard from Mongols that the autumn flood
water on the Etsin-gol should not reach the western temple
on the banks of the Möruin-gol for another ten days, so
that Yew should have no difficulty in crossing the last-
named stream. He would have to force it because our
store of 300 gallons of petrol, with a quantity of other
baggage, was east of the stream at Nogon Deli's headquarters. The only risky thing was to make such a long
journey with only one car, for if this got out of order it
would be irretrievably lost. As we had often done before
on the expedition, we staked everything on one card. The
baggage was divided into two piles ; one was to go east
with us, the other Yew and Serat were to fetch on their
way back from the Etsin-gol. Both parties could easily
be given petrol enough. The price was the same as at
Anhsi—three and a half dollars a gallon, three times as
much as in Shanghai.

Now that the high dignitaries of the town had entertained us, the representative of Eurasia did not wish to be
left behind, and served up twenty-seven dishes at the dinner
he gave us. Our journey through Kansu was like a
triumphal procession ; in every town we had to eat as
many dinners as possible. All this hospitality was kindly
meant, but the eating of dinners was both trying and a
waste of time. It is good form, according to Chinese
etiquette, to entertain distinguished foreigners travelling in
the country, and if the victim is good-mannered he simply
cannot refuse an invitation.

After dinner we made a little expedition to Chiu-chüan,
" Wine Spring ", situated outside the east gate of the town.
Here a spring rises in a walled-in basin. In old days it
was pure wine. Close by is a once beautiful and well-
kept temple, which, we are told, had been destroyed by
Ma Chung-yin 'for the army's camp-fires.

The town of Suchow seemed full of life, with many
people and plenty of movement in the streets, especially
in the trading quarter, where there was a press of carts
drawn by horses, oxen or mules, while trade caravans, with
camel-bells jingling, were arriving from Kwei-hwa and

the Etsin-gol. The Suchow oasis was believed to have
84,000 inhabitants, 10,000 of whom were within the walls
of the town. We were told this by the mayor himself.
There were said to be scarcely a hundred East Turkis
living in Suchow. Mongols came now and then to buy
and sell goods. The garrison was put at 2,000.

Marco Polo passed through Suchow in 1273. The Jesuit
father Benedict Goës, who had been sent by the mission
at Goa to Central Asia, by way of Kabul, Kashgar, Aksu
and Hami, to find out whether Cathay and China were two
different empires, was detained at Suchow for eighteen
months and ended his days there in 1607. The Mohammedans of the district treated him as an enemy and burned
his doubtless rich and valuable diaries.

On December 30 we and our Chinese friends assembled
in the mayor's court-yard, where Yew got into Serat's
lorry. Li and Liu Chia belonged to the Etsin-gol party.
Liu Chia had been engaged on the Etsin-gol for the outward trip and was now to return to his home for good.
He received both pay and a bonus and thanks for keeping
good watch. Then all the gear that was to go east with
us was loaded up on to " Edsel "—last of all beds, tents,
fur coats, basins, spades and other indispensable rubbish,
which grew shabbier and more ragged as time passed.

We drove through the drum-tower, the centre of the
town, and out through the south gate. Our road led along
the southern wall of the town to the south-eastern corner
tower, and then we were out in open country again.

We met strings of carts bound for Suchow ; they were
laden with fuel underneath and hay above. Just there we
left the classical Imperial Highway on our left. It issues
from the east gate of the town, while we were driving
south-east along a road which joins a number of villages.

The afternoon sun blazed into the car. We drove
through the village of Hsi-tien-sze, with a smallish temple.
The district became more cultivated ; clay houses and
groups of trees occurred more frequently, and we often
crossed water-courses and irrigation canals by small bridges.
We had only to stop for a moment to be surrounded by a
crowd, poor wretches groaning under twenty different

taxes and living below the starvation line. A school we passed had seventy pupils and four teachers.

An uneven piece of road made the lorry give such a violent jerk that San Wa-tse, who was sitting on the top of the load, lost his balance and fell off, accompanied by Chokdung, who had made a vain effort to keep the lad from falling. They broke neither necks nor legs, but San Wa-tse sprained his wrist and was excused work for a short time. He received attention when we reached the day's camp, no. 148. The place bore the name Ying-erh-pu, " Young Soldiers' Camp Village ". The district had a bad reputation as a resort of thieves, for which reason our most valuable boxes were taken into the tents for the night.

On the last day of the year the Nan-shan, in the morning light, formed an infinitely charming background to the trees and houses of the village. The mountains themselves appeared in quiet colours, only a shade darker than the sky which vaulted its pale blue arch over the white strips of snow-field on the crests. The men and boys of the village crowded round the cars in silent wonder when we were preparing to start, leaving them in their poverty and submissiveness.

The road soon forks ; the left branch, which is identical with the old Imperial Highway, runs through a belt of dunes of drifting sand, the other—which we followed— soon leads out into barren desert, real *gobi*, with hard, in places gravelly, soil. Farther on were scanty tufts of vegetation. The watch-towers stood like sentries along the road. Chang-san-li-maio was a little temple, whose dumb gods might perhaps give tired wanderers a ray of hope.

Shang-ho-ching, " Clear Upper River ", was a village of scattered houses by a town wall with picturesque corner towers and gates. No one lived inside the wall. We crossed three water-courses from the mountains, sunk deep in the soil and provided with bridges ; and went on through fresh villages, over tiresome little irrigation canals and dry channels of mountain streams, and through a chaos of terraces, ridges and ravines.

The village of Ching-shui-pu, " Clear Water Village ", was surrounded by a wall and had two gates. As usual, the road ran right through the place, in at one gate and out at the other. But these gates were kept shut at night to keep out thieves and robbers. There was, therefore, a stone barrier a foot high right across the road, deeply and firmly rooted in the ground. These barriers had often given us trouble; we had often made inclines to get over them; but those of Ching-shui-pu were too high for our cars. Most fortunately, there was another road south of the village.

As early as 7 a.m. on January 1, 1935, Effe paid a New Year visit to the tent shared by Chen, Kung and myself and lit a splendid fire in the stove. We were dressed in a few minutes and went over to the boys' tent to offer them our *kung-hu-hsin-nien*—good wishes for the New Year. On New Year's Eve Chia Kwei had given us a finer dinner than usual—soup, ham omelette and chocolate pudding, with coffee and cakes. Our New Year camp was on a farm on the outskirts of the village, where they used to thresh corn, so that the ground was as hard and level as a floor. A villager had been appointed watchman.

The *hsien*, or administrative area, of Suchow consisted of seven districts, of which Ching-shui-pu was the most easterly. The population was said to be as much as 1,200 families. Most of these seemed to be about when we started. The height above sea-level was 5,200 feet. The first day of the year greeted us with brilliant sunshine. We drove through nothing but ploughed fields and scattered farms. But soon the country grew more lonely, and became desert again.

We stopped for a while in the village of Ma-yang, on the other side of a wide gully, to change guides. As no one volunteered for the task, the *chia-chang*, or headman, of Ma-yang himself offered to show us the way to Kanchow. He took us first to a deep-cut canal with a bridge, so bad that not even an empty car could cross it. He then declared that there was a stronger bridge over the canal lower down. But on closer examination one of its two piles was found to be broken. Then we returned to the first bridge, and mobilized the occupants of a number of carts to help us pull the bridge to pieces, use the timber to fill up the canal, and level the tops of the canal banks with our spades. We got across after great labour and made honourable compensation for the damage we had done.

The Pei-lung-ho was a fair-sized river-bed just east of camp no. 150, and Ku-shui, or " Bitter Water ", was a gully between low hills, crossed by a bridge.

Four antelopes were grazing by the roadside. Effe stopped the car and crept up to them with his gun. He disappeared among the rough ground. The antelopes' attention was entirely fixed on the car, and they did not notice him. A shot rang out, and three antelopes fled towards the mountains ; one had fallen. Chia Kwei and Chokdung jumped off Georg's lorry and ran to the wounded beast, which they killed and carried to their car.

Soon afterwards we passed two antelopes, and again Effe stalked them. One fell to the first shot ; the other stayed faithfully by the fallen beast, which lay motionless, and presumably was already dead. Another shot, and the survivor fled, but only to fall after a few steps. These two also were carried to the lorry, and we had fresh meat for several days.

It clouded over and grew dark behind us, as if a snow blizzard were coming on. We pitched our camp no. 150 in the wilds not far from the village of Yüan-san-tou. It began to snow in the night, and was still snowing at eight the next morning. We were not doing long daily runs by any means, usually only 25 or 30 miles. This was due not so much to the badness of the road as to the time-wasting map-making work. In the level, open desert, where we could take long compass bearings, the work went more quickly. But in inhabited areas, where houses and walls, trees, terraces and ravines obstructed the view, the bearings were quite short and we moved forward hopelessly slowly.

With a new guide and under a clearing sky we drove to the Taoist temple of San-kwan-miao. To eastward rose an isolated hill, called Yü-mo-shan, " Poplar Mountain ". Now and again the road crossed a gully with a gravel bottom. Now we were driving through desert and could see to the north the infinitely remote horizon of the Gobi, like that of the sea. The earth was striped white, yellow and grey—snow, sand and gravel. Everywhere were farms and trees, men, small caravans, wayfarers and carts. A string of several carts came along, laden with rough boards intended for coffins. At a farm where we stopped to buy fuel there was a romping crowd of boys in ragged blue blouses and red breeches, and one or two pretty little girls in red jerseys and green trousers. We encamped in the village of Yang-hsien, 47 miles from Kanchow and $4\frac{3}{4}$ miles due south of the little town of Kao-tai. The headman of the village came to see us and got us two night-watchmen. The evening was brilliantly clear. Sirius suddenly flashed up over the top of a wall, and shone over the earth with wonderful brilliance.

On the night of January 2 the temperature fell to $-7 \cdot 8$. The whole countryside lay white under hoar-frost, sparkling like diamonds in the bright sunshine. When this Imperial Highway is frozen the surface is good enough, but it must be awful in spring and autumn, especially for loaded cars. For then the canals are full of water, which in places floods the road for miles, and then one has to drive through endless marshes and swamps. This road can be of no use for motor traffic without real road-making and properly regulated canals and dykes.

The little town of Kao-tai has a mayor and a Catholic Mission. Between Kao-tai and Kanchow there is another administrative area (*hsien*), formerly called Fu-i, but now Ling-tsei.

The country became more open and the cultivation scantier. Every family had its farm surrounded by a wall. Now we drove through the village of San-tsian-pu, " Three Communities' Village ".

Here too some work had been done on the road ; the track was from 23 to 26 feet wide, and on some stretches there were ditches a foot deep, while on others they were hardly there at all. The road we were following ran south of the Imperial Highway, which we should not touch again till Kanchow. There the Imperial Highway follows the Great Wall.

The road cut deeper and deeper into a narrow yellow clay defile; rather picturesque country. It opened out again, and we had the village of Sa-ho-pu before us. At times the road ran along an avenue. In the eastern gateway of the village were hanging three small wooden cages for criminals' heads—they were now empty. Three hundred families were living in the village. The school was closed for lack of funds. Outside the gate was a pretty temple, which a caravan of twenty camels, laden with wheat, was just passing. Just outside the eastern gate, Tung-kwan, we passed the bed of the Sa-ho, " Sandy River ".

Another night with a temperature of — 8·5, and another day of brilliant sunshine. It was bitterly cold in the open air. Our camp was in the district of Hsi-tou-hao, " Number One in the West ", which stretches as far as Kanchow. We were, therefore, already in the Kanchow *hsien*, or under the jurisdiction of Kanchow; the boundary runs along the Sa-ho. We were now on the Imperial Highway, with the telegraph line on our left. An avenue of trees stretching from Honan to Anhsi had been planted fifty-six years before at Tso Tsung-tang's orders, and hereabouts many of the trees were still standing. In the village of Sa-chientsi we drove right past a theatre. At open-air performances of the kind most of the spectators actually stand in the road. We had mountains to north and south of us, those to the north at a considerable distance. The whole countryside was covered with snow; only the road was clear of snow and generally sunk six feet or more.

The surface of the ground was cut into typical *yardangs*, just as by Lake Lop-nor; the sharp clay ridges were as much as nine feet high. The traffic increased; the villages were full of carts, cows, calves, pigs, dogs and people. Our direction was south-east; to our left extended the Kanchow oasis, running eastward. Our road ran along a dry water-course and brought us to the left bank of a fair-sized stream, where a cart was stuck fast in the ice above the axles, not an encouraging spectacle for us. The river is called Hei-ho, or " Black River ", and is the eastern source of the Etsin-gol.

It took us two good hours to get over the arms of the

river. It was obviously impossible to attempt a passage where the high road crossed them. Caravans and carts moved away to the northward, where possibly a bridge had been made. We followed them; but a mail-carrier on his way to Suchow advised us to try lower down.

We lost ourselves in a hopeless labyrinth of canals, canal-banks, small bridges, winding streams and dry beds, and felt our way gingerly over the treacherous water-courses. At last there remained only a little wooden bridge on three caissons. It was too high and too rickety. One or two carts were just coming the other way. They despised the bridge and drove straight out into the stream, 20 yards wide but not more than 18 inches deep. We chose the same way; and at last we too had successfully crossed the Black River.

The soldiers at the north gate of Kanchow received us with the utmost calm, and even gave us a military salute. They were satisfied with our cards and declared that orders had come from Nanking saying that we were coming and giving orders about our reception. Accordingly we drove to the mayor's *yamên*. He welcomed us, and handed us over to a couple of understrappers, who showed us the available rooms. These were impossible, and we preferred to pitch our tents in one of the inner court-yards of the *yamên*, where two policemen were ordered to keep watch over the cars.

A law has been passed in China for the abolition of the old Chinese New Year and the celebration of the New Year at the same time as in Western countries—i.e. the solar instead of the lunar year. We had already, at Suchow, seen the red New Year notices pasted up on pillars, doors and house-walls. And here, at Kanchow, the festival was in full swing. There were performances in the theatres, demonstrations and processions in the streets, where there were swarms of dressed-up clowns and gaily costumed boys on long stilts. The festival was to continue for several days. But this does not prevent the old Chinese New Year from being celebrated as before when its time arrives, usually in February. It is not easy to root out old manners and customs.

We stayed three whole days at Kanchow to repair our

cars and replenish our stores. One day we went to an early dinner with Father Haberstroh and Father Frisch. Their mission station, with houses, schools and a church with stained-glass windows, was established about fifty years ago by the Belgian Sheut mission. We also paid a brief visit to the four German nuns who have their own Sheut house and chapel and an orphanage for sixty girls of different ages. It was the girls' free time, and they were playing in the yard.

That the time was ripe for the introduction of motor traffic into the heart of Asia we had already seen at Kwei-hwa, where merchants had established a " bus company " with lorries running to Hami and Suchow. We heard at Kanchow that a similar company had been started at Liangchow; it had six motor-lorries, which ran between the two towns twice a month. They were said to cover the distance of 137 miles in two days, or a day and a half if the road was dry. It cost 160 Mexican dollars to hire a whole lorry from Kanchow to Liangchow; and 180 Mexican dollars from Liangchow to Lanchow, where the traffic was busier and the distance 162 miles. The lorries carried for the most goods, not often passengers. A lorry would carry 3,200 catties, a camel 300 catties. It was thus, with the road conditions so primitive, a good deal cheaper to use camels.

The Fathers told us that Kanchow had about 30,000 inhabitants. The mayor's *yamên* put the figure at 9,000 families. A few Ujgurian communities lived in the remote valleys of the Nan-shan. The Ujgurians, we were told, visited the town only when they had butter, sheep, wool or horses for sale.

The town, like other towns in Kansu, made an impression of poverty and decay; but some of the streets were picturesque, with their gaily coloured houses, painted portals and elegantly carved wooden roofs. There are some fairly large temples, including Ta-fo-sze, " Great Buddha's Temple ", with a recumbent Buddha 40 paces long. A pagoda called Mu-ta, nine storeys high, towered over the city. About 70 li away, in the mountains to southward, was the lama monastery of Manti-sze.

On the afternoon of January 5 the town authorities themselves contributed to the series of New Year performances in a repulsive manner, characteristic of the province of Kansu. A trial scene was enacted before tightly packed masses of eager spectators in the court-yard of the *yamên* which was nearest to ours. A gang of criminals had murdered a rich man and looted his property. The actual criminals had escaped, but eight others who had abetted them had been denounced by the people of their district.

We were so close that we could not help hearing the horrible screams and yells that echoed through the walled-in court-yards of the *yamên*. They did not sound like human voices, but more like the bellowing of tortured animals. Between the cries we could hear the chief tormentor's words of command : " Harder ! " followed by blows, and fresh torrents of inarticulate confessions.

Georg and Effe had a look into that hell upon earth, where the poor wretches stood bound and stark naked but for a loin-cloth—but I cannot describe this horrible scene of torture, nor the refined, devilish ingenuity of the torturers. At last the victims' sufferings reached a point at which they lost all control over their cries of pain ; they laughed and cried at once, they bellowed with an undertone of entreaty which would have melted a stone. One stout fellow would not let himself utter a sound under the intensified torture. He remained perfectly silent, but a cold sweat poured from his forehead, and at last he collapsed and lay insensible on the ground. Another, who was uttering fearful yells, suddenly became silent ; he had fainted. In an hour or two the court-yard was silent again.

The reason why we did not see much of the mayor of Kanchow was that his valuable time was occupied in administering this kind of justice. On the coast torture is abolished and prohibited. But here, in the interior of Asia, it flourishes just as in old times, or perhaps worse, for public order and discipline were higher then than now. When we asked questions about it, the answer was given that only cruel, terrifying punishments had any effect on the rogues who murdered, looted and robbed. It was also said that the robber bands themselves applied torture to the well-to-do farmers and peasants they attacked. There were even modern Western names for different kinds of refined instruments of torture, such as " riding on the engine ", " the telephone " and " the aeroplane ". I refrain from describing the procedure.

The mayor, Liao, had telegraphed later to the governor-general at Lanchow and asked whether the eight malefactors should be shot or not, but no answer had yet been received. The wretched men, torn, flayed and shattered, had therefore to spend another night in uncertainty. One would almost have thought, after the bestial treatment they had received, that death would have been hailed in their prison as a welcome guest.

During the civil war, the last stages of which we had witnessed in Sinkiang, another civil war had been raging in the regions east of the Gobi proper. Sun Tien-ying was a robber general of whom we had often heard when we were last at Kwei-hwa. He and his bands were then on the north-western bend of the Yellow River. He had been commissioned by Nanking to march to the province of Ching-hai or Kuku-nor, conquer it, colonize it with his army and " develop " it. But the Tungans' " Big Horses ", Ma Pu-fang at Sining and Ma Hung-kwei in Ninghsia, did not approve of this. So Sun had first to beat Ma Hung-kwei, because the province of Ninghsia was on Sun's way to Sining.

War broke out, and Ma Hung-kwei was at first defeated. In their extremity the Tungans sent envoys to Nanking begging for support. Thereupon Nanking forbade Sun to carry out his plan, but he did not obey and continued to make preparations for his march through Ninghsia. Then Nanking took strong measures and sent aeroplanes, guns and troops to support the Tungans. At the same time General Fu Tso-yi at Kwei-hwa-cheng received orders to attack Sun from the Paotou direction. He did so ; Sun had to give way before superior numbers, and finally agreed to withdraw to Peking and Tientsin.

The Government, by its energetic intervention, had strengthened its authority among the Tungans, and there were fears that Nanking would demand as a recompense that the Tungans should conquer and pacify Sinkiang. The Tungans would resist any such plan for fear that the coup would lose them their mastery over Kansu. But the Fathers thought that Ma Pu-fang at Sining would sooner or later march against Sinkiang, more probably on his own account than Nanking's.

If it had not been for the cars we should not have stayed another day in Kanchow, that hideous purgatory. Yet one more evening we had to listen to cries of pain from the neighbouring court-yard. This time it was from less serious offenders who had been brought before the court. They were farmers who were accused of not paying tax for the grain they had harvested. The prisoner was placed by a stool to which his hand was fastened palm upwards ; the court usher then struck him on the hand with a switch— ten cuts, then another ten, and so on till the poor wretch confessed. The usher counted the blows in a sing-song tone, and the delinquent yelled in time to the blows. One stubborn peasant did not utter a sound, and we could hear only the blows and the counting.

With this sort of thing going on close by, we were thankful when silence fell once more upon the court-yards where these barbarous scenes were enacted. After Korla, where we ourselves had so nearly lost our lives, no place where we stayed in the interior of Asia left so painful an impression in our minds as Kanchow.

XXI

ALONG THE GREAT WALL

THE immensely long main traffic route we were following through the interior of Asia is divided into
stages, or posting stations, for caravans and ox-carts.
From Urumchi to Hami eighteen stages are reckoned, with
inns and caravanserais; from Hami to Suchow eighteen
days; from Suchow to Lanchow eighteen days, and from
Lanchow to Sian likewise eighteen days. The mail-
carriers needed only half this time. A letter from Anhsi
to Shanghai usually took eighteen days.

We left Kanchow on January 8, 1935. We drove down
its comparatively clean and wide main street, with plenty
of life and a lot of business being done at open booths.
The Chinese towns usually have a drum-tower and a clock-
tower, but at Kanchow drum and clock were combined in
one and the same tower, through which we drove. We
drove under the double rchway of the south gate and
through the gate in the outer wall. Here we were stopped
by the guard, who questioned us and remarked that Georg's
lorry, "Edsel", did not carry a flag bearing the official
title of the expedition. Both cars carried a Chinese and a
Swedish flag.

Outside the gate too the road was still a street, with
shops, and formed the Nan-kwan quarter. We passed a
theatre and a temple, Chang-shao-sze. An open stream,
12 yards wide and crossed by a bridge, flowed by its
southern gate. A few miles away to the left rose a
quite short mountain range in changing hues of violet.
The road was fairly good, and ran between occasional
farms and trees. It was from 30 to 40 yards wide. The
watch-towers still followed us faithfully.

A funeral was going on outside the village of Ying-fachuan ; there was a band containing no instruments but shrill pipes. Near the village of Erh-shih-li-pu, " Twenty li Village ", rose a quite new gateway, or *p'ai-lu*, which possibly marked an administrative boundary. Then we drove across sandy ground, in which the road was sunk several feet. Neither trees nor farms were now in sight. The Nan-shan to the south seemed to be about 20 miles away, the mountains to the north 5 or 6 miles. We drove on through a landscape of yellow clay, past several ruined walls and gates and over frozen canals and water-courses, with or without bridges.

Parts of the Great Wall now began to appear on the southern slopes of the neighbouring Pei-shan, and at their foot. The stretches of wall became plainer as we went on, but were often interrupted, probably by floods from the mountains. We were only three-quarters of a mile to the south.

The road ran for some way deeply sunk between clay terraces—for 10 or 12 feet, like a corridor. When we emerged again from the narrow passage the next village, Tung-lu, with its walls, gates, *p'ai-lus* and temples, was right in front of us. Then the road ran along the left bank of a river, with a perpendicular rock wall, some 16 feet high, on its right. Several villages followed, and new bits of fairly wide sunk road. We pitched our camp no. 154 at the village of Mi-hwang-tien, 5,500 feet high. We were here on the banks of the San-tan-ho, which runs to the Kanchow-ho. Here too we had engaged two night-watchmen. As long as we were awake we heard them pacing to and fro outside the tents.

The night temperature dropped as low as 3·7. On the morning of January 9 it was blowing hard from the east and it was bitterly cold. I hurried into my fur coat and immediately after breakfast got into the small car, which offered the best protection against the wind.

The temple Yü-wang-miao, dedicated to the Emperor Yü by the Hsia dynasty, was quite close to our camp. Yü had worked for thirteen years to control the floods of the Hwang-ho and Yangtse, and had allowed no obstacle to deter him. His beneficial activity had extended as far as the region where we then found ourselves. Three times he had passed his open door without looking in—the work must be completed first. When this had been done he would withdraw into solitude and undisturbed peace. But the whole people wanted him as emperor and forced him to ascend the throne. There are many temples erected in his honour on the two giant rivers and in Kansu.

We went on through villages, over canals, past farms and trees and along sunk roads, and after a run of an hour and a half we crossed the river San-tan-ho, divided into two narrow arms with bridges over them. Soon after we had the foot of the mountains on our right and a frozen canal on our left. The picturesque temple Ta-fo-sze, " Temple of Great Buddha ", stands low down on the mountainside. We stopped and went into its courtyard, where stood vessels containing incense; in a pavilion were three images of Buddha with altars. Buddha himself, 68 feet high, sits dreaming and smiling in the main building of the temple.

We moved farther away from the mountains again, reached the town of Shan-tan-hsien and drove along the main street, which had an open canal down the middle, crossed by many bridges. There were open booths along the sides and plenty of people about. We paid a hurried visit to the mayor. He advised us not to travel by night, as the district was not safe.

Just outside the town we came up to the Great Wall. It is built of sun-dried brick, double in places but usually single, about 6 feet thick at the base and 3 feet at the top, and nearly 20 feet high. These measurements vary a great deal. A little farther on the thickness was about the same but the height rather less. At this point a large watch-tower was built into the wall itself.

All day we saw the Great Wall on our left as a straight yellow line, interrupted here and there. I never tired of looking at that fantastic piece of building, which had grown up in the desert tracts of inner Asia at the bidding of mighty emperors. It ran sometimes higher, sometimes lower; its shape changed at times as the result of varying powers of resistance to wind and weather and running water; the lights upon it changed as the hours of the day passed, and so did the position and shape of the watch-towers.

We pitched our camp no. 155 at San-shih-li-pu, " Thirty li Village ". It was thought safer to encamp within the walls of the village than out in the open. But our police-men from Suchow always got a couple of night-watchmen. Now we had a boy of seventeen, who was newly married. His wife of nineteen had gone home to her mother five months before, and the young husband was allowed to visit her only now and then. The ill-treated lover poured out his troubles to our boys, and they chaffed him merci-lessly. In those parts most of the women, even the Tun-gans, cramp their feet.

We continued our journey south-east, with an almost isolated mountain spur, Tai-hwang-shan—" Rhubarb Mountain "—standing up ahead of us.

It is said that 90 per cent of the population of Kansu is afflicted by the pernicious vice of opium-smoking. Is it surprising that they are so poor and life is a burden to them ?

The Great Wall followed our road, not far to the left, with unshakable fidelity. Three watch-towers were in sight at the same time. To the right was a mountain peak called Yen-tze, " the Red ", after a red colouring substance with which Mongolian women formerly painted their lips. The mountains to the left were called the Chi-tu-shan, farther on by the usual name of Pei-shan. A desolate plain with a sunk road followed. A few antelopes flashed past, an eagle was gliding earthwards. Once the road passed between two watch-towers that almost touched. The name of the next village, Feng-cheng-pu, " the Village of the Rich Town ", had an ironical ring when one thought of the twelve poor families that lived there.

Now the old Imperial Highway led us into a narrow gravel valley shut in between low mountains. The Great Wall wound about a hilltop to our left and then ran down steeply to the valley bottom. The Imperial Highway preferred the mountains because there were men's habita-tions and water there. The level country to the north was empty waterless desert.

We climbed higher and higher and were soon 8,000 feet up. The Great Wall was again winding about the mountain peaks immediately to our left; and again it plunged down to the bottom of the valley. One admires the patience of the people and princes who built it. And those compact picturesque watch-towers were ever with us. The wall had collapsed over certain sections, but fragments of sun-dried brick lay in heaps where it had fallen.

At this point we reached our greatest height, 8,775 feet. More open country followed, with an extensive view. The sun sank, and dusk fell on that romantic country with its ancient towers and its endless wall. At camp no. 156 we had descended to 7,800 feet.

After a temperature of 0·7 in the night we continued our journey on January 1, steering south-east, and reached Shui-chüan-yi, " Water-spring Station ", a decayed town with picturesque gates, now ruined. Sixty families lived there.

A peak to the right of our road was called Ching-lung-shan, " Green Dragon Mountain ". The country was broken; at times we were driving among low hills. The watch-towers did not stop, but the Great Wall was interrupted in places. The road was sometimes good but often ruined by heavy rains and by deep cart-ruts. We drove up hill and down dale, over troublesome erosion gullies that ran across the road—now we were in desert or steppe, now again among cultivated land or villages. At this point the Great Wall swung away to the north-east in the direction of Chen-fan. Near the village of Shih-li-pu there was an unbroken line of trees on the right-hand side of the road—memorials of the energetic Tso Tsung-tang.

At the western gate of Yung-chang-hsien we were stopped by soldiers, who asked the usual questions. They were not satisfied with cards, but wanted to see our passports. While the commander had gone into the town to report our arrival we had to wait at the gate, guarded by soldiers with fixed bayonets. After twenty minutes' delay permission was given, and we drove past a few *p'ai-lus* and through the drum-tower to the town authorities' *yamên*. The mayor himself came out to have a look at us and our

cars.   He was a spruce old fellow with close-cut white hair
and had served for several years at Urumchi under Marshal
Yang.   He gave us a new policeman and let us go on.

After passing a few more arched gateways and another
party of arrogant soldiers we at last came out of Yung-
chang and encamped at a farm.   The town's name means
" eternal prosperity ".   Five hundred families were living
inside its walls and about a thousand outside.   No prosperity was noticeable ; everything was poor and run to
seed.   Our policeman got two night-watchmen and well
water from a farm opposite.   We had bought fuel in the
bazaar.   It had been blowing hard all day.   The faces of
cart and caravan drivers whom we met were ash-grey from
the whirling dust.

And it was blowing just as hard next morning.   Visi-
bility was bad, and the compass bearings for the map-
making were again short.   The road ran first through a
burial-ground, the graves in which were marked by conical
mounds.   The coffins are laid in the earth only 2 or 3 feet
deep.   Several memorial tablets were erected in honour of
dead persons who had earned gratitude or admiration.
Among them was a young widow who after her husband's
death had never married again—which is regarded as a
proof of character, loyalty and devotion.

The road hereabouts was excellent.   It was laid in
1928–29 by the troops of the " Christian general ", Feng
Yü-hsiang.   His principle was that the soldiers should
always be kept at work.   A few of Tso Tsung-tang's trees,
but only a few, were still standing near a couple of old
watch-towers.   The dust of the road was flung up in
whirlwinds by carts, donkeys and camels.   We did not see
them till they were quite close, and the camel bells rang out
melodiously amid the howling of the storm.   The road
was from 21½ feet to 27 feet wide.   It had ditches 3 feet
wide and 18 inches deep.   For long stretches it was washed
away by heavy rains.   All the bridges were broken down,
and at times we had to make troublesome detours alongside
the road proper.

The mountains disappeared altogether in the wall of dust.
We were crossing a stretch of desert.   When we stopped,

we heard the little national flags beating against the cars as they fluttered, and the complaining of the storm.

Small children, half-naked, frozen blue, with dripping noses, swarmed round the cars as soon as we stopped for a moment. We gave them chocolate and bread, and felt the grip of their little ice-cold fingers. The people warned us against the river which we should have to cross just east of the village.

We drove on. The road was covered with frozen water for long stretches. We reached the first arm of the river, where we met three Chinese Catholic nuns in long black cloaks and black head-cloths.

At the third arm a cart was stuck fast in the ice. This was the cart in which the nuns had been driving. Effe drove straight out into the water, but was soon hopelessly stuck. Georg had to unload his " Edsel " and tow us back. It was getting late in the day. We pitched camp while " Edsel " dragged the nuns' cart out of the broken ice. The river was called the Chieh-ho and the little village where we encamped Chang-lu-pu. We were there 5,500 feet above sea level.

On January 13 it cost us four hours' hard labour to get the cars across the river. First the small car stuck and had to be towed out, then " Edsel " came to a stop among boulders and gravel and ice-floes. There were several arms. At the last, called the Tu-lan-ho, the whole of the luggage had to be unloaded again and taken over in a cart. At this arm, too, the small car got immovably stuck. But we mobilized people from a village, who dragged us out with long ropes. Then the ice was cut away from our tyres and the engines warmed up with embers. Meanwhile " Edsel " was loaded up, and we continued our journey. The road was now horrible ; it was under water for long stretches, and several small streams had to be crossed.

In the ploughed fields at the sides of the road we sometimes saw a block of ice standing on end ; we were told it signified a prayer to the gods for a good harvest. Now and again we drove through a village. One of the villages was unprotected, but each farm had its own wall. It is said that in the time of the Mings Mongolian robbers attacked these places, which had, therefore, to put themselves in a state of defence.

Conifers appeared by the roadside. It was past five when we drove into a street which led to the north gate of Liangchow. Here we were stopped as usual and allowed to drive in when the guard were convinced that we had no evil intentions. We went to the mayor, who received us well and invited us to stay in his *yamên*.

Liangchow was said to contain 4,080 families, or 25,000 souls. In the whole district there were 32,000 families. Three thousand persons had been killed in the earthquake of 1927.

On the following morning, the 14th, I had a letter from Yew with the good news that he had reached our last camping-ground, the village of Chang-lu-pu, the evening before. Less good news was that Serat, in crossing the first river, had broken a front spring and then smashed the differential, which put his lorry out of action. He therefore wanted various spare parts and tools from us, and Georg was sent to his help with " Edsel ", Chokdung and two policemen. Our visit to Liangchow was unfortunately not to be as short as we had hoped.

I drove in a rickshaw with Kung and Chen to the eastern gate of Liangchow, and the five li on to the new town. The tower-houses on the gates of the old town, which had been a picturesque ornament of the town wall when I visited the place before in December, 1896, were now missing. The new town was just a square wall, and its west gate, through which we drove, was simply a double opening in the wall. There were no houses inside it but the new barracks and officers' quarters, where the general in command, Ma Pu-chin, and his staff were living. In front of their house was a barbed-wire entanglement, at which we got out and handed our cards to the sentry. We were taken to a waiting-room, where, among others waiting for audience, we discovered a Tibetan.

An officer conducted us to the reception-room. General Ma Pu-chin, a little man of forty in a field-grey uniform, was elder brother to the mighty Ma Pu-fang at Sining.

He received us courteously, asked us about our plans and our mission, invited us to dinner the same day, and rose after half an hour's conversation round his brazier.

We then visited the representatives of the Eurasia Company, who had 3,000 gallons of petrol, so that we were able to get our supply renewed without difficulty by means of telegrams to Messrs. Walter and Li at Shanghai.

At the evening's entertainment the senior aide-de-camp did the honours. The general was a Mohammedan and might not eat with unbelievers.

On the 15th I went to call on the missionary of the China Inland Mission, Mr. John Stanley Muir, and his wife, in the same house where I had spent the Christmas of 1896 with Mr. and Mrs. Belcher. The house had scarcely had a coat of paint since then. Belcher had built a large church to hold 300 persons. On its outside wall were memorial tablets to Susie Belcher, who died in April, 1929, and William Belcher, who followed his wife the same year. He was carried off by typhus when tending the sick during a severe epidemic. "Blessed are the dead that die in the Lord." The church had a fair-sized bell, which had fallen from the tower in the earthquake of 1927 and passed through two wooden floors undamaged. Mr. Muir told me that the conduct of the mission was passing step by step into Chinese hands, and that it was intended that the organization should become entirely native.

I felt some emotion at seeing again, after thirty-eight years, a place where I had been so kindly received by English missionaries, and it felt strange thus, so long afterwards, to make a pilgrimage to their graves. Georg Söderbom had met them in 1928, and they sent me a friendly message, which did not, however, reach me till they were both dead.

At the Catholic mission I met Father Alois Baecker and Father Oberle, of the Societas Verbi Divini. Three others were employed in some of the mission's schools. Four nurses were serving in their ambulance. A little way outside Liangchow there was a station, 90 li west of the town, where I visited a splendid church in 1896. The mission was then in Belgian hands, and my visit was mentioned in the records.

The fathers told me that the rains had been inordinately heavy in their season during the last three years. The harvest had been destroyed over wide areas. The present winter had been abnormally mild. They thought the summer rains would be the worst enemy of the proposed motor route. The road would be destroyed and the bridges washed away by the rain. Moreover, passing travellers would steal the timber of the bridges. Only cement would resist the weather and thieves.

On the afternoon of the 16th we heard the noise of a motor engine ; it was Yew returning from his trip to the Etsin-gol. The enterprise had been successful ; Serat was bringing back the lorry, even if knocked about and in need of repair. Yew brought with him a reinforcement to our provisions ; of the things he brought, butter and orange marmalade were specially welcome.

We thus obtained, reluctantly, a few more days of rest at Liangchow for the carrying out of repairs. A large part of our time was wasted on dinner-parties with Chinese dignitaries and the missionaries, calls and return calls. Our room was usually full of visitors.

We heard from several sources how the people were oppressed with unreasonable taxes they simply could not pay. Many gave up their farms and fields and went to lodge with friends to escape the tax. Others had to borrow money at from 4 to 10 per cent a month. Well-to-do farmers who owned 400 *moo* (fifty acres), and who had daughters, had at last to hand over all their land plus their daughters to some rapacious scoundrel who had plunged them into debt.

Hardly anything but opium was being grown around Ping-fan ; in the Liangchow region this was rather less so. The price of wheat had fallen to half what it was before, so that it did not pay to grow and export it. The situation was absolutely impossible. The country was being impoverished. Proper irrigation and decent roads were unknown. It was the rival generals' struggle for power which was sucking China dry.

On January 19 Kung started with Georg and " Edsel ",

Jomcha and San Wa-tse, and one policeman. He was to take the shorter route via Chung-wei on the Yellow River, which, it was thought, might be the most suitable for a railway between Sian and Liangchow. Our plan was that we should meet at Lanchow.

When they had gone Yew told me of his experiences on the way to and from the Etsin-gol, and I made notes of all that he said. It was interesting to know that the Torgut prince on the Etsin-gol had heard in April, from travellers from Hami to Suchow and to his camp, that the whole of our expedition was lost—we had all been killed by Big Horse's men. He had given up all hope of seeing us, and had therefore been most astonished when Yew and Serat turned up in his camp. A tax-collector who came to see us at Liangchow said :

" You've been nine months in Sinkiang and have got out without losing a single man ! Incredible ! "

XXII

THROUGH PERILOUS MOUNTAIN REGIONS

THE night temperature seldom fell below 7·2. On the night of January 20 it was as high as 8·4. And now at last we were ready to start. We hurriedly paid our farewell visits. But it always took time to get away from a big town. It was not until late in the afternoon that we drove out. At Tung-kwan, the east town gate, we were stopped by a camel caravan—tall, regal beasts with thick dark winter coats and noble heads. They looked wonderful in the half-light of the gateway.

Chin-kwan, "Golden Gate", was a fine name for a village in that poor country. We twice crossed the Chin-shui-ho, a river with several arms. Here we met a man with two yaks ; he had come straight from Tibet. Firs were growing in several places, an unusual sight. We pitched camp on the other side of the village of Ta-ho-yen.

We had watchmen at night. They received as pay 650 coppers, little Chinese bronze coins with a square hole in the middle, six or seven hundred of which went to one silver dollar at Liangchow. All night we heard the rattling of wheels and carts, and people talking.

And so we began a new day's journey on the road to Lanchow, the last stage but one on the endless road to Sian. Not till we reached Lanchow had we a definite feeling that we were approaching civilization.

Ho-tung-pu, " the village east of the river ", had plain gates without arches. Here too the people looked poor. Their clothes smelt foul—never washed, steeped in the dried sweat of years, and full of lice. Hungry children ran about on legs as thin as matches. The poor creatures were left to fend for themselves by the local authorities and the military command, who had no thought but for their own profit.

We came into an open gravel plain. A whole village lay in ruins; it had been destroyed by earthquake and looting combined. Ching-pei-yi had once had elegant brick town gates, but now they lay in ruins, and along the main street we saw only the heaped ruins of fallen houses.

The mayor of Liangchow had warned us against the village of Ku-lan, because the country round about was infested with robbers. We ought to drive quickly through the critical area and not spend the night near Ku-lan. At that day's camp we had neither night-watchmen, police or soldiers. A Mr. Sun, of the Ministry of War, whom we had met at Suchow, had been attacked between Ping-fan and Ku-lan on his journey westward and robbed of everything he had—draught animals, money, food, even the clothes he wore. But he had escaped with his life.

I was awakened in the middle of the night by Yew calling loudly for Chokdung. I raised myself out of my sleeping-bag and asked what had happened. " There's someone on the lorry," Yew replied. Chokdung hurried out, and at the same moment a thud was heard, as of someone jumping down to the ground from a height of several feet. The thief disappeared behind a wall or into a ditch. As far as we could see nothing was missing. Chokdung was ordered to keep watch till daybreak, and the rest of the night passed quietly.

As soon as we had left the village the road ran into a corridor again and ran on, 25 feet wide, between terraces and hills. We approached the dangerous village of Ku-lan, and were stopped by soldiers without rifles. On our asking why they were unarmed, they replied that if they carried rifles they would at once be disarmed by robbers. We drove through the village without any adventures, and into a valley, on a road serpentining along the left bank of a partly frozen river which wound 30 feet below. The mountain slopes on both sides ran steep to the valley. The valley became wilder and more picturesque. At a point where it grew broader we met six carts with

curved straw roofs ; they contained a circus or a troupe
of acrobats.

In the afternoon we met a still more unusual party—
fifteen men in a Chevrolet lorry, which ran as a bus between
Liangchow and Lanchow.   The bus company had been
started by Ma Pu-chin.   The buses did not start till all the
seats were occupied ; so that the earliest buyers of tickets
(18 dollars) had to wait.

Up and down hill we went, among boulders and gravel.
Sometimes there was not much space between the boulders.
Then we went into a kind of gutter along the slope, with
a protecting wall that hid the view.   There was a fair
amount of traffic—carts, donkeys, tramps, traders, and
boys carrying on flexible sticks two baskets containing a
sort of glass pipes, which made a noise like a cuckoo if one
blew into them.

The valley became wilder and wilder, with steep cliffs
and delightful views.   The evening light on the mountains
was magnificent ; the peaks shone out a brilliant orange as
we serpentined sharply along that extraordinary road,
which was certainly not made for cars.   It is called Ku-lan-
hsia, " the hollow road of Ku-lan ".   Where the road
crossed small side valleys or clefts there were curves so
short and sharp that it was a hard job to get a lorry round
the bend without plunging over the precipice.   A stone
tablet with an inscription had been set up to the memory
of a worthy man who had given money towards the upkeep
of the road.

We crossed a side valley by a bridge and climbed again on a
narrow, dangerous winding cliff road, sloping steeply
towards the precipice.   We wondered all the time how long
we should be able to keep the cars on an even keel.   One
error, and we should have dashed down the slope and been
crushed to a pulp.

Fifteen yaks were grazing on a slope opposite.   The
slopes which the sun did not reach were covered with snow.
The road was too narrow for the small car, and the lorry was
a foot wider—I could not understand how we could possibly
manage to get along without disaster.   The Great Wall
descended from the right-hand side of the valley.

Sometimes we were down in the valley and in contact with its belts of ice, but each time we went up again on to the winding cliff road. In one place, where a massive rock wall projected, the road was fearfully narrow. We stopped and waited for the lorry. We examined the spot, took it carefully, and got past. A cart appeared on a rise ahead of us. Luckily the driver stopped in time ; a meeting on that narrow shelf was unthinkable.

Our boys, Chia Kwei, Li and Chokdung, had a philosophy of their own. When the lorry, on the top of which they were crouching, approached the most dangerous places, they threw their fur coats over their heads so as at least not to see the catastrophe if they were hurled to a violent death. It would have been better to jump off, but perhaps that was often easier said than done. While we were resting for some time—Serat had had a puncture—a young man passed and asked us a great many questions : how many were we ? how many rifles had we ? and so on. Effe thought he was a spy from a robber band which was going to attack us during the night.

We drove past a row of elms on the bank of the ice-bound river. The place must be lovely in summer. We encamped 6,800 feet up near the village of Hou-shui, " Watersmeet ".

It was bitterly cold on the morning of January 24 ; the night minimum temperature had been -3.3. A party of horsemen came riding through the valley in the direction of Liangchow. We wondered what sort of people they were, but they were only soldiers, who stopped and asked us a lot of questions. They told us that a band of about thirty robbers had been captured the day before, fettered and chained together. They were now being hustled off to Liangchow to be tortured and sentenced.

We drove down to the river, which at that point flowed from the south-west and was 35 yards wide. It was mainly frozen, but there was a narrow strip of open water in the middle. The small car got through. The lorry tried to cross at a spot where the river was 60 yards wide and carried several layers of ice with water between. It had not got far when it broke through the ice ; this was a gradual process owing to the different layers of ice, and the bump on the bottom was not very severe.   But the baggage had to be unloaded and carried across the ice to *terra firma*. The whole incident cost us two hours.

Then we went up a hill on the left of the valley.   Boulders 18 inches thick had been moved to the side of the road. We came to another sunk road 12 feet wide.   We met wandering Tungans and Chinese peasants and merchants. Nearly all of them wore blue clothes or sheep-skins which had once been white.   They wore felt stockings and shoes, with fur or little felt caps.   We crossed a transverse gully in a deep-cut ravine with a bridge.   Then came another hollow road in loose strata of clay and gravel.   Here we met two carts with curved straw roofs, accompanied by several horsemen.   One of these was a bridegroom on the way to fetch his bride.   His retinue included three more carts.   In these carts he was to move his own goods and chattels and the contribution of his bride's parents to the new home.   Poor as people may be, life runs its course ; they marry, produce children and die.

A fearfully steep winding hill took us down to the bottom of the valley again.   How loaded carts could ascend it was beyond understanding.   We were at a height of 7,150 feet.   Here and there springs formed sheets of ice, shining like metal in the sun, on the walls of the valley.   Lung-kou-pu, " Dragon's Mouth Village ", consisted of only a few huts.   We crossed a few patches of ice, one 10 yards wide ; the ice bore.   We passed several lovely spots with groves of trees ; conifers grew on some of the slopes.   At Nan-yüan, " South Farm ", there were two watermills on the river-bank.   There were old watch-towers all the way ; lama temples and temples of Buddha were to be seen here and there.

We halted at 5.30 and pitched camp no. 163 at a height of 8,450 feet.   Hard by was the village of Nan-nien. A rich man who lived there owned 200 sheep, which were driven down to the folds at evening.   The rich man promised us two night-watchmen, who appeared at dusk and made friends with our boys at once, talking, laughing and telling stories.   Every quarter of an hour during the night

we heard their cries, intended partly to scare away thieves and
robbers, partly to show us that they were keeping awake.

We were all freezing cold on the morning of January
25 ; the thermometer had reached — 3·6 in the night, and
it was blowing hard from the south-east.

We set off and went on climbing. The valley was
swarming with rock doves. Patches of snow and sheets
of ice lay here and there. Higher and higher we went.
The mountain-tops grew rounder. Young Chinese came
along swinging large baskets rhythmically and gracefully
on bamboo poles, in time with their steps. At 10.45
we reached the pass, 9,000 feet high. Right at the
head of the pass, Wu-shao-ling ("Black Mountain-top")
a little temple had been erected, Han-tsu-miao, "the
temple dedicated to Han's ancestors". This was the
greatest height we reached on the whole expedition. An
old priest with a long pointed beard came out of the temple
and looked at us. The pass forms the boundary between
Ku-lan and Ping-fan.

We had seen several more sections of the Great Wall
before we reached the pass. Now, when we began to
descend, we had the Great Wall on our left. It was triple
at that point ; we were outside the middle wall, and inside
the outermost. The valley was fairly open. To our left
we had for the most part rounded hills on which flocks of
sheep were grazing, to our right higher mountains. Here
we met eight mounted Tungans with bundles on their
horses. It was impossible to tell whether they were
merchants or robbers.

In a short time we were outside the Great Wall, which
here is interrupted in several places. Near the village of
Chin-chang-yeh we crossed the river Ping-fan-ho on the
ice, and an open arm by a bridge. We were going south-east
along a fairly wide valley, with the huge snow-covered
mountain chain to our right. The Great Wall is here
built of blocks of clay and sun-dried brick, and is about 10
feet high. The Ping-fan-ho is a fair-sized river, and where
the valley was broad and open it formed large ice-floes. In
several places we saw the ruins of fortifications, houses and
walls. We crossed a frozen tributary from the lofty range

to the south-west. The Great Wall crosses the main stream at this point. Afterwards we had it now to the right of our road, now quite close by on the left. The towers seemed more frequent than before.

In places the Great Wall was only a few yards to our left. It sometimes gave the impression of being crenellated, but this was only because time and weather had worn away its top. At one point where it was undamaged it was 14 feet high, 2 feet 9 inches wide at the top and rather more than 6 feet 6 inches wide at the base.

We encamped in the village of Fou-chong-pu, 7,150 feet up.

Another cold night, with a temperature of — 2·8. A village dog stood and barked at us as long as the lights were lit in our tents. But when we had put out our lights and the camp had become quiet he executed a change of front and barked at travellers on the road. He went on all night and barked himself hoarse. I thought at first of driving him away; but no, he had volunteered to watch over us while we slept, presumably thinking—and rightly —that it was rash of us to encamp close to a high road without a night-watchman.

The road ran between trees along the river-bank, and the valley was rather narrow. The river was ice-free and swift-running, with floating ice-floes and the banks frozen hard in places. We continually enjoyed magnificent views. At the village of Wo-shen-yeh the river was wider and frozen over, and resembled a lake. We crossed the river, now squeezed into a narrow channel, on a high, short plank bridge.

Beyond the village of Feng-pu we drove through another sunk road, 12 feet deep. Luckily we met no carts there, though the traffic had increased, and there was more than we had ever seen since we left Kwei-hwa nearly a year and a half before. The sunk road soon became 18 feet deep and more, and wound this way and that. There was another road up on the hill to the right, but it could not be used by traffic. At one place a little wooden bridge crossed the sunk road. A road which had been worn so deep into the ground must have attained a respectable age.

When at last we emerged from this corridor we had the Great Wall on our left a hundred yards away. When we had passed the village of Shi-li-tien-tse, " Ten li Shelter ", we were in open country and the river was out of sight. We passed a Taoist temple with a pretty roof and reached the north gate of Ping-fan, where we were stopped by soldiers. They just looked at our cards and let us pass. In a short time we were with the mayor, who begged us insistently to stay to dinner. But we asked to be allowed to go on after we had had a cup of tea in his *yamên*. The mayor told us that the district or *hsien* of Ping-fan had had 100,000 inhabitants thirty-eight years before; now it had only 70,000. Twelve hundred families lived in the town —Chinese, Tungans, Manchus, Mongols and Tibetans.

Then we drove under some quite pretty *p'ai-lus* and out through the south gate, which was double, with a separate gateway outside. Thirty-eight years before, coming from Tibet and Sining, I had entered the town through the west gate. I now came in again along a road which I had never before travelled.

Then we lost ourselves in a hollow road 24 feet deep, filled with whirling clouds of dust. We pitched our camp no. 165 close to the village of Teh-chen-pu, 6,175 feet high. Close to the camp was a *kwei-sin-kou*—a tower with a wooden superstructure consecrated to the god Kwei-sin, who, in the days when examinations were so popular under the Manchu dynasty, used to decide who would get the highest honours.

On January 27 we went straight into a hollow road 15 feet deep. We met several carts drawn by nervous mules, which either reared or simply turned round. All the dust that was thrown up was enough to choke one. A bridge led over a tributary. From the right bank of the river the mountains rose to a considerable height, while on our left we had only low hills.

At the village of Kao-chin-tse the road ran between a row of houses and the ice-bound river, to which a bank some 20 feet high fell sheer. Charming avenues of big trees adorned the banks.

Another hollow road, with a plank across it. The dust

lay thick on the road and was flung up by wheels, hooves and feet. Everything was grey upon grey. One could not pick up a thing in the car without a grey cloud of dust rising. In those tortuous labyrinths of houses, walls, terraces and trees, and in that dust-laden atmosphere, the bearings were at most 20 yards long, and we crept forward like snails. Strange that people could live on a road over and around which thick clouds of dust continually hovered ! They got dust into their lungs for whole days on end ; only at night did they get a few hours' release.

On the night of January 27 the temperature fell to — 5·4. We went on between yellow clay hills past the temple Kwan-yin-sze. The Great Wall cropped up to the right of our road ; we must have crossed it unknowingly in a section where it was interrupted. The river, the Ping-fan-ho, was also to our right. That road must be very dangerous for cars after heavy rain ; one would slip over the edge as if it were greased and plunge into the depths. The road between Liangchow and Lanchow was beyond comparison the most difficult and dangerous we had travelled on the whole motor expedition. The country was mainly loess clay, though solid rock emerged here and there. In the evening the sky grew dark and some snow fell. We had encamped on a little flat surface between little cones, where eighteen dead had settled before us—a burial-ground.

We set off, and passed through a cañon-like ravine with curious yellow clay pillars. There was plenty of traffic ; the fields were cultivated everywhere ; flocks of sheep were grazing here and there. From a ridge we had an extensive view over the savage contours of the country to the south-south-east.

A piece of a perpendicular clay wall had fallen the night before and blocked the road. The carts drove right over the debris, but we shifted a few obstructive small boulders out of the way. Soon after we went through Hsiao-lu-che, " Little Basin ", a small village, where the people were sweeping out and cleaning up their houses for the year's second New Year festival. All the women had cramped feet.

Another pass lay ahead of us. The ascent began, and became horribly steep, with very sharp zigzag bends. We sat with our hearts in our mouths, wondering whether the gear would hold, or the car would run backwards over the precipice. But at last we were up, after climbing 195 feet in a little more than half a mile. On the other side of the pass we went on east-south-east along the winding cliff road on the other side of the valley. A cart had over-turned and spilt oil on the roadway; the drivers were trying to pick it up with their hands. Effe stopped and helped them scoop it up.

The carts had large copper bells hanging under them. The donkeys too wore bells, so that the valleys were full of a melodious jingling and tinkling. A few grottoes appeared on a slope to the right. Ahead of us a red bluff resembling a palace rose high above the valley—an Acropo-lis with tall columns, perplexingly like a work of man's hands.

The road ran between steep grey mountains with a good deal of new-fallen snow. The sunk road grew ever narrower, deeper and colder. Picturesque red mountains reappeared at the end of it. Savage, impressive scenery; the two cliff walls were only from 50 to 70 yards apart. Suddenly we saw the end of the hollow road, emerged from the mountains and had the Hwang-ho valley immediately in front of us to the south, bordered by pale-hued mountains.

We drove east-south-east between wide ploughed fields, with mountains to our left. To the south-west the Yellow River gleamed under the setting sun. We came to Erh-shih-li-pu, a name which indicated that it was only 20 li, or 6 miles more to Lanchow, the capital of Kansu. To the right we caught a glimpse of the Great Wall and as before, watch-towers with or without surrounding walls.

We reached the Yellow River at 5.30, and the road ran from 30 to 45 feet above it. We drove through a turreted gate into the town, and followed a street that led to yet another gate. Our camp no. 168 was pitched in the *yamên*.

On the following day we paid a visit to the governor-general, Chu Shao-liang, who received us very politely and told us that he had received orders from the Premier, Wang Ching-wei, to help us in every way and give us protection on our journey to Sian.   On all dangerous sections military detachments would be told off to escort us.

Then we visited the Catholic mission, a magnificent establishment with a large church, and several houses, of simple and dignified architecture.   Bishop Buddenbrock received me with all the warmth and kindness which his letters to me had breathed for several years past.   At Dr. W. Haude's request and my own he had assisted us with important meteorological information about Kansu.   I now sat with him for a long time.   He had spent thirteen years at Lanchow and before that had worked in Shantung for seventeen years.   The mission had four fathers, four lay helpers and fourteen sisters.

The China Inland Mission also had an important station at Lanchow, where we met Mr. Keble and his family.

To our great pleasure Kung and Georg had already arrived from Chung-wei ; they had had various adventures on their journey.   On January 31 we had a regular European lunch with the governor-general Chu.   He was the only man who could keep the " five Big Horses " in check.

We paid another visit to the China Inland Mission and met there Dr. and Mrs. Vaughan Rees and Mr. and Mrs. Thomas Moseley—Mrs. Moseley was from Skåne.[1]   The English hospital, of which Dr. Rand was formerly in charge and after him Dr. Rees, lay on high ground on the north bank of the river.   From its windows there was a splendid view across the Yellow River.   A week or two earlier it had been possible to drive across the river on the ice ; now only narrow belts of ice and drifting floes remained.   The river was crossed by an iron bridge with five spans, which did not suit its surroundings ; it was 240 feet long and 26 feet wide.

[1] The most southerly province of Sweden.

XXIII

LAST DAYS ON THE SILK ROAD

ON February 2 we said good-bye to our new friends at Lanchow. But as usual it was an eternity before we were ready, and not till 3.45 did we roll through the crowded streets of the big, handsome city, where the red placards and the swarms of people showed that the Chinese New Year was only two days off.

We drove out through the double southern gate and, after a bend to eastward, through the Tung-kwan gate. Outside the town we passed innumerable graves with stones, beneath which generations of Lanchow Chinese sleep their last sleep. We followed the wide valley of the Yellow River, bordered by mountains of a fair height. But in half an hour's time we drove up into a little side valley to the right between rounded hills. The road was wide and in good condition. Then we went up and down over ridges, ledges and little valleys. The slopes were fairly steep. The country became more open, but in certain places the road was sunk again. There was more snow in the ravines and in places sheltered from the sun. When we pitched camp after a two hours' journey, we had covered 24 miles. But we were doing no map-making now; the country was well known. Our camp bore the number 169 and the district, 6,800 feet high, the name Ma-chia-chai.

As the road wound about the sides of the loess hills, we wondered what was the object of the truncated clay cones which had been left standing here and there in the middle of the track. They showed how much of the clay soil had already been taken away, while square wooden labels on their sides indicated how much could still be taken away or filled up before the gradients of the road had been sufficiently levelled.

With dales on both sides we drove up a ridge to a pass, where we were surrounded in every direction by wide spaces, yellow rounded clay hills with no solid rock. On both sides lay ploughed fields, striped white by the snow that remained in the furrows after the ploughing.

We saw no one and seldom met travellers. A golden eagle hovered over the desolate country. For some way the road kept to the hill-tops; up there the ground was pretty flat, but on both sides of us we had what looked like a sea of great yellow waves.

Then we descended a long, steep, fearfully winding hill to a good-sized valley. The difference in height between hill-top and valley bottom was about 975 feet. We went along a hollow road for some way and then uphill again along another. There we met a Dodge lorry. Its passengers told us that they had been a fortnight coming from Sian and had had fights with robbers all along the road.

A bridge ran over a frozen water-course in the valley bottom, but it had a gap in the middle to prevent carts from using it; they had to drive across the bed of the stream. From time to time we passed a village or farm. The bridge at Ting-hsi was not fit for use, and we too had to drive through a muddy river-bed, in which we stuck.

The mayor of Ting-hsi, on whom we called, declared that the road was fairly safe for about 18 miles ahead, but after that we must be on our guard against attacks. He therefore gave us an officer and two men as an escort.

We were climbing a fearfully steep hill. The car could not get up; it stopped and ran backwards, the brake would not hold, we gathered speed and ran towards the edge of a precipice. At the last moment Effe turned and drove at full speed against the perpendicular clay wall. It was soft, and the car suffered no damage worth mentioning.

We drove on up and down nasty gradients. We sat with our hearts in our mouths, rejoicing every time we got across a side valley or round a bend.

Serat was not to be seen. Had anything happened to him? We waited. Ah, now we heard his engine. It was getting dark. One ought not to drive over such country after dark; so we stopped at the village of Hung-tu-yo, camp no. 170, having covered 72 miles. We were 6,500 feet above sea-level. The inn yard was cluttered up with a long train of carts loaded with telephone poles for a new line from Sian to Lanchow. So we put up at a separate farm large enough for our three cars and our two tents.

After 2·5 degrees in the night we proceeded at daybreak on February 4. We were told that we had a tolerable road as far as Hua-chia-ling and that the country was quiet, but after that the road became bad and there was danger from robbers. A short time before we started our three soldiers sat on a tower outside the village and did a little target-shooting. They were evidently practising and testing their rifles to be ready to meet an attack by robbers.

From the village we drove headlong down a horribly steep and narrow sunk road and then slowly ascended a valley, in the bottom of which we crossed a frozen brook several times. Then another precipitous slope faced us. Six men pushed. We made a few yards. Blocks of wood were placed behind the wheels. The small car's piston-rings were loose, the engine had no power. It was very dangerous to drive in such conditions ; I preferred to walk up the ghastly hills. And this road was a new one ! The old road, which ran higher up, was even worse.

I stopped some way up and waited and waited. No one was to be seen, but at times I heard shouts and the sound of blows. I was anxious and ill at ease. Had anything happened ? Should I hear that a car had gone over a slope or been smashed up ?

Ah, now I could plainly hear the noise of engines ; the small car was coming. Yew ran up a slope and reported that the road looked awful.

Effe hurried downhill on foot to help Serat. We waited. We heard shots. Were robbers about ?

Then the ten carts laden with telephone poles came grinding up the hill. When a couple of them had reached the summit where we stood, the two front horses were unharnessed and taken down to help their comrades pull up the heavy loads.

Yew came back. At a sharp bend he received a blow

from a bundle of telephone posts, lost his balance and rolled a few yards down a slope, but recovered his foothold.

At last Serat and his lorry appeared and we went on up to a pass (7,150 feet). A village surrounded by ploughed fields lay on a slope. These Chinese farmers are wonderful ; they do not waste a scrap of ground fit for cultivation.

After that we remained for a time on the hill-tops. The curves were fearful, but the hills were not difficult. Now and again we passed through a village. We left a square fort on our left and reached another small pass, from which there was an immense view in every direction. Everything was yellow—hills, houses and walls.

A small donkey caravan appeared. The animals had their ears decked with red paper ; they were celebrating the New Year. And here were twenty camels without loads, being led eastward. The soft hillsides were everywhere striped with plough.

We had been warned that the country which was infested with robbers started at Hua-chia-ling. The road, we had been told, now ran through wilderness for over 50 miles. We had four soldiers with us, and they and we kept our fire-arms in readiness.

We drove over a few conspicuous ridges. Streams of melted snow ran down over the road from snowfields higher up, so that it became slippery. The region was after all not entirely wilderness. We passed through one or two villages, and ploughed fields were common.

A solitary tree stood by the wayside ; otherwise the country was bare. Now and again we saw a shepherd with his flock of sheep and goats. The road was as slippery as ice, owing to the melted snow that ran down over the yellow loess. We continually expected the cars to slide over the edge of the road into an abyss. The wreck of a lorry lay by the roadside.

That road was horrible, especially when it was wet. There was a change of scene every minute, and yet the landscape was rather monotonous. The small car often stuck in the mud, and we had to wait till Serat came and helped us out.

We had to drive for more than two hours longer through

the pitch-dark night in that dangerous country—an exciting journey indeed ! Now we were on the top of a ridge with a sheer drop on both sides, now on a steep hillside, with at least one abyss always beside us, and the edge of the precipice and certain death 3 feet away.

There was more and more snow as we left the parched interior of the continent behind us and drew near to the coast and the moist sea breezes. The snowfields shone white even in the darkness. I for my part could not see how Effe was driving, and sometimes had a feeling that he had lost the road. I asked him if he could see it clearly. He was, as usual, as cool as a cucumber ; he drove cunningly down into a transverse gully and up on the other side. It was worse on the steep, winding uphill stretches. If the engine and brakes failed, and the car ran downhill as it had done the day before, Effe would not be able to see the road in the darkness, and the car would run over the edge and fall into the depths.

In a short time we met three night walkers who told us that we had three li to go, and we crept on in the dark. At last we saw a few trees and some houses ; we drove into the main street of a village and encamped at a farm. We had driven 165 miles from Lanchow and had another 86 to go before we reached Ping-liang. On our way there we should have to cross the Liu-pan-shan mountain range, to reach the top of which we had to ascend 3,250 feet. Then we should be going downhill all the way to Sian.

Close to the village of Ma-chia-pu was a watch-tower with five small pyramids ; it was a long time since we had seen one like it. Here too there was an avenue, which continued, with many interruptions, until we entered a small valley, where the road was good, but winding and hilly.

We surmounted a few hillocks and descended again into the valley bottom, where the road was good and about 25 feet wide. We drove into the little town of Ching-ning. Here we changed escort. All the shops were shut for the New Year festival.

It took an eternity to get the new escort. The mayor

sent message after message, but received the answer that the officer in command of the garrison was not to be found, and no soldiers could be had without his consent. And we must have an escort, as the road we were going to travel was very unsafe.

Meanwhile the mayor gave us a good deal of information. There were 60,000 persons in his *hsien* and 14,000 in his town. There were thirty-six schools in the district. A regiment 3,500 men strong was there, which squeezed 150,000 dollars a year out of the population. The soldiers were recruits taken from robber bands.

"It's a good thing for you to have fellows like that for your escort," he said, "for they are on good terms with the robber bands and the people under their escort are not attacked. All the way from Lung-teh the garrisons are taken from the Central Government's troops, and they are reliable."

He added: "If you meet six men, or more, together on the road, look out, for they're more likely to be a robber band than not."

When we complained of the bad road, the mayor replied: "You ought to see what it's like in two months, when it's all become one sea of mud. Now it's frozen hard."

We got away at last after a few hours' wait and drove out through the east gate.

We descended through a deep, narrow sunk road to the bottom of the valley, which was covered with snow and ice-floes. The road was good; it wound along the slope above the valley, and had a fence.

A New Year's procession came along with a large yellow paper lion at its head and carrying several flags. They looked contented and happy, those poor farmers getting a bit of amusement out of the year's chief festival. But they did not like the new road, which deprived them of a strip of land without any compensation.

The road sometimes ran between trees. We met 131 camels laden with goods, a pleasant and picturesque sight in the wintry landscape.

The wide and well-kept road was now accompanied by two rows of splendid alders. A large herd of black pigs were being driven to Sianz. The *chaussée* was wonderful, though it shrank now and then to a narrow sunk road.

The traffic was very small, as it was the day after the New Year festival. The larger shops are kept shut for a fortnight, the smaller for a week only. Wooden columns and door-posts had strips of red paper pasted all over them. Even the caravans were decorated for the feast. Red ribbons hung from the pommels of the pack-saddle of the first camel in each string.

It was beginning to get dark when we reached the gate of Lung-teh and made for the mayor's *yamên*. He received us in a study of the usual type, indescribably simple—a table heaped with papers by the window, a smaller table for teacups, seven chairs, and by the inner and shorter wall a *kang*, on which he slept at night. The window had a wooden lattice pasted over with white paper—one never sees glass panes in that part of the world. By one wall was a primitive stove with a pipe. A tin basin stood on a wooden wash-hand stand. The little room was thus in reality at the same time office, reception-room, sitting-room, washing-room and tea-room, and was the only one in the whole *yamên* that was heated. All the mayors in Kansu, even in the big towns, live in an equally modest style—in cramped quarters, poorly furnished, cold, dirty and dark.

While we were sitting talking to the mayor two officers came in and asked if they might come with us in our cars. We replied that they were welcome in the capacity of escort.

We were told that Lung-teh had been looted by robbers nine times in the last two and a half years and, therefore, was still to a large extent in ruins. The last time this had happened was scarcely a year ago. Some of the inhabitants were killed, the rest fled. Some of them had now returned. Merchants were, generally speaking, the most likely people to be attacked on the road ; official or military cars were left alone.

The distance to Ping-liang was estimated at 43¾ miles, 10 of which ran over the Liu-pan-shan range. The road, we were told, was not so steep and difficult as those over the passes we had left behind us, and it was hardly ever blocked with snow ; but it was often damaged in summer, slippery and dangerous after rain—indeed, it was not infrequently quite unfit for traffic for several weeks or more.

Like several of the mayors we had met before, the mayor of Lung-teh told us that the peasants were endeavouring to reduce their house and landed property to a minimum in order not to be bled with taxation. They did not send their children to school either, because school cost money.

The little town was inhabited by 300 families. There were 6,000 families in the Lung-teh administrative area. The Central Government kept a garrison of 250 men in the place.

It snowed the whole evening. On the morning of February 6 it was still snowing. The mayor, in whose *yamên* we had stayed, came out himself and said good-bye to us. He insisted on our taking seven soldiers with us, because the region was considered very unsafe.

We picked up the escort at the barracks and rolled out into the blinding white countryside. A party of thirty men was going off eastward, probably to deal with a robber band.

The snow lay on the high road several inches deep. So long as the road was tree-lined it was easy enough to find our way, but when the trees stopped the road was hidden by the snow. We felt our way forward through several villages, following the tracks of the donkey caravans.

The ground began to rise. The cars slipped and swayed on the hills and at the bends. The snow became thicker. We put temporary snow-chains on the small car's back wheels. Now we went uphill in real earnest, over solid rock. The road wound about in small zigzags; it was well and carefully laid, and had a low fence. An impenetrable curtain of snow enveloped the chalk-white countryside; we could not see clearly for more than 30 yards ahead. And the snow went on falling.

At one or two steep places the road was not finished. The track was quite narrow, and stone ledges had not yet been blasted away. The car could not get on. Chia Kwei placed stones behind the wheels to prevent it from running back downhill again when it had made a few yards. The snow lay in heaps and had to be cleared away.

Three pedlars, with baskets swinging on bamboo poles carried over their shoulders, were the only travellers we met; most people keep indoors in such weather.

After a few good-sized bends we reached the pass, about 8,400 feet high, and zigzagged downhill. The snow fell thicker; whole masses of snow slipped off the roof of the car.

In a little while the snow became less dense. We saw a village in the valley beneath, with groves of trees. Its name was Ho-shan-pu. We crossed a bridge where a camel caravan had rested. Pheasants were running about in the snow quite near the houses. The seven soldiers who had been with us jumped off.

We passed another camel caravan. The boxes it was carrying contained tobacco from Lanchow. We followed a fair-sized valley, into which side valleys ran. There were hundreds of pheasants about. They sat on the road and flew up a few yards ahead of us.

The valley grew narrower. At one point where it was quite narrow were the three little temples of San-kwan-kou, very picturesquely situated in a cleft. Here the road ran on the right-hand side of the valley; it was well-built and fenced.

At 3 p.m. we drove in through the west gate of Fing-liang and followed a long street, in which the China Inland Mission had a station. We stopped outside the town authorities' *yamên*. But there was no one at home, and we went on, now in company with Serat. The immensely long street was one sea of mud; the snow was shovelled out into the middle of the road and obstructed traffic. All was wet, dirty, poor and uninteresting.

Outside the east gate we crossed a solid bridge. We halted in the twilight at the village of Sze-shih-li-pu, where we were 4,050 feet up. Although we had been driving for nearly eight hours, we had done no more than 60 miles.

On the morning of February 7 the same dark, gloomy weather prevailed, and the thermometer had therefore not fallen lower than 18·7 degrees.

And on we went, through the broad valley, between

hills which now became lower and lower. We drove through villages and along avenues, past farms and copses, and over bridges. Hsü-chuang was a biggish village with empty streets; everyone was indoors, playing *ma-chang*, drinking tea and smoking opium. A motor-bus had been attacked there a few days before, and the passengers robbed of their money, valuables and clothes; but the bus had been allowed to go on.

The avenue was now continuous, but the road ran outside it. The snow lay in regular drifts. We often drove over bridges. The road was wretched; we bumped up and down all the time; it had been much better in the mountains.

About noon the road swung off to the left at a right angle and ran down to the river, the Ching-ho. We crossed several frozen arms of the river. Then Effe drove out into the main stream, where the car sank deeper and deeper until the water was running through it. The things which were lying on the floor had to be rescued in haste. We had to put up our legs on the back of the front seats, and there we sat with the water surging through the car. Luckily we had not to wait long before Serat came and towed us out.

In a little while we had to cross the river again, and the same manœuvre was repeated twice. Serat helped us, but once nearly upset himself.

We drove into the town of Ching-chüan through a ruined gate and went down the narrow main street, which soon became a sunk road. We were on the wrong road; we had to back and turn, and were directed to Tung-kwan, the east gate. Then we drove along the foot of snow-covered hills on our right. The valley grew narrower. Reddish-yellow clay cliffs rose on our right. We had the river on our left, and crossed a bridge over a side valley. Then the road went up unpleasant slopes to a ridge, the view from which was obscured by mist. The loess cliffs had assumed picturesque shapes—houses, walls, fortresses and towers.

We went on climbing. The trees in an avenue were covered with hoar-frost and looked like alabaster. Then the road kept to the hill-tops for a time. It was cold up there, and the snow lay fairly deep. The avenue had come to an end, and it would have been impossible to find the way if a few Chinese lorries had not been by.

The boundary between Kansu and Shensi runs right through the village of Yao-tien. We drove past some solitary farms, through a village, by a grave with a headstone, and passed a tobacco caravan of 200 camels. We descended through a long, gently sloping sunk road to a fair-sized valley with a river flowing through it which led to the Ching-ho. We crossed the river by a bad bridge.

Twilight had turned into darkness when, after a day's run of 90 miles, we drove to the mayor's *yamên* in the town of Ping-hsien, which, we were told, had 3,000 inhabitants. It lay 2,600 feet above sea-level.

We went on up and down through a red clay landscape, and were once more enwrapped in a mist of falling snow. We passed one herd of pigs after another, on their way to the slaughterers at Sian.

But now we were running downhill again; the hills became lower and drew back on either side, and we came down into flat country. At the gate of the village of Chien-chun we were stopped by soldiers, who asked the usual questions. The long strain was over now. No longer need we sit with our hearts in our mouths on the brink of gaping abysses and in expectation of robbers in ambush. There was more and more traffic; we passed or met both carts and motor-lorries. A flock of wild geese flew overhead from south-west to north-east.

We drove across a plain which ran on all sides to where a wall of mist formed the horizon.

Again we drove through villages and gateways and were questioned by soldiers. In one village they said that three cars containing foreigners from Sweden were expected. But as nothing had been seen of Georg and his lorry since we left Lanchow, we were only two, so that the number did not tally and the soldiers became suspicious. But after a good deal of palaver they let us pass.

At 2 p.m. we passed the town of Hsien-yang and its great walls. We drove through three towered gates to the wooden bridge over the Wei-ho, a really big river. It was 3 p.m. when we reached the west gate of Sian or Chang-an, as the town is now called again, where the old Silk Road can be said to begin—and for us to end.

We put up at the North-Western Hotel (Hsi-pei-fan-tien) in tiny semi-Europeanized rooms.

Sian, "the Western Peace", the famous capital of the Han and T'ang dynasties, was thus the last camping-ground of the long motor expedition and bore as such the number 175. February 8, on which we covered 80 miles, was our last day of travel on the Silk Road.

So my account of our journey must end at Sian.

After a few days' stay in the town we took the train to Nanking, where the Government gave us an almost royal reception. I myself had the honour of being received by the veteran president of the Republic Lin Sen, and of being invited to visit the great Marshal Chiang-Kai-shek, who then had his headquarters at Hankow. The Prime Minister, Wang Ching-wei, invited the whole expedition to dinner, and made a speech in our honour in the presence of his colleagues which we shall never forget. At another festivity, at which the Prime Minister and 250 members of the Government and officials were present, I had an opportunity of submitting a first report on our journey in the form of an address. The kindness and attention which I received on my seventieth birthday are also among the proudest and most precious memories of my stay in the Far East.

I then went to Shanghai with Dr. Erik Norin, who had met us at Peking. The Swedish Consul-General, Lind-quist, received us there with the utmost hospitality. We then started home via Peking, where many old friends paid their tribute to us. We travelled through Manchuria to Novo Sibirsk; there we were for one day the guests of the German Consul, Herr Grosskopf, who during the past eight years had given our expeditions such powerful support.

From the moment when, on April 15, 1935, we again set foot on Swedish soil, we were hailed by the people of Sweden all the way to Stockholm, where relations and friends, who had so long been kept in anxiety, were there to meet us. All the members of our expeditions living in Sweden were present at a party in my home the same evening, and I could not be humbly thankful enough that they were all alive, and for their loyalty they had shown me during the past years.

It was just fifty years since I had left home for the first time to devote a whole lifetime to the exploration of darkest Asia.

APPENDIX

SO much for our own observations on the spot in 1934. It seems impossible to obtain any reliable information about events in Sinkiang from places outside the frontiers of the province. Not even in China is anything definite known about what is happening there.

The Eastern frontier, where the old caravan routes from China and Mongolia enter the country, are barred. The only two countries which have consuls in Sinkiang, Russia and Great Britain, must have definite first-hand information in the Foreign Offices in Moscow and London, but this, for obvious reasons, is kept secret. The missionaries—the Swedes at Kashgar and Yarkend, the China Inland Mission, and the German Societas Verbi Divini at Urumchi—must for their own sakes be careful about what they report. Now and again, a casual news paragraph or a vague rumour about events in these hermetically sealed regions of Central Asia appears in the English press, and very rarely scraps of information are to be gleaned from travellers' narratives, scarcer than ever in the political conditions now prevailing—for example, those of the British women missionaries, the Misses Cable and French, and the newspaper correspondent Peter Fleming's book *News from Tartary, a Journey from Peking to Kashmir*, published in 1936, while Owen Lattimore's excellent accounts were written before the rebellions broke out.

The best book which has been written about conditions in Sinkiang from the time immediately after the rebellions reached their climax is Sir Eric Teichman's *Journey to Turkistan*, published in 1937 and containing an account of a motor journey in the tracks of the Sino-Swedish motor expedition from Beli-miao through the Gobi, across the Etsin-gol to Hami, Urumchi, Turfan, Kara-shahr, Korla and Kucha, and thence via Maralbashi to Kashgar. Georg Söderbom helped in the organization of this expedition, and Teichman engaged my two Mongolian drivers, Serat and Jomcha, and took over one of my motor-lorries, a 1933 Ford. Teichman had been in H.B.M. consular service in China for about thirty years, spoke Chinese fluently, had a thorough knowledge of the Chinese psychology, and was a master of the diplomacy and tact without which no one can achieve anything with the Chinese.

Teichman's journey was made during the last four months of 1935, and thus immediately follows the events described in my books *Big Horse's Flight*, *The Silk Road* and *The Wandering Lake*.[1] In a survey of recent events in Sinkiang it is, therefore, of the greatest importance to give a brief résumé of the main features of Teichman's narrative.

He described the situation in 1932–33, when the Turkis and Kirgises made common cause with the Tungans against the Chinese in Eastern Turkistan. At the beginning of 1933 the Turkis got the upper hand in Kashgar and besieged a Tungan force in the new town, Han-cheng, where the Chinese citadel was situated.

After Ma Chung-yin (Big Horse) had been defeated in the spring of 1934 he retreated, as has been said, to Kashgar, where he relieved the Tungan garrison, overthrew the Turki authorities and himself took over the government.

But the Tungan rule in Kashgar did not last long. In July, 1934, the provincial troops—a combined force of Russians, Manchus, Turkis and Mongols—advanced to Kashgar and drove out the Tungans, who retreated, without offering battle, to the Yarkend-daria and Khotan. To the general surprise Ma Chung-yin, having made an agreement with the Russian Consul-General and probably received a guarantee of his personal safety, fled into Russian Turkistan, where he and his escort of 120 men were disarmed. It was rumoured that he had been taken to Tashkent and thence to Moscow. After Ma Chung-yin disappeared from the scene Ma Ho-san took over the command of the Tungan forces.

In 1935 there were no active hostilities between the Tungans and Chinese, and Sinkiang remained comparatively quiet under its military governor-general Sheng Shih-tsai, who then held sway over the whole province except for its southern part between the Yarkend-daria and Charkhlik, not far from Lop-nor.

It was, therefore, thought a suitable moment to send a diplomatic mission to Urumchi to negotiate about conditions on the frontier between India and Sinkiang under its new regime. The most important matters to be discussed were Indian trade, the conditions on which Indian merchants might reside in Eastern Turkistan, peace and security on the Indian North-West Frontier,

---

[1] *Den vandrande sjön*, not at present published in English, dealing with Dr. Hedin's journey to Lake Lop-nor.

and British trade communications between the Chinese coast and Sinkiang.

British India had been represented in Sinkiang by a Consul-General at Kashgar since 1890. The first occupant of the post had been Sir Francis—then Captain—Younghusband, well known as leader of the invasion of Tibet and the capture of Lhasa under Lord Curzon's auspices in 1903–4. In 1890 I had spent Christmas Eve with him and Sir George Macartney at Kashgar. In 1935 the Consul-General was Colonel J. W. Thomson Glover. He was instructed to meet Sir Eric Teichman at Urumchi. After their negotiations with Sheng Shih-tsai they were both to return to Kashgar, whence Teichman would go on to India.

Teichman found the relations between Urumchi and Nanking as cool as we had found them in 1934. In theory the province was under the Central Government at Nanking, but in practice it was autonomous, as is usual with the remote provinces on the periphery of China. After Marshal Yang's death the independence movement in Sinkiang had become more and more pronounced. Sinkiang is separated from China proper by vast expanses of desert, and it is a consequence of its geographical position that the province should turn its back on China but hold out its hand to its Russian neighbour, on whom it is economically dependent. The further circumstance that people of the same race and language live on both sides of the Russo-Chinese frontier has prepared the ground for a political *rapprochement*. Sheng Shih-tsai told Teichman frankly that in his life and death struggle with Ma Chung-yin he had received no help whatever from Nanking, but, on the other hand, ungrudging support from Russia.

Between 1932 and 1937 Kashgar and the surrounding district were sorely tried, and the Swedish missionaries with their schools and hospitals were almost continually in the greatest danger.

When Teichman reached Kashgar at the end of 1935 the nominal power was in the hands of a triumvirate, strictly controlled from Urumchi, consisting of General Liu Pin, who had come to Urumchi in 1934 with the army beaten by the Japanese in Manchuria, the weak *tao-tai*, Hsü Lien, and an elderly Turfan merchant named Mahmud.

The Russian Consul-General Teskuloff was a strong and influential man. The British Consul-General supported China and opposed the Russian influence as best he could. Teichman thinks that the Russian pressure on Eastern Turkistan was stronger in Tsarist days than it is now; but I cannot agree with him on this point. Russian influence has certainly become stronger and stronger since 1928, and since the Russians helped the Urumchi government against Ma Chung-yin in 1934 with motor-lorries, arms, ammunition, aeroplanes and troops, there is no question that their political power in the province has been almost unlimited. It was the Russians who defeated the Tungans, not Sheng Shih-tsai. Without Russian help the war between the Chinese and Tungans would have taken quite a different course.

Some people feared in 1935 that Sinkiang would suffer the same fate as Outer Mongolia and become entirely dependent on Russia. The Russians themselves, of course, deny that they have any intention of occupying the province. I obtained in 1934 a strong impression that they would be content to get the whole trade of the province into their hands and take over the direction of its economic affairs. And if they succeeded in this they could spare themselves all the expensive apparatus that a military occupation involves—the guards, the construction of military roads, the setting up of a civil administration, and much else.

But the situation has changed very much since 1934 and 1935. Since then the Japanese have conquered Chahar, Sui-yuan and Shansi—the provinces of Northern China in which the great trade and caravan routes to Sinkiang start. If the Japanese refurnishing in Asia proceeds in the same direction as now and at the same pace, Sinkiang may become a bone of contention between Japan and Russia.

Like Switzerland, Sinkiang is situated in the heart of a continent and, like Switzerland, it is surrounded by powerful states with divergent interests. But, unlike Switzerland, Sinkiang cannot stand on its own legs. Its military forces are a negligible quantity, and there is therefore increasing friction between its neighbours on its frontier, British India, Russia, China and Japan—which, since the occupation of the northern provinces of China and the caravan routes, can be counted as one of Sinkiang's neighbours.

Trade with India is moribund and can be ignored. Russian trade is already almost omnipotent, and has driven out Chinese trade. For Russia, which is close both to Kashgar and to Urumchi, and has developed certain trade routes to the provincial centres, it is an easy and agreeable task to manœuvre competitors out of the field. Even in 1934 the influence of Russia in Sinkiang was stronger beyond all comparison than that of the Central Government at Nanking. And since the outbreak of the present war, it is safe to say that the influence of Nanking has been almost paralysed.

But the greatest and most important change which has taken place since 1934 and 1935 is in the strategic position. This has been a natural consequence of the war between Japan and China. It is probable that Japan, which has already conquered Manchuria, Jehol and Inner Mongolia, will seek to bring Outer Mongolia also under her domination in order that she may thence outflank Siberia and the Trans-Siberian Railway, which is the principal line of communication of the Russian Far East. For this outflanking to be complete and effective it must also include Sinkiang—i.e. the Altai and Dzungaria against Siberia, Semipalatinsk and Sunirjetschensk, and Eastern Turkistan against the Russian Pamir, Ferghana and Russian Turkistan.

Russia in 1930 completed the Turksib (Turkistan-Siberia) railway between Tashkent and Semipalatinsk, which runs along, and not far from, the north-western frontier of Sinkiang; so that it is easier for her to dominate Sinkiang strategically than for Japan, whose long lines of communication, so long as no railways exist, run through the Gobi desert.

But the inaccessibility of the province will not be an insuperable obstacle to either Japan or Russia if, either now or at some future time, the stake of battle is the mastery of Asia. Sinkiang was often the scene of bloody wars in ancient times, and the members of the Sino-Swedish motor expedition of 1934 had an opportunity of seeing with their own eyes the fighting going on within its borders. It no longer sounds fantastic to predict that in the near future it will be possible to bring war camels, loaded with arms and ammunition, to drink on the banks of the Kum-daria and Lake Lop-nor—to a region where in the spring of 1934 we were the only people in an area of 125,000 square miles. But it will be strange to think that it was we who in 1934–35 prepared and mapped out their roads through deserts and mountains.

We have already seen that Britain, as much as seventy-five years ago, desired that Yakub Beg's dominion, which coincided with the greater part of the province called Sinkiang, should be strengthened and should serve as a buffer state against the Russian advance. After Yakub Beg's kingdom had been recaptured by the Chinese, it became, in the same way, a British interest that China should maintain and strengthen her power over the province. To Britain, Japan is just as unwelcome as Russia as a neighbour on the North-West Frontier of India. But now, when China has been manœuvred out of Sinkiang, and the rivalry between Russia and Japan will probably grow more acute, Britain is powerless, and must content herself with the role of a spectator. For, in the first place, there is a limit to the possibilities of conveying troops, artillery and motor transport over the Gilgit and Karakoram; in the second, it looks as if Great Britain had too much trouble within the frontiers of India to be able to risk any Hannibalesque adventures over the mountains to the north.

To return to events in and around Kashgar during recent years, we can obtain from Swedish sources a good deal of information supplementary to that cited above.

It was in April, 1934, that the two Tungan generals Ma Chung-yin and Ma Ho-san came to Kashgar with the remnants of their defeated army. Ma Chung-yin had paid several visits to the Swedish mission, had played tennis with the missionaries with skill and enjoyment, and shown himself polite and attentive. He had several talks with the Russian Consul-General, and had probably let himself be persuaded to cross the frontier at Irkeshtam. Ma Ho-san disapproved of this, but when Ma Chung-yin stuck to his decision and actually carried it out, Ma Ho-san had become commander-in-chief of the Tungans and brought the country between the Yarkend-daria and Charkhlik under his domination. Khotan was his headquarters as recently as August, 1937.

In 1936–37 the Red Russians began their " godless " propaganda in Eastern Turkistan. The older East Turkis and the *bais* (merchants) in Kashgar resisted this movement, while the younger elements succumbed to it. Mahmud Si Yang, or General Mahmud, a brother to old Mossul Bai, one of our friends in Turfan, was the leader of the Turki population of Kashgar and at the same time an opponent of the Red Russians and their Chinese henchmen, who were all on the side of Urumchi.

Mahmud Si Yang and his East Turki troops had joined forces with Ma Ho-san and his Tungans. The combined armies were 15,000 men strong, and with his force Ma marched against Kashgar. The old town surrendered, whilst Han-cheng, the new town, which was surrounded by a high wall, held out against the siege for three months. Ma Ho-san, himself driven in a lorry, led his troops by way of Faisabad and Maralbashi to Aksu, which he captured, though the new town held out. Now the Red Russian propaganda bore fruit; the Tungans and East Turkis quarrelled and split, but withdrew to Kashgar and Yarkend. A large number of Tungans went over to the Reds.

In the spring of 1937 Mahmud Si Yang told his followers that he was going on a shooting-trip in the mountains, and went off in the direction of Yangi-hissar. When he had gone the whole of his East Turki army, which had been in garrison in Kashgar, set off for Yarkend. Outside Yarkend Mahmud Si Yang met his troops and handed over the command to one or two of his right-hand men. He himself departed to India, accompanied by Mossul Bai.

The Red Russians, combined with the Chinese and a number of deserters from Ma Ho-san's Tungan army, now dominated the western part of the country, Yarkend and Kashgar. The East Turkis, who are fanatical Mohammedans, hate Bolshevism and refused to go over to the Reds. They were therefore slaughtered in numbers. A thousand or so, who were endeavouring to reach Khotan, were overtaken in the desert and mown down with machine-guns to the last man. All the Turkis in Kashgar who had assisted the adversaries of the " godless " propaganda were massacred, including all the rich merchants in the place, who were sought out in their houses at night and disappeared. Many of them were hustled into a pit and buried alive. Innocent people, who did not know what it was all about, were included in this cruel and barbarous purge.

When Ma Ho-san, our friend from Turfan and Korla, found himself abandoned by most of his generals and troops, he saw that his position was untenable and fled over the Karakoram pass to Ladak with a bodyguard of a thousand men. On the way there he had reason to suspect that his chief of staff was a spy in Russian pay, and shot him down with his own hand.

At Ladak the British Joint Commissioner forced Ma Ho-san to leave his troops, which had to bivouac in the mountains around Leh. He himself was allowed to go on to India, but the 300 lb. of gold-dust he brought with him was confiscated. The English took the view, and rightly, that this gold had been stolen from the Chinese Central Government, which still ruled over Eastern Turkistan, at least in form.

The capable young White Russian Vorotnikoff, who had joined our expedition at Urumchi in 1928 as assistant to Drs. Hummel and Haude and afterwards, till 1933, to Dr. Nils Ambolt, went, on leaving us, to the mission at Kashgar and worked in the mission printing works, where a new translation of the New Testament was being printed. It looks as if Vorotnikoff had on various occasions been incautious and made remarks criticizing the Red regime, the neglect of education, and so on. One day in the summer of 1937 a Red Russian came to see Vorotnikoff in his room at the mission ; he was politely received, sat down and had a chat over a glass of tea. He had hardly been gone a quarter of an hour when the mission was surrounded by about fifty East Turkis in the service of the Tcheka. Eight of them had gone into the young Russian's room, seized all his books and papers, and ordered him to accompany them. The prisoner, understanding what was in the wind, had begged to be allowed to kneel down and say his prayers. His request was granted; the Turkis respect prayers (*namas*). Then he was taken to the Turki prison. The missionaries did all they could to get him freed, but were quite unable to keep in touch with him. They were told later by the British Consul-General, Glover, who came to Kashgar with Sir Eric Teichman, that our young Russian friend had been taken to Aksu by the Red Russians and shot.

This episode gives an idea of what is going on now at Kashgar. On one occasion 150 prisoners were taken out at once, but they were hardly in the open air before the executioners opened fire and shot them down; only twenty escaped.

In other respects the new lords treated the mission with a certain consideration, probably because they found that the missionaries did not concern themselves at all with politics. About a hundred converts belonged to the mission, seven of whom had been converted in the last year. Most of the Christian Turkis disappeared during the massacres.

In his admirable and exciting book, *D-Anoy conquers the Pamir : a daring German Exploration Flight*, which came out at the beginning of the year, Baron C. A. von Gablenz gives us a fleeting glimpse of the conditions which prevailed in Southern Sinkiang in August and September, 1937. He and his two companions had to make a forced landing on August 28 near the village of Lop-bazar, on the eastern edge of the Khotan oasis, on account of engine trouble.

The Germans, who had flown from Tempelhof to Sian to open the regular air line between Berlin and Shanghai—a line farther south than that which I had undertaken to map out for the Luft Hansa in 1927–28[1]—were on their way home to Berlin when the accident at Lop-bazar led them right into the Tungans' claws.

They were held as prisoners for a month in the fortress of Khotan, but during this time they were able to pick up one or two pieces of news and find out for themselves what was going on. They heard that there had been fighting recently at Aksu

---

[1] This was the origin of the Swedish-German-Chinese expedition, which started in the spring of 1927.

between troops from Urumchi and Kashgar, and saw the defences of the fortress of Khotan being strengthened with feverish energy. Soon, too, shots were heard near by and dead soldiers were carried into the fortress.

The prisoners learned that "the great general" was soon coming from Kashgar; they also heard that it was the commander of the 36th Tungan Division, Ma Ho-san, our friend from Turfan, who had gone from Kashgar to Aksu to fight the troops from Urumchi. Later he had been defeated himself; his troops had deserted him and marched via Guma to Khotan, intending to go via Cherchen and Charkhlik to Korla and join rebel formations in that area. These statements of von Gablenz confirm previous reports from other sources.

Ma Si-ling, the general in command at Khotan, who had detained the Germans after their forced landing and till now had been under Ma Ho-san's orders, abandoned him on hearing of his defeat. When the fleeing troops reached Khotan, he had refused to let them enter the town. This was the cause of the firing, and the dead men being carried into the fortress.

The "great general" who was expected at Khotan, and on whose disposition the Germans' fate depended, was called Ma Shing-wei,[1] and it was he who had defeated Ma Ho-san at Aksu.

At last General Ma Shing-wei arrived at Khotan and ordered the German aviators to be set at liberty. They were thus able to return home after a month's captivity.

A short time before von Gablenz's adventures at Khotan, another German, Dr. W. Filchner, who had been out on an expedition taking magnetic observations, arrived there and was also detained as a prisoner for some time. He returned to Germany quite recently, and no details of his experiences are yet known.

In the middle of February information is understood to have been received showing that the Swedish missions were in no immediate danger. But there seems to be no doubt that the Kashgar-Yarkend region is seething with unrest and that Russian influence is advancing eastward, the Red Terror in its most barbarous form. If the murders at Kashgar are repeated in other Central Asiatic towns with a Mohammedan population, a life and death struggle is to be expected between the Mohammedans—

---

[1] Ma is a very common name among the Tungans, who are Mohammedans. It means Mohammed. In Chinese the word means "horse"; and when some years ago there were five leading generals in Kansu named Ma, they were called "the five Big Horses". (See page 40.)

who, as I have said, are among the most irreconcilable enemies of Bolshevism—and Red Russia.   A war of religion may spread like a steppe fire to Russia's Mohammedan possessions in Western Turkistan and the Tungans in Kansu.   As Russia is the only Power from which China is receiving effective help in her desperate struggle against Japan, it is not surprising that the Chinese sympathize with the Bolsheviks, even if an alliance with them may involve China herself in certain dangers in the time to come.

As a man of culture, a Christian, and a man of gigantic moral stature, Chiang Kai-shek is *a priori* a sworn enemy of Bolshevism. He has held sway over the largest nation in the world for eleven years and enjoys his people's unbounded confidence.   The result of the war now going on depends on him.   His own people look up to him and have a blind faith in his strength of character. No one but he can save the old Middle Kingdom, and it is comprehensible that the Japanese have insisted on his disappearance as their first condition of peace.

The war in the Far East, whose repercussions extend to Sinkiang in the interior of the continent, is a chain of dramatic events of fantastic magnitude.   It is a duel between the most determined and energetic people of our time and the man who, as strategist, statesman and patriot, is the greatest of contemporary leaders.

A telegram received on December 22, 1937, from Shanghai stated that the Chinese had decided to make a motor-road through the heart of Asia to the Russian frontier for the transport of arms and ammunition from Russia to China.   The proposed road was to start from Szechuan and run via Lanchow, the capital of Kansu, to Hami, the first town in Sinkiang, and on via Urumchi, the capital of that province, to the Russian frontier.

The only road which connects Lanchow and Hami, and can be used for the purpose indicated, is the famous old Silk Road which linked up the China of ancient times with the West.   In old days the part between Sian and Chia-yü-kwan, the westernmost gate in the Great Wall, was called the Imperial Highway ; it continued thence by way of Lop-nor, " the wandering lake ", and Lou-lan to Korla, Kucha and Kashgar, and went on through foreign countries till it reached the coast of the Mediterranean. The appellation " Silk Road " was given to it in later days ; the reference is to the vast quantities of Chinese silk which for 500 years were carried along the Imperial Highway to the West.

The eastern section of the Silk Road was single—the road Sian–Lanchow–Liangchow–Kanchow–Suchow–Tun-hwang ; but at the last-named oasis it divided into three branches, the middle road running by Lop-nor, the northern via Hami, Turfan and Korla, and the southern via Charkhlik, Cherchen and Khotan. All three met again at Kashgar.

The road mentioned in the Shanghai telegram leaves the Imperial Highway as early as Anhsi, and then follows the northern branch to Hami and Turfan, where it leaves the Silk Road and runs off to the right to Urumchi.. Thence it continues north-west to Manas and north to Chuguchak, quite near the Russian frontier. The first place in Russian territory is Bakhti, 180 miles from Ayagus station, quite near Sergiopol, on the Turksib (see page 299).

The distance of 3,000 miles between the Chinese and Siberian termini of the proposed road, mentioned in the telegram, seems rather exaggerated, though it depends on what the termini are to be. On the Swedish expeditions of 1927–35 I drove by car all along this road, along some of the northerly sections several times. The distance from Sergiopol to Bakhti and Chuguchak is, as I have stated, 180 miles ; from Chuguchak to Urumchi 372 miles, and from Urumchi to Lanchow nearly 1,200 miles. The total distance from the Russian railway at Sergiopol to Lanchow is thus about 1,800 miles. The simplest plan would have been to go on from Lanchow to Sian, but this town is too near the Hwang-ho and too much exposed to Japanese flank attacks, and that is probably why the telegram speaks of Szechuan.

But one cannot read this without a certain feeling of surprise and doubt ; for the road from Lanchow to Cheng-tu, the capital of Szechuan, runs through the Min-shan and other mountainous regions, where long and laborious work would be needed to convert the tracks into passable roads for heavy vehicles, let alone motor-roads.

The whole of the road from Sergiopol to Lanchow, 1,800 miles long, is described in my books *Riddles of the Gobi Desert* and *Big Horse's Flight*, and especially in the present volume. I need not, therefore, discuss its merits as a motor-road. The fact that my Swedish, Chinese and Mongolian comrades and I were able to get our motor-lorries along it, with loads of over two tons per lorry, is sufficient proof that this road can perfectly well be used for the transport of heavy goods, especially in winter.

If what the telegram says is true—that 700,000 workmen, fore-men and experts are being mobilized to make the road, repair it and keep it working to its full capacity—it is clear that enormous importance is attached to this gigantic road-making enterprise. To transform a road 2,000 miles long, intended for camel caravans and two-wheeled carts drawn by oxen, horses and mules, into a

modern motor-road is an attempt which cannot but excite admiration, and which speaks volumes for the strength of will and
resolution of the Chinese supreme command. The rulers of a
country do not mobilize 700,000 men for a colossal undertaking
in mid-winter unless they are determined at all costs to ward off
invasion by superior forces, and unless they are convinced that
they can rely on the people's readiness to make every sacrifice
for the national defence.

I cannot refrain from pointing out the apparently predestined
and at all events curious connexion between this expedition and
the great road-building enterprise of which the telegram speaks.
For all the way from Lanchow via Hami to Urumchi, along the
motor-road to be, the tracks of our wheels have been imprinted
in the ground, and perhaps even now, in valleys protected against
wind and weather, where the earth is fairly soft, are visible as
faint depressions in the soil.

The fact that the Prime Minister Wang Ching-wei in August,
1933, charged me, a foreigner, to lead a motor expedition from
China to Sinkiang and lay down two main routes through the
desert, might suggest that he foresaw or guessed what would
happen and realized that in certain circumstances it might be a
good thing to have motor-roads to Sinkiang, the most westerly
Chinese province, which marches with Russian territory to the
north and west.

Of course, when the plan for the motor-car expedition under
my leadership was drawn up in the summer of 1933 I did not
dream, much less think, of the possibility of a war with Japan,
and least of all that such a war was so imminent. In any case it
would have been wise of the Chinese to start work on the road
at once in accordance with the proposals we submitted after our
return to Nanking on February 12, 1935. If they had done so,
the road to Urumchi would have been completed in time, before
the beginning of the war.

Now the work will have to be done with feverish haste. Will
the road be completed before it is too late? The undertaking
requires a tremendous organization. Presumably convoys of
lorries, filled with men and gear, will be flung right into the heart
of Asia, and the working population of the oases will be mobilized,
so that work can be carried on in sections at the same time all
along the route.

Certain stretches are already quite complete, and need no
further improvement, or very little. The road between Sergiopol
and Chuguchak—in the Russian area—is first-class; indeed, the
railway planned there may already be running. The section

between Chuguchak and Urumchi is presumably being constructed by the Russians, and it may be taken for granted that the Russians will supply Amo cars as in the civil war. During the four months and a half for which Yew and I were detained at Urumchi in 1934, we had an opportunity of observing how deeply rooted Russian influence already was in the province. It is possible that Russian engineers and workmen are being used on the section Urumchi–Turfan–Hami; perhaps, indeed, even farther.

In Kansu, between Suchow and Liangchow, there are pieces of road laid in 1926 by the " Christian general ", Feng Yü-hsiang, with an eye to motor traffic. One difficulty about road-making in the winter is that the ground is frozen. But it is a great advantage that the hundreds of irrigation canals, which may flood the road during the warmer seasons of the year, are then covered with ice.

The statement in the telegram that the whole route—assuming it to be in good order—can be covered in a fortnight is no exaggeration. The Chinese are skilful drivers.

I little guessed, during the long and wearisome months I spent on the Silk Road, that this motor route would become of historic importance in three short years. I must be forgiven if I was thrilled to receive the message from Shanghai, and if I follow the course of the work in the tracks of my old cars through the world's greatest continent with closer attention than any other white man in the world.

Two expert Chinese engineers, Irving C. Yew and C. C. Kung, were members of my expedition. It was their task to map, study and describe in detail the routes we proposed, take measurements of all the water-courses, irrigation canals and ravines which needed bridges—in short, to include in their reports all the material required for a start to be made on the road.

Yew sent me a letter dated December 25, 1937, in which he told me that he had received orders to go to Sian, to follow the Silk Road thence in our old wheel-tracks all the way to Urumchi, and then return to Sian by air. At Urumchi, where we had been detained three and a half years earlier and subjected to so many annoyances, he had now met with nothing but amiability and hospitality from Sheng Shih-tsai.

Reports from different sources agree that in the autumn of 1937 the representatives of Soviet Russia dominated Turkistan, not only commercially but also politically. A telegram to *The Times* dated Delhi, February 10, confirms these reports. It says :

"Russian influence in Sinkiang is being consolidated as a result of the Sino-Japanese hostilities, and the Tungan military leaders recently in revolt against the Provincial Government at Kashgar [1] are now preparing to support the Chinese forces.

"General Ma Chung-yin, former leader of the Tungan forces in Kashgaria, has arrived in Sinkiang from Moscow, where he has been detained by the Soviet authorities for some time, and is proceeding to Kansu to assist the Chinese. His half-brother, General Ma Ho-san, who recently fled to Calcutta when the Tungan rebellion collapsed, has also been invited to assist the Chinese. His departure for Kansu is regarded as a certainty.

"It is also reported that 150 Sinkiang boys now being educated under Russian auspices at Tashkent are being transferred to the military college there, where they are expected to be joined by another 200 Sinkiang lads shortly."

So that most interesting personality Ma Chung-yin, after nearly four years' internment in Moscow, has suddenly reappeared in the wide spaces of Central Asia.

A telegram states briefly that he " has arrived in Sinkiang from Moscow ". Which route did he take ? Probably the railway to Semipalatinsk and Sergiopol and Russian motor-cars thence to Bakhti and Urumchi. He, who at the beginning of 1934 so nearly captured that town and fought a desperate battle with Sheng Shih-tsai, resulting in his own defeat, has now presumably been received by the latter as an honoured guest and an ally.

The other Tungan general who is mentioned in the telegram from Delhi, the cavalry commander Ma Ho-san, who is not Ma Chung-yin's brother, though probably a relative, is also mentioned in *Big Horse's Flight*. He had been wounded by a splinter from a Russian aeroplane bomb in the middle of February, 1934, and was attended at Turfan by our doctor David Hummel, who probably saved his life, as gangrene had already set in. At Korla too he was attended by Hummel, and he accompanied Big Horse and his fleeing army to Kashgar in one of our lorries.

When Ma Chung-yin (Big Horse) abandoned his army at Kashgar against Ma Ho-san's wishes and advice, and crossed the frontier into Russia, Ma Ho-san, as related above, took over the command of the defeated Tungan army and brought under his authority the whole of the southern part of Turkistan, from the Yarkend-daria to Charkhlik, not far from Lop-nor. Then, late in the summer of 1937, he came up against Urumchi troops near Aksu and was defeated. In those parts Soviet propaganda, in alliance with the Chinese in Kashgar, had got the upper hand

---

[1] The correspondent means the provincial government at Urumchi.

and became all-powerful. Most of the Tungan generals and the greater part of Ma Ho-san's troops abandoned him and went over to the Russo-Chinese *bloc*. Ma Ho-san, betrayed by his own men, fled over the Karakoram pass into India with a thousand loyal supporters. He was interned there by the English, his bodyguard having been detained at Ladak (see page 301).

And now the Delhi telegram says that Ma Ho-san, in Calcutta, has received an invitation to go to Kansu and support the Chinese, and that he will certainly obey the summons.

The great stage, the desert of Central Asia, is ready and waiting ; the two chief actors have taken their places in the wings. The drama can begin.

It would be interesting to know the reason for the Russians' desire to obtain possession of the Tungan general's person. Presumably they realized that he might be a valuable piece in the great game of chess whose prize is Central Asia. And now the moment has come to play him—in the war between Japan and China.

If the much-discussed telegram from Delhi is correct, the English in India, who, like the Russians, are on China's side in the war, have followed the Soviet example and given Ma Ho-san permission to return to Kansu.

I wrote cautiously in *Big Horse's Flight*, page 247, " Whether he (Ma Chung-yin) will bob up again one fine day in the heart of the deserts—it is no use prophesying in a country where anything may happen, in a time in which all things are possible ! "

But now he has come back, and not only he, but also his general of cavalry and friend Ma Ho-san. What will happen now, and what will the next move be ?

As far as one can judge, the Chinese are resolved to hold out to the uttermost in defence of their country. The tenacity which, without any first-class military achievement, has enabled the Chinese people to maintain itself for 4,000 years, while the rest of the great world of antiquity has collapsed, seems to be going to count for something in this war as in the past.

When will the Chinese acknowledge themselves defeated and willing to conclude a peace that will make the country helpless ? When the Japanese have captured the whole of the northern part of the country and all the coast provinces ? It does not look like it. The Chinese seem to be determined to continue the war even when this has happened.

Is it too daring to suppose this ? No, it is not, if one collects and compares the various pieces of information which from time to time emerge from the fog of war.

It is estimated that the new motor-road will be ready in a month—the road which starts from the coast of the Indian Ocean and runs through Burma, Yunnan and Szechuan to Cheng-tu, capital of the last-named province.[1] At that town it joins the road which is now being made to Lanchow and which is identical with the Silk Road. It will then be possible to drive in a car diagonally right across Asia, from Rangoon on the coast of the Indian Ocean to Leningrad on the Baltic—a companion to the road I dreamed of a few years ago, from Shanghai to Boulogne or Bremerhaven, the most important link of which was likewise to be the Silk Road.

In short, the road now being constructed from Burma to the frontier of Russian Siberia at Chuguchak will give the diminished territory of China two wide entrance-gates for the supplies which will enable her to continue the war on interior lines.

If the last stage of the war is really fought out in Central Asia the invading armies will be set a task which is beyond their powers. One needs only to think of the immense length of the lines of communication and the Russian flank to the northward.

These are the circumstances in which General Ma Chung-yin, our friend Big Horse, and his cavalry general Ma Ho-san have been presented with their new opportunity.

June 1938.

---

[1] I learned from a very reliable Chinese source on June 1, 1938, that the whole road from the Russian boundary at Chuguchak to the coast of the Indian Ocean is now in running order. On the Central Asian section of the road 1,000 lorries are said to be running. From the Russian frontier to Urumchi there was a great deal of snow last winter, but thousands of natives were mobilized to keep the road clear, and there was no interruption of traffic.

INDEX